BUYING TIME

BUYING TIME

ENVIRONMENTAL

COLLAPSE

AND THE

FUTURE OF

ENERGY

KAZ MAKABE

Foв E E D G E

ForeEdge

An imprint of University Press of New England

www.upne.com

© 2017 Kaz Makabe

All rights reserved

Manufactured in the United States of America

Designed by April Leidig

Typeset in Arno by Copperline Book Services

For permission to reproduce any of the material in this book,

contact Permissions, University Press of New England,

One Court Street, Suite 250, Lebanon NH 03766; or

visit www.upne.com

Hardcover ISBN: 978-1-61168-931-0

Ebook ISBN: 978-1-61168-932-7

Library of Congress Cataloging-in-Publication Data available upon request.

5 4 3 2 1

CONTENTS

CIVILIZATION IS ABOUT ENERGY

Modern civilization is about energy abundance. Few things illustrate this more dramatically than nighttime satellite photos centered on the Korean Peninsula. Everything north of the thirty-eighth parallel and south of China is swathed in darkness, with only a pinprick — sometimes not even that, if there is a brownout — representing the capital city of Pyongyang. Contemporary popular fiction such as the recent U.S. television series *Revolution* depicts a world in which electrical devices are no longer usable, and a nasty and brutish Hobbesian world ensues. In testimony to a U.S. Senate subcommittee in 2005, the commissioner of the congressional EMP (electromagnetic pulse) Commission pointed out that the destruction of the U.S. power infrastructure for an extended period could result in the death of 90 percent of the population and set America back a century or more as a society.[1] Power infrastructure in densely populated regions can also be severely damaged for many months or even years by geomagnetic storms caused by solar activity. The impact on today's overwhelmingly digital world of another "Carrington Event," a powerful solar storm that knocked out telegraph systems in Europe and North America in 1859, would be catastrophic. It is not an exaggeration to state that, when the lights go out for a long time, civilization as known by many of the world's people ceases to exist — literally.

My own brush with the fragility of modern civilization came following the earthquake and tsunami that struck northeastern Japan on March 11, 2011. I was comanaging a multi-strategy fund for a Japanese sponsor, and energy was of interest only in regard to our ownership of oil futures and related equities, given the potential impact of the "Arab Spring" on supply. I was walking back to our office in the Roppongi section of Tokyo from the building next door when the ground started swaying and gradually intensified to a level akin to sailing on a sea with moderate waves: better to sit down, or hang on to something while standing or walking. Since crossing an open plaza to go back into a building seemed unwise, given the possible danger of being filleted by falling glass, I stayed put under a solid awning until the main temblor subsided, then made my way to our office tower to retrieve the car. Although voice cell phone service was sporadic at best, text mail and landlines were working reasonably well, and I was able to contact my wife at the building complex where she worked and where our one-and-a-half-year-old daughter attended day care. But with many elevators in eastern Japan stilled as aftershocks continued and elevators had to be inspected and reset, carrying a child up forty-one flights of stairs to get home after we safely arrived at our apartment building highlighted the appalling inconvenience of modern urban living without the trappings we usually take for granted. We were very lucky: many workers in the capital either walked, all night in some cases, to get home through exceptionally congested streets, or stayed put at their workplaces or temporary shelters until some public transport was restored.

Though serious enough, the immediate effect of the earthquake on the greater Tokyo metropolitan area was light compared to the devastation and loss of almost twenty thousand lives wreaked by the quake and subsequent tsunami near the epicenter. But the aftershocks were not only seismic: the meltdowns unfolding at the Fukushima Daiichi nuclear power plant, about two hundred kilometers from the capital and only sixty kilometers from the city of Sendai, kept the nation and the world on edge for weeks afterward. With food supply chains disrupted and refineries damaged, staples quickly disappeared from supermarkets, and gas stations stayed open for only a few hours a day (if at all) to serve drivers who waited for hours in long lines. Distributors around the world of iodine tablets and syrup, designed to inundate thyroid glands, particularly those of children, so that they would not absorb radioactive iodine, were out of stock (as I found out) within a day or two of the event. Not only were Japanese privately concerned about their families and less than confident about the government's ability to distribute these essentials effectively, but American West Coast residents, concerned about fallout from across the Pacific, stocked up as well. Some expatriate managers of foreign companies, understandably concerned for their families' safety, headed home or decamped to other Asian capitals as soon as possible, earning the sobriquet *flyjin* — a play on *gaijin*, or foreigner. Rolling blackouts were instituted to prevent complete, widespread blackouts, as Tokyo Electric Power (TEPCO), the operator of Fukushima Daiichi, was able to provide only three-quarters of the power usually supplied to its service area. During the summer following the disaster, residents and businesses in TEPCO's service area were urged to set thermostats higher and conserve electric power, and television news programs carried spare grid capacity forecasts daily. Cities were noticeably darker at night in the absence of the familiar massive neon signs usually ubiquitous in Japan. By May 2012, all nuclear power plants in Japan were shut down for inspections and recertifications.

In net energy self-sufficiency, Japan ranks among the lowest among major industrialized countries, at around 15 percent in 2010 before Fukushima, and now a mere 4 percent. Nuclear power provided about 27 percent of Japan's electricity before Fukushima, and planned new construction would have seen the share increase to around 50 percent by 2030.[2] The planned reliance on nuclear power, combined with increasing emphasis on energy efficiency and renewable energy, was supposed to allow Japan to meet its targets to reduce its carbon output according to the terms of the 1997 Kyoto Protocol (Japan subsequently decided in 2012 to not participate in the second commitment period, starting in 2013). In the absence of meaningful economically efficient sources of fossil fuels — coal was mined until 1986, when the government decided to close almost all domestic mines and import coal instead — Japan had made nuclear energy a national priority since the Atomic Energy Basic Law was passed in late 1955, to help provide the much-needed energy for postwar economic reconstruction and development. Despite a couple of "lost decades" following the bursting of the real-estate bubble during the early 1990s, Japan remains a highly urbanized, power-hungry industrial society. Japanese public opinion, so long apathetic toward or accepting of nuclear power, has turned against it following the Fukushima meltdown. Former prime minister Naoto Kan, on whose watch the Tohoku earthquake occurred, stated during a May 2012 parliamentary inquiry into Fukushima that, with metropolitan Tokyo and its thirty million residents having been brought to the brink of evacuation, "experiencing the accident convinced me that the best way to make nuclear plants safe is not to rely on them, but rather to get rid of them."[3] More recently, in September 2013, former prime minister Junichiro Koizumi of the Liberal Democratic Party, the party under which the country's nuclear energy industry was coddled for decades, expressed his opposition to the continued use of nuclear power in Japan.[4]

Despite the introduction of a feed-in tariff system for renewable energy in July 2012, the process of shifting the nation's power mix has been far from smooth: most of the capacity added since then has been solar photovoltaic (PV), as wind, geothermal, and hydro all require extensive and lengthy environmental impact reviews and are stymied by bureaucratic overlaps.[5] Even for solar PV, the Ministry of Agriculture is loath to de-categorize disused agricultural plots (often abandoned by those too old to work the fields and without heirs to stay on and till the family plot) to allow them to be used for electricity production, ostensibly to preserve food self-sufficiency while maintaining barriers to entry for imports and more efficient agribusinesses. Meanwhile, Japan's structural trade balance turned negative — a record deficit of 13.7 trillion yen ($134 billion) — in fiscal year 2013, mainly due to the massive amounts of imported fuel needed to make up for idled nuclear power plants: not a good place to be when a country is also running a staggering national debt of close to 240 percent of GDP and rising. Japan's commitment to meet greenhouse-gas reduction targets has been a casualty as well, as total emissions increased 2.7 percent year-on-year in 2012 and 1.6 percent in 2013, to a level 10.6 percent higher than 1990, the base year used for the Kyoto accord.[6] Determined to kick-start the economy after decades of deflation and stagnation, the Liberal Democratic Party, under the leadership of Prime Minister Shinzō Abe, appears set on restarting as many nuclear plants as possible, a slow process requiring extensive safety reviews.

Shortly after the Fukushima Daiichi disaster, my reflexive response was that Japan should shut all nuclear power plants and forgo further deployment. But doing without nuclear power in any form would mean that Japan's high structural dependence on imported energy, and inability to reduce its carbon footprint pending extensive rollout of renewable power sources, would continue for some time: this realization made me examine the broad topic of energy and resilience further. Japan's energy problems are but a microcosm of a key issue facing the world today: How do we secure enough energy to support the complexity of modern civilization without breaking the bank and jeopardizing our environment? Humanity is increasingly depleting cheap energy resources, faces significant global environmental degradation caused by fossil fuel use, as well as other factors, and is engaged in a race to develop a portfolio of cost-efficient alternatives. Too often given short shrift in discussions about our future, plentiful energy — efficient, resilient, and clean — is the key to sustaining the positive trajectory of our civilization.

Civilizations die from suicide, not murder.
—**Arnold J. Toynbee (1889–1975)**

I think God's going to come down and
pull civilization over for speeding.
—**Steven Wright (1955–)**

1

WAITING FOR THE WINDSHIELD

In 1860, French naturalist Henri Mouhot came across a set of enormous and complex ruins amid the Cambodian jungle. Though other Europeans, including a Portuguese monk during the sixteenth century, had visited the Angkor temples earlier, Mouhot is credited with evocatively describing their grandeur and piquing tremendous international interest. Mouhot, who died of malaria during another expedition a year after "discovering" Angkor Wat, was invoked thereafter by the French, in their quest for colonies, as the symbol of a heroic (white) explorer uncovering a long-lost civilization before succumbing to the jungle. During the decades since, archaeologists and historians pieced together that the complex had been built by the Khmer Empire, which lasted from the ninth to the fifteenth century and ruled most of mainland Southeast Asia at its peak.

The capital of the Khmer kingdom, Angkor was a city of over 750,000 inhabitants sprawled over an area the size of New York City, making it one of the most extensive urban centers in the preindustrial world. Estimated to have been built in just three decades, the huge central temple complex

Angkor Wat occupies 208 hectares (500 acres) and is 213 meters (699 feet) at its highest point, over 60 meters higher than the pyramids at Giza. Khmer engineers built a remarkable system of hundreds of canals and reservoirs, spanning over 1,500 square kilometers, to tame the monsoons, which not only typically dumped almost 90 percent of the annual rainfall during six months but varied greatly from year to year. The managed, predictable water supply allowed for significant increases in food production, supported a large population and a developed bureaucracy, and bestowed legitimacy on the ruling classes.

But recently researchers have discovered that Khmer engineers faced increasing difficulty in repairing and maintaining a water management system that had grown in complexity and had become increasingly vulnerable to extreme climate events. During the fourteenth century, as Europe was experiencing the onset of what scientists have come to call the "Little Ice Age," from about 1350 to 1850, there are records in Asia of colder conditions and famine as well (for example, major famine in China from 1333 to 1337 and in Japan from 1459 to 1461). Based on their study of tree-ring records in Southeast Asia, scientists from Columbia University's Lamont-Doherty Earth Observatory believe that there was a mega-drought in the region from the 1330s to the 1360s, followed by a shorter but more serious drought from the 1400s to the 1420s, punctuated by extremely intense rainy seasons that may have damaged Angkor's irrigation system. The second drought was recorded shortly before Angkor succumbed to invasion in 1431 from the Ayutthaya Kingdom in present-day Thailand.[1] So the Khmer appear to have suffered an energy (food) crisis precipitated by changes and irregularities in the climate patterns to which they had skillfully adapted, a crisis that rendered them less capable of maintaining complexity and leaving them vulnerable to predation by neighbors.

Civilizations have come and gone throughout the arc of human history. Though the collapses of many civilizations are associated with dramatic precipitating events, factors that set the stage for decline can be discerned over decades or centuries beforehand. Prior to the Industrial Revolution, humanity was merely one of many denizens of the Earth, and our impact on the environment writ large was limited. Civilizations were shaped, limited, and in some cases destroyed and dispersed by the seemingly capricious forces of nature. Despite the most remarkably advanced irrigation, engineering, and land-management technologies, demographic shifts and environmental changes rendered such diverse civilizations as the Western Roman Empire, the Mayan city-states, and the Khmers increasingly vulnerable to decline. Gradual increases in complexity during their development eroded their net energy surplus, undermined their resilience, and set the stage for a confluence of factors — major climate shifts, wars, pestilence — to drive the nails into their coffins.

Of all the examples of socioeconomic decline, the Western Roman Empire has probably captured the interest of historians and the public most, with myriad explanations offered such as barbarian incursions, currency debasement, pestilence, and the adoption of Christianity. Perhaps some of the intense contemporary interest stems from the nagging perception that there are parallels between ancient Rome and the modern world — particularly the United States as a unitary hegemon after the fall of Soviet communism but followed by costly wars in Afghanistan and Iraq, the Great Recession, and the rise of China — an example of Mark Twain's anecdotal observation that "history does not repeat itself, but it does rhyme." But many of the traditional explanations for the Roman Empire's decline appear more like symptoms of systematic vulnerability or, at best, contributory or proximate causes that do not explain the decline adequately.

In *The Collapse of Complex Societies*, anthropologist Joseph Tainter makes a powerful case that, like other societies that experienced collapse, Western Rome was doomed by declining returns on investment in socioeconomic complexity, which rendered it increasingly vulnerable to shocks from which it had successively less capacity to recover. The Roman policy of territorial expansion from the third century BCE was highly successful in terms of marginal return — the additional output from a unit increase in an input, which in this case was conquest. But once the difficulties of administering distant lands, given the technologies of the era, dictated that expansion end at around the reign of Augustus (bracketed around zero CE), the accumulated spoils of conquered lands were no longer available for incorporation, and just maintaining the status quo thereafter took up an ever-increasing share of the empire's resources. Tainter makes the argument that "once a complex society develops the vulnerabilities of declining marginal returns, collapse may merely require sufficient passage of time to render probable the occurrence of insurmountable calamity."[2]

Another empire of much fascination regarding its decline and, more recently, an ancient calendar that some claimed to portend a very bad outcome for the world as we knew it in 2012, Mayan civilization spanned much of Central America and lasted for roughly three thousand years before experiencing rapid collapse during a period of a century and a half between about 750 and 900 CE. Though the Mayans were originally seen as a peaceful, low-density, agrarian civilization with impressive religious centers inhabited by priests and a small ruling class, advances in understanding the hieroglyphic language and archaeological fieldwork over the past thirty years have changed our understanding of the Mayans dramatically. The prevailing view today is that the Mayan civilization was much more urban than previously understood, with high-density population centers supported by labor-intensive farming and highly developed irrigation technologies, and engaged in frequent warfare.

Paleoclimate records from ocean sediments indicate that successive multiyear droughts occurred between 760 and 910 CE, affecting the Yucatán Peninsula inhabited by the Maya, and coinciding with their demographic decline during the period called the Terminal Classic Collapse.[3] Given the importance of irrigation and water control for maintaining political power and legitimacy, these dry conditions probably had devastating effects on the stability of Mayan society. The complexity of the Mayan socioeconomic system left it increasingly vulnerable to synchronous shocks to food production across regions, and "when a number of local groups each experience lean times concurrently, their behavior is largely without option, and is entirely predictable: competition, raiding, and warfare."[4]

Why, then, are we fascinated by the collapse of these once-thriving civilizations? The most obvious causal parallels between the expansion, hegemony, and decline of ancient Rome on the one hand and, on the other, Great Britain during the seventeenth through the twentieth centuries, or between either of them and the United States, never fail to appeal to our curiosity. The implications of globalization for the increasingly synchronous nature of the world economy reminds us of ancient Mayan city-states and their descent into warfare and collapse when things went wrong for all of them at the same time. The ancient Khmers' attempt — very successful for a time — to manage the seasonal monsoons' impact on their major rivers cannot help but conjure images of Hurricane Katrina overwhelming successive efforts by the Army Corps of Engineers to tame the Mississippi River through "whack-a-mole" redirections and construction of extensive canals, levees, and floodwalls. But more importantly, the collapse of civilizations illustrates the fragility of socioeconomic systems when investment in ever-increasing complexity results in diminishing marginal returns and, over time, renders these civilizations more vulnerable to insurmountable shocks and a significant reduction in complexity: a reversion to what some would argue is a more normal (but pretty scary to most of us) state of affairs in the long span of human history.

Complexity and Limits to Growth?

A key component of society's vulnerability to ever-increasing complexity is the possibility that technological progress and innovation are yielding diminishing returns. As a species, human beings have exhibited a remarkable knack for adaptation and survival, though some anthropologists suggest that, during the peak of the last major ice age, the global population of our ancestors may have fallen to the tens of thousands — perilously close to extinction. Many optimists would argue that humanity, with our tremendous capacity for adaptation and innovation, will continue to provide the conditions needed for growth, pointing to such relatively recent developments as AI/robotics, genetic mapping, and nanotechnology.

But some economists argue that the marginal return from investment in research and development has fallen steadily after reaching peaks some years ago (more on this later). Perhaps the perceived innovation slowdown in some sectors is part of the ebb and flow of technological adoption and change: it took roughly six decades after the first successful powered flight for technology to enable mass air travel, but most aspects of the air travel experience have not changed that much since. It may yet take several decades for information technologies to fulfill their full potential, or for many of today's emerging technologies to diffuse and enable substantial economic invigoration. If, however, those who argue that truly game-changing innovations have been slowing are correct, we must question how long the exponential socioeconomic growth of our civilization can continue.

As an observable phenomenon, declining marginal returns on investment apply to a broad range of human endeavors on which long-term growth depends. Governmental organizations become more complex and costly tools of socioeconomic management, and command increasing (non-market-priced) shares of output in many countries over time. But they seldom shrink, unless confronted with stark budgetary realities or threat of sanctions (as in Europe today), and even then only very reluctantly and painfully. Education is a notable area in which the United States has increased spending considerably over the past three decades, only to see high school graduation rates and measures of learning decline. Conversely, vast advances in education for small investments can still be found in the poorest of nations. Energy and mineral extraction provide classic examples of diminishing returns on investment, as easily accessed and highest-quality resources are tapped first, and the costs of extraction gradually rise while the quality of product falls, even given technological advances. Despite the miracles bestowed by the "Green Revolution" of the post–World War II era, agriculture also follows a pattern of the most productive land being exploited, then decreasingly productive land being created through deforestation and supplemented extensively through fertilizer use, with unintended and potentially severe consequences for the global environment.

When I started out in banking almost three decades ago, some of the earliest lessons in the graduate training program covered the power of compounded interest. The instructor would point out that if one reinvested the interest from a bond paying 10 percent annually at the same rate (rates were very high back then), it would take only about seven years to double your money: so start saving now — sage advice that all but the most astute ignored until much later in their careers. At a more "macro" scale, economic orthodoxy in the last half century has been based on the fundamental assumption that constant growth should be the norm and the ultimate goal of economic endeavor. When U.S. GDP growth — a problematic measure itself, which we'll touch on later —"stagnates" at around 1.7 percent as it did in 2011, public consensus calls for growth to be brought back to a more "normal" 3 percent level or higher. Or commentators often have fits about

China's GDP growth rate when it falls below 7 percent, the level below which many fear potential social unrest.

But take a step back and think about the compounding effect of growth, and assumptions about constant growth take on a different hue: a 3 percent growth rate would imply a doubling of nominal GDP in about twenty-three years, and only nine years at 8 percent, the basis for frequent citations that China's economy will overtake that of the United States during the next decade. Even after adjusting for inflation, real GDP in developed countries has followed dramatic, nonlinear paths. Looking at the United States, real GDP in 2005 dollars has grown from about $50 billion in 1850 to about $13 trillion in 2011, an almost 270-fold increase, with much of the outright increase taking place from about $1.1 trillion in 1939 on the eve of World War II to the present level.[5] We generally expect this type of growth to continue indefinitely, based on limitless technological advances and the assumption of near-perfect substitutability of inputs. But does a worldview of endless growth realistically reflect sustainable levels of resource consumption needed to limit, or even help undo, environmental degradation?

Neo-Malthusians versus Cornucopians

It is easy to dismiss talk of limits to resource exploitation and growth as alarmist, and many point to the power of human ingenuity in overcoming past constraints to growth. The Reverend Thomas Robert Malthus was the eighteenth-century British scholar found in many economic history syllabi and the namesake for the term "Malthusian," referring to the idea that overpopulation would lead to unsustainable resource depletion and environmental stress (but more generally directed nowadays at party-poopers who stress limits and thresholds). Writing around the time the Industrial Revolution got into full gear, in *An Essay on the Principle of Population*, Malthus held that unchecked population growth would eventually outstrip the ability of the earth to sustain humanity. Critics like to argue that he was proven wrong, given the subsequent exponential population growth and general improvement in living standards the world has experienced.

The basic idea that Earth's resources are limited and cannot support endless human population growth is not unreasonable, but critics point out that Malthus focused too much on mouths to be fed instead of their owners' abilities to innovate. Although he did not make any firm predictions, Malthus's timing was also pretty awful, as he articulated his theories just before the broad use of fossil fuels triggered a dramatic revolution in the amount of cheap thermodynamic energy available to improve the human condition. Combined with major advances in agricultural productivity through scale and the use of fertilizers, the use of fossil fuels allowed for a steady increase in Great Britain's population from twenty-four million in 1830 to forty-one million in 1900, and even faster increases in other countries undergoing industrialization at the time (the United States, which grew from thirteen million to seventy-six million during the same period, was a particularly impressive outperformer because of immigration).

Scientific and technological advances in medicine, agriculture, and the use of fossil fuels to generate power account for much of the tremendous economic growth and many enhancements in quality of life experienced in the developed world since the middle of the nineteenth century. These advances have allowed developed and developing economies to shift from heavy reliance on the primary sector (agriculture, fishing, and mining) to the secondary sector (manufacturing) and, increasingly, to the tertiary or service sector for economic growth. But just because about 63 percent of gross world product is currently driven by the service sector today (80 percent in the United States), with manufacturing at 31 percent and the primary sector at 6 percent,[6] does not mean that the tertiary sector — including the information sector, which some call quaternary — can drive endless growth by itself. Given how far removed most of us are from the means of physical production, it is sometimes easy to overlook that the value of a highly structured financial product is quite marginal without enough food, water, and energy to sustain us. Some futurists, however, envisage the convergence of genetic engineering, robotics, and nanotechnology as setting the stage for a world of practically limitless growth.

In 1968, ecologist Paul Ehrlich warned in *The Population Bomb* that, by the 1970s, the world would face catastrophic starvation and broad unrest as global population outstrips the available food and other resources needed to support it. Agricultural productivity continued to increase, however; governments and nongovernmental actors were somewhat successful in encouraging family planning in emerging nations (the most infamous example being the one-child policy of the People's Republic of China); global trade liberalization ameliorated food shortages and increased productivity; and critics of Malthusianism were once again able to congratulate themselves on the power of human ingenuity.

Economist Julian Simon, who criticized the view that population growth would engender resource scarcity, argued that increasing wealth and technological innovation make resources more available, markets inspire substitution for increasingly scarce resources, and growing populations represent expanded markets and sources of innovation. In 1980, Simon proposed and entered into a famous wager on resource scarcity with Ehrlich, in which they respectively bet that the inflation-adjusted prices of copper, chromium, nickel, tin, and tungsten would fall or rise by 1990. Simon won the bet, as all five metals fell in inflation-adjusted terms during the period, once again providing inspiration for anti-Malthusians. But if the wager had been for a longer period, to 2011, Ehrlich would have won the bet for four of the five metals, reminding us that, like stand-up comedy, making prognostications is all about getting the timing right.

In contrast to the suboptimal predictive ability of *The Population Bomb*, particularly in light of the hype and controversy it inspired, the Club of Rome (a think tank focused on a range of global political issues) commissioned a group of scholars at the Massachusetts Institute of Technology focused on system dynamics theory and computer modeling to study where then-current socioeconomic trends might lead humanity in the future. The result was *The Limits to Growth* (henceforth abbreviated to LTG), a bestselling 1972 book that modeled, in aggregate, the effects of five variables — world population, food production, industrialization, pollution, and the consumption of nonrenewable resources — under three main scenarios. The pioneering work incorporated feedback loops and lags, the impacts of exponential consumption growth of limited resources (while allowing for some substitutability), and the cumulative effects of resource utilization and environmental degradation offset against their rates of recovery.

The outputs of the model, named World3, consisted of the following: global population, birth rates, death rates, services per capita, food per capita, industrial output per capita, nonrenewable resources remaining, and persistent pollution. The scenarios were "standard run," business-as-usual socioeconomic policies along the lines of 1900 to 1970; "comprehensive technology," in which resources are effectively unlimited, 75 percent of materials are recycled, agricultural land yields double, pollution is reduced 25 percent from 1970 levels, etc.; and "stabilized world," where deliberate socioeconomic policies to control population and shift consumption patterns are implemented in addition to technological solutions to achieve more sustainable equilibrium. The first two scenarios suggested that things will end badly, with "overshoot and collapse" for the model's outputs. Although economic growth would continue through the late twentieth to early twenty-first centuries, the "standard run" suggested that resource constraints would begin to be felt starting during the early twenty-first century, until the outputs of the model (except persistent pollution) collapse dramatically by sometime during the middle of the twenty-first century. The "comprehensive technology" scenario only managed to delay the reckoning to later in the twenty-first century.

The authors of LTG published updates of the original study in 1992 and again in 2004, in which they point out that, though it was not designed to be a predictive model as such, "the highly aggregated scenarios of World3 still appear, after 30 years, to be surprisingly accurate."[7] In 2007, Australian researcher Graham Turner[8] compared historical aggregate data from 1970 to 2000 against the World3 model outputs and found that actual data fit remarkably well with the "standard run" business-as-usual model. The study provides additional, independent validation of the systems dynamics approach taken for LTG and beckons us to take the model outputs regarding the next fifty years seriously.

More recently, in 2012, Jorgen Randers, one of the authors of the original LTG, published a fortieth-anniversary revisit to the systems trend analysis pioneered by LTG in his book 2052: A Global Forecast for the Next Forty Years. Randers's new study revises the peak for population growth downward to eight billion and brings it forward to 2042,[9] owing to extensive urbanization and falling fertility, and estimates that growth in humanity's impact on the environment will slow marginally because of slowing economic growth (partially caused by the diversion of economic resources to mitigating the impact of environmental deterioration and climate change) and increased use of renewable energy. Although he posits that the pace of humanity's impact on the environment is slowing somewhat compared to the "business as usual" scenario of the original LTG, Randers nevertheless feels that the more significant impact of positive-feedback climate change will occur during the decades following 2052 as the world warms more than 2°C.

Cheap, abundant energy has been the basis for much of the phenomenal aggregate socioeconomic growth since the beginning of the Industrial Revolution. Starting with coal (which still produces over 40 percent of electric power globally), supplemented significantly by liquid fuels, particularly for transport, and increasingly by natural gas, fossil fuels and their derivatives (petrochemicals) have been the key resource enabler for the exponential economic and population growth the world has experienced over the past two hundred years. But like all resources bounded by the amount stored in the earth and the means (current and prospective) to extract them, the highest-quality and most accessible are consumed first, followed by progressively more challenging, lower-quality sources.

Coal is generally classified according to energy and moisture content, reflecting the stage of conversion from plant matter into fossil fuel, and is roughly divided into "hard" and lower-quality coal. Hard coal is further classified into anthracite, the highest rank and scarcest (about 1 percent of production), and bituminous, the higher grades of which are used for coking coal to produce steel. At the dawn of the twentieth century in the United States, high-quality coal was used in power stations in New York City and much of the Northeast, but lower-quality coal was used extensively from Pittsburgh and most points west: as a result air quality in the latter cities was correspondingly lower. Lower-quality bituminous coal (also called thermal coal), along with sub-bituminous coal, is used for power generation, cement production, and other industrial uses. Lignite, the lowest-quality coal (also called brown coal and a step above peat), is largely used for power generation but has only about half the energy content of bituminous coal. Germany, which has been replacing much of its nuclear capacity with coal, has the world's largest reserves of the stuff. The world's estimated coal reserves are roughly divided between high and low quality, but many coal-producing countries have experienced a steady decline in the quality of coal recovered over the past several decades, according the

IEA Clean Coal Centre.[10] This quality decline means that coal is becoming dirtier to burn without costly treatment or carbon capture; unfortunately, there is still enough of it recoverable out there to last over a century.

Crude oil followed a similar but more dramatic pattern, with sweet light crude being steadily supplanted by sour (high sulfur content), harder-to-process crude as the extraction costs rise. And tapping "tight," hard-to-recover oil and gas through new technologies has basked in the spotlight over the past several years as a means of supplementing traditional sources of fossil fuels. But there are indications that the productive lives of wells using the new techniques are far shorter than for conventional drilling, requiring constant investments in new wells. Moreover, the technique's environmental effects remain uncertain in light of proprietary chemical cocktails used and the massive amounts of water needed, particularly problematic in regions of water scarcity. Of course, the environmental effects of extraction and consumption for all fossil fuels obviously need to be treated not as "externalities" but factored in to determine the true costs of these resources — a concept that has been around for decades but slow in catching on as a convention in national and corporate accounting.

The Importance of Energy Return on (Energy) Investment

Even given advances in extraction techniques and the discovery of reserves in areas previously underexploited, like the deep seabed or the Arctic, growth in global energy demand implies that the cost, both in terms of prices and environmental impacts, of fossil-based energy will trend up over time, with higher likelihood of volatility. The energy cost of extracting resources, captured in the key concept of energy return on energy investment (EROI), is often more important than mere data and conjecture about how much is left in the ground. EROI, also often abbreviated as EROEI, is *the ratio of energy returned over the energy used to get it.* In early societies, the energy output from agriculture was generally not much more than the energy input — both from food — and a subsistence farmer's life was neither long nor joyous. With the introduction of irrigation, the plow, and animal power, the energy output from agriculture became a multiple of the inputs, leaving an energy surplus to enable the trappings of organized society, with merchants, craftspeople, warriors, and leaders who did not have to worry about growing their own food. When the use of fossil fuels began to revolutionize how goods were produced and transported, seams of coal were easily accessible and oil was literally oozing out of the ground in the areas that would become major producing regions, making the EROI of the fuels very high at first. But as the most accessible sources were depleted, the energy required to extract them from more challenging places steadily increased, eroding EROI accordingly.

Though very useful, EROI can be a slippery concept, as it can vary widely depending on what boundaries are used. For example, it takes almost one hundred liters of water on average to produce one kilowatt-hour of electricity in the United States.[11] Among other applications, a lot of water is used to extract oil and gas from the earth, generate steam to turn turbines, cool plants, and to scrub exhaust. Getting all that water has an energy cost, which can be substantial, and a reason why so many power plants are contiguous to bodies of water. Or nuclear EROI looks significantly higher if the energy used for fuel enrichment is excluded, a criticism levied against some numbers offered by nuclear proponents. So incorporating the energy associated with indirect inputs or externalities in the production process can have a very big impact on EROI.

Most early studies on the topic focused on EROI measured at the mine mouth (or wellhead). An aggregated version can be called "societal EROI," and researchers also have expanded the concept to "EROI point of use," which consists of the energy used to find, produce, refine, and deliver energy. Systems ecologist Charles Hall, a pioneer of this approach who, with two colleagues, articulated the various forms of EROI, points out that the EROI point of use for oil in the United States is about 40 percent less than its wellhead EROI when adjusted for the energy costs of extraction, refining, losses to other petroleum products, and transportation.[12] An even broader measure is "extended EROI," which incorporates the energy required to use as well as deliver the energy returned. But EROI cannot be the exclusive criterion for making rational decisions about a society's desired fuel mix: coal and hydropower are the highest narrow EROI sources at 80 and 100, respectively, but the former is the biggest source of carbon emissions, and the latter, when using traditional dams, presents significant environmental

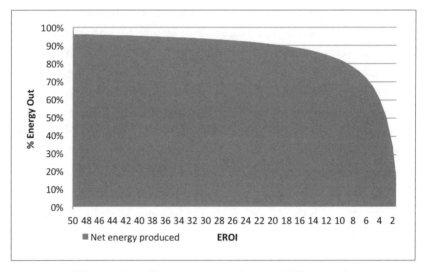

Net energy cliff (first published by Euan Mearns at http://theoildrum.com).

problems. Moreover, there are still very few alternatives to liquid fossil fuel for air transport applications (bio-kerosene has been used experimentally by the U.S. Air Force and commercial airlines, but not yet at large scale), so society would be forced to continue to use gasoline and kerosene for aviation even if their EROI were to fall below 1:1.

It is worth noting that EROI is a unit-less construct that does not actually represent the net energy produced by a given energy source or aggregate set of sources, but is merely a ratio of the energy delivered over the energy used to get it. But by looking at the percentage of energy delivered as net energy and the percentage of energy used to produce it as a function of EROI, we end up with a graph that resembles a cliff for net energy output when EROI falls below 8.

The important takeaway is that an energy technology with an EROI of 80 does not make it twice as good as another with 40, as both deliver well over 90 percent net energy; but a drop from 10 to 2 EROI would mean a change in net energy output from 90 percent to 50 percent of the gross energy involved. So the important thing for society is to ensure that, given sensible boundaries and paying sufficient attention to the depletion of nonrenewable resources, its extended EROI is comfortably above the "net energy cliff" and to avoid adding technologies with EROI below 8 where possible.[13]

Since humanity requires aggregate EROI of significantly more than 1:1 to support growth, corn-based ethanol (0.8–1.6) or hydrogen-based economies look quite poor given current and near-term technologies (but sugarcane ethanol is potentially much better at as high as 10). Hall and colleagues point out that the resources required to acquire energy in a lower EROI world would crowd out other investments and economic activity, and they describe how delivering one unit of oil-based fuel for use by the final consumer requires about three units to be extracted, with two being used in energy costs to refine and deliver it, suggesting that the minimum extended EROI needed for any energy system to make a net positive contribution to society is about 3:1. Illustrating how, with oil at $70 a barrel, the United States expends one-tenth of economic activity to secure the energy that allows the rest of economy to function, the authors state that their "guess is that we would need something like a 5:1 EROI from our main fuels to maintain anything like what we call civilization."[14] So when thoughtful commentators talk about "peak oil" (or peak anything in terms of finite resources), they are not just referring to the actual situation in which over half the known reserves have been consumed, but are incorporating the future costs of extracting the resources as key inputs into the global economy.

Many of the scholars involved in the study of EROI are ecological economists who owe their intellectual roots to, among others, Frederick Soddy, a Nobel laureate in chemistry who worked with famed physicist Ernest Rutherford on figuring out how radioactive elements decay into other elements. During the 1920s and '30s, Soddy offered an unconventional take (and much derided at the time) on economics, based on the laws of thermodynamics, which preclude perpetual motion machines. Debt growth cannot continue indefinitely: when it significantly outpaces the growth of physical wealth, an economy must adjust through inflation or, in its absence, debt repudiation. When societal EROI, perhaps better expanded to a monetary rather than energy concept in this illustration, falls below a sustainable level, a society can make up the shortfall for a while through debt, which cannot grow indefinitely and ultimately must be repaid or repudiated. This idea has become even more relevant in the wake of the debt-fueled Great Financial Crisis of 2008 and its profligate (in money-printing terms) aftermath.

So how do renewable energy technologies come into the broad picture? With ever-increasing efficiencies and perhaps improving EROI, renewables have made notable progress in both developed and developing worlds. Denmark is often touted as the poster child of renewable energy, with wind power accounting for a record 39 percent of the electricity consumed by the nation in 2014.[15] Moreover, the Danish government has set an ambitious goal of deriving 100 percent of its energy — including that used for heating, transport, and industry — from non–fossil fuel sources by 2050. (That Denmark can continue to export fossil fuels from its North Sea fields while becoming independent from them is another story.) In contrast, the renewable energy story in some parts of the developing world is more about local, decentralized efforts. For example, private initiatives are providing rural African and Indian communities with the means to recharge cell phones through portable solar rechargers, allowing them to leapfrog development through access to communication and knowledge through the World Wide Web.

But practical considerations, such as the amount of real estate needed for truly large-scale solar and wind power generation in many developed countries, the "not in my backyard" (NIMBY) issues, or cost-effective energy storage to smooth intermittencies, raise questions about how quickly and effectively solar and wind can offset the decline in nuclear generation and its replacement by high-emissions coal in the OECD countries. Global energy demand, driven by rapidly urbanizing emerging economies, has also been growing too fast for renewable technologies to keep up and play a significantly larger role in global aggregate energy consumption. And nuclear energy, the great unfulfilled hope of the 1950s and 1960s in the United States, provider of about 75 percent of France's electricity, and still the hope of rapidly developing economies around the world (particularly in Asia outside Japan), poses challenges regarding safety, uranium supplies for traditional fission, nuclear proliferation potential, and disposal of radioactive waste.

Times They Are a-Changin'?

Many observers of technological innovation point out that the lives of even the lowest-income denizens of the advanced world are orders of magnitude better than those of the most exalted aristocracy two centuries ago. They would list access to modern medical care, electricity, and mobility as being among the most important improvements and, most recently, unfettered access to a tremendous trove of digitized knowledge. But others would argue that the pace of technological change seems to have slowed over the past several decades. We feel this intuitively when watching views of the brave new future in the popular media of four decades ago, from *The Jetsons* to *2001: A Space Odyssey*, and note that our primary mode of transport is not the flying car, and we are not staying at the Hilton in orbit around the Earth on our way to a permanent presence on the moon. As technology entrepreneur Peter Thiel and colleagues put it on their venture capital firm web page, "Instead of Captain Kirk and the USS Enterprise, we got the Priceline Negotiator and a cheap flight to Cabo."[16]

Take a step back and ponder how our daily lives have changed during our lifetimes, at least in the developed world. For me at age fifty, many essential technologies such as clean running water, electricity, telecommunications, and transport are not fundamentally different from when I was a small child. This is not to belittle tremendous advances such as computing (and Moore's Law), the Internet, gene mapping, and nanotechnologies. But a person from the developed world who entered a state of suspended animation since the middle of the twentieth century would wake up today and find that most of the changes to daily life are, with a few notable exceptions in computing and perhaps biotechnology or medicine, evolutionary (the toilets, at least in Japan, mostly come equipped with convenient little sprays for washing one's behind) rather than revolutionary (I don't have to leave the house to hit the cold and smelly outhouse anymore). But imagine living through the mid-nineteenth century to the beginning of the twentieth century in the industrializing world, when many of these basic, life-changing technologies were being widely introduced, and the world must have changed very dramatically over a lifetime indeed.

Some studies focused on innovation and its impact on the social and economic realms suggest that genuine, life-changing innovations have been slowing over the past century. If true, this trend would follow an increasingly familiar pattern: as socioeconomic complexity grows and "low-hanging fruit" have been harvested, the costs of introducing the next innovation become ever larger. Although tremendous progress in such areas as AI/robotics, genetic engineering, and nanotechnologies promises to keep changing our lives, perhaps even in revolutionary ways, we need to keep in mind that these innovations must also help enable fairly rapid productivity and efficiency advances in primary sectors — food production and resource extraction, broadened to encompass overall energy production — to sustain exponential economic and population growth. And on the flip side, automation through software and robotics — one of the most pervasive accelerating phenomena — threatens to eliminate many jobs permanently and challenge the very structure of the mass-market capitalist system that has served us well since the Industrial Revolution.

In the quest for exponential growth, humanity faces a plethora of major challenges: population growth, urbanization, food production, resource depletion, and an ecological "footprint" that is growing ever larger than the ability of Earth to support the activity. As a species, we already exceed the Earth's sustainable carrying capacity by 50 percent or more, and would need about two Earths by 2030 if current demographic and resource-use trends continue. But for the economically advanced world to suggest that developing nations should, for the sake of the Earth, minimize or forgo stages of industrial development common in the West — "leapfrog" is the positively spun jargon — smacks of outrageous egocentrism. On balance, and despite the optimism I share about innovation, I feel that those who ring alarm bells about our civilization today have the upper hand. Thanks to two centuries of exponential growth powered by extensive fossil fuel use, our complex socioeconomic and environmental cycles are becoming increasingly synchronized to make chaotic disruption more likely — disruption that will almost certainly be accompanied by great cost in blood and treasure.

Against this backdrop, clean and abundant energy is the most important enabler to help preserve our civilization. Ancient cultures and societies collapsed because of growing complexity and reduced resilience, particularly in maintaining high production growth in their main source of energy: food. We still face considerable challenges — incredible waste, arable land availability, productivity plateaus, regional water availability and groundwater depletion, just to list a few — in securing the food we will need in the future to feed the next two billion mouths as well as the billions whose dietary patterns are changing rapidly. But if we single out a factor today that would help nudge humanity away from overshoot and collapse, it is the availability and growth of clean, cheap, and abundant thermodynamic energy to supplement and rapidly supplant energy currently derived from dirty fossil fuels.

Significant game-changers for energy are needed, if not to overcome decline by themselves, to at least buy time to tackle the array of interconnected challenges facing humanity.

Nuclear Technologies Forgone and to Be Decided

From the 1950s to the 1970s, scientists and engineers at Oak Ridge National Laboratory in Tennessee developed and tested nuclear reactors designed to be eventually fueled by thorium, an element much more plentiful than uranium and which, as it very slowly decays, accounts for much of Earth's internal heat. Although inherently stable and requiring a kick-start from a small dose of uranium, thorium-fueled reactors can produce, for a given amount of fuel, over thirty times the power of reactors powered by enriched uranium, while leaving only a small fraction of the waste behind — waste that requires a couple of centuries rather than thousands of years to decay to background radioactivity levels. They could also be used to burn nuclear waste currently piling up around the world looking for permanent homes. And compared to the uranium-fueled, large-scale light water reactors generating power around the world today, well-designed thorium reactors would be immune from the danger of catastrophic meltdown, and would be very unsuited for producing weapons-grade fissile material. So why is thorium-based power not a major and growing portion of the power generation mix for humanity?

Perhaps the effective disappearance of thorium-based power for forty years can be traced to the impetus behind developing the atomic bomb, its military-run provenance, subsequent geopolitical setting, and the nuclear (and nuclear-powered) arms race. The slow recognition of thorium as a promising new avenue for developing a major power source, particularly in the United States but in other countries as well, presents an illuminating case study of promising innovation that was neglected by entrenched, conservative business and bureaucratic interests.

Thorium-based power, along with other modern reactor technologies that are far safer, more efficient, and more proliferation-resistant than the light water reactors (LWRS) commonly used today, is a significant potential game-changing technology for alleviating humanity's slow-burn crisis of fossil fuel use driving undesirable planetary change. The benefits of cheap, reliable, and abundant power with minimal carbon emissions are profound: it can meet the accelerating demand for power from countries eager to approach the current living standards of the developed world, be used to desalinate oceans cost-effectively to provide plentiful water for industry and agriculture, and perhaps someday even make a cost-effective "hydrogen economy" possible.

Developing and deploying the means of providing clean, reliable, and sufficiently high EROI energy is as close to a panacea for the world's challenges as we are likely to find, if we recognize that electorates, politicians, and consumers have very limited attention spans, particularly for highly complex, interrelated issues calling for fundamental and painful changes in the way we live (or aspire to live, for the developing world). And the plethora of technologies and computing power that may well help save humanity from decline is in a race against growing complexity, resource depletion, and environmental degradation.

A notable success in global efforts to address the adverse impact of humans on the environment was the Montreal Protocol on Substances that Deplete the Ozone Layer. Signed in 1987, in force since 1989, and revised seven times, it has been ratified by 197 states, widely implemented, and atmospheric concentrations of the substances covered have leveled off or decreased since it came into effect. But the agreement was such a notable success because of its specificity, the handful of companies who accounted for the bulk of chlorofluorocarbon (CFC) production, and the rapid development of safer substitutes, although the most common of them still pose problems as greenhouse gases. The treaty incorporated supportive measures such as the development of action plans or financial assistance that could be taken in the event of noncompliance by a signatory; encouraged the transfer of technology to reduce CFC emissions; and provided financial mechanisms to help ease the transition to substitutes. Also instrumental was U.S. leadership, notably absent in the current climate change agenda until very recently.

Difficulties in negotiating and implementing the broad-ranging Kyoto Protocol, which the United States has never ratified, and its follow-on agreements represent a stark and disturbing contrast. Humanity, in its rapidly growing socioeconomic complexity, urgently needs abundant sources of efficient energy, both in terms of energy return on energy invested and environmental cost. In conjunction with increased energy efficiencies and further deployment of renewables, safer, cheaper, more proliferation-resistant nuclear power is a game-changer.

As for the constant dispute between, for the sake of simplification, the neo-Malthusians and the Cornucopians, each camp makes eminently valid points that are not necessarily mutually exclusive: that the Earth is subject to physical limits and cannot support limitless exponential growth, but technology may be accelerating at a pace that will allow us, in currently unimaginable ways, to overcome many limits and prevent or undo some of the damage we cause. But there is little doubt that, in largely conducting business as usual, humanity is like a bug waiting for a windshield: the passing traffic of problems will eventually lead to an unfortunate outcome. It therefore behooves us to focus on currently feasible ways to mitigate the most pernicious effects of the Anthropogene age while humanity slowly but, one hopes, surely devises more permanent solutions for living on the only home we have.

Smoke lowering down from chimney-
pots, making a soft black drizzle, with
flakes of soot in it as big as full-grown
snow-flakes—gone into mourning, one
might imagine, for the death of the sun.
—**Charles Dickens (1812–1870)**

It's good to be in something from the
ground floor. I came too late for that and
I know. But lately, I'm getting the feeling
that I came in at the end. The best is over.
—**Tony Soprano (1959–2007?)**

2

JOULES ARE A SOCIETY'S BEST FRIEND

A ghostly little island dots the sea off the coast of Nagasaki, Japan. Gun-kanjima, or "Battleship Island," was once a thriving but now abandoned coal mining community. A ragged concrete city rising from the sea, it served as the model for arch-villain Raoul Silva's lair in the 2012 James Bond film *Skyfall*. Residents of the island next door had been using its exposed coal as a household fuel for centuries, but the first mine shaft was not dug until 1886, during the frenzied effort of the Meiji era to catch up with the West. During the 1890s, ownership passed to the Mitsubishi Company, which dug additional shafts, built infrastructure such as living quarters and a school, and began expanding the island. The local Nagasaki paper began calling it Gunkanjima instead of its official name, Hashima, in 1921 because its profile and gray concrete hue resembled that of the battleship *Tosa*, being built at the time at the Nagasaki shipyard. The battleship was never completed and scuttled to adhere to the Washington Naval Treaty of 1922, half a century before its namesake island was abandoned.

Gunkanjima, August 2014
(photo by author).

Like any coal mine, Gunkanjima was a dangerous place to work: miners descended six hundred meters before digging coal out of seams at the end of shafts beneath the seafloor, some as deep as one thousand meters, and accidents claimed over a thousand miners' lives. As able-bodied Japanese men were sucked into the maws of the military machine during the Second World War, about seven hundred Chinese and Korean laborers were forced to dig the coal under appalling conditions and starvation rations — it is said that over a hundred died. Some forced laborers, unable to bear the conditions, threw themselves off the seawall or drowned trying to swim back to the mainland.

Gunkanjima benefited from the rapid industrial reconstruction of Japan following the war. By the late 1950s, supported by all the amenities of a small city — schools, stores, hospital, restaurants, a movie theater, betting parlors, even a temple and shrine — the island's population reached a peak of over five thousand. The 6.3-hectare (16 acre) island's population density was nine times that of metropolitan Tokyo, and perhaps the highest ever recorded in the world. The work was hard and hazardous, but the pay was better than on the mainland, and the living was tolerable, if cramped. But as oil and gas replaced coal as the main fuels powering Japan's industrial growth, the mine was closed, and all inhabitants were evacuated over the course of three months in 1974. Gunkanjima is not only a relic of Japan's coal age but, like Pripyat next to Chernobyl, an eerie example of a modern community that quickly lost all its residents. It is also a cautionary tale of what happens to cities, wholly dependent on bringing in food and essential goods from outside, when they lose their reason to exist.

Before the advent of internal combustion mechanization, civilizations and empires needed a lot of energy to build cities, roads, and aqueducts, as well as maintain internal peace and defend or expand territory. The means of capturing and distributing this energy was predictable, efficient agriculture, through which the sun's energy would be harvested as storable and transportable food to power society. Grains provided the core of human diets, while plentiful animal fodder enabled draft animals to provide the supplementary kinetic energy necessary to build and maintain complex civilizations. In his book *The Upside of Down*, Thomas Homer-Dixon points out that, though the causes often cited range from failure of governance to barbarian invasion, the decline of ancient Rome was very much an energy crisis brought about by the inability of food production and distribution to keep up with the demand from inefficiencies and increasing complexity, rather than merely the oft-cited and vague politico-economic concept of imperial overstretch.[1]

Prior to the development of a reliable steam engine, horse and other animal power were, along with limited uses of wind, water, animal/vegetable fats, wood, and stored kinetic energy (think windup clocks or ancient catapults), the primary means of preindustrial civilizations to harness and utilize energy. The diffusion of technologies to increase output dramatically from concentrated reservoirs of stored energy — coal in particular — set the stage for the Industrial Revolution and humanity's increasing, nonlinear impact on the state of the Earth. It is difficult to overstate the impact of this shift from agriculture-based energy to the significantly higher energy density of fossil fuels.

Joule is a standard measurement of energy, work, or heat, named after James Prescott Joule, an English brewer and physicist who published much of his work during the mid-nineteenth century, a less-specialized era when running a brewery and producing seminal works in physics were not mutually exclusive, but perhaps even complementary (how does one use heat most efficiently in brewing?). Specific energy is defined as energy per unit mass (joules per kilogram), and energy density is the energy stored in a unit of volume (joules per liter). Though sometimes used interchangeably, energy density is particularly important in transport, as gases must be compressed under very high pressure to be used efficiently as fuel.

Humanity has accessed ever more powerful sources of energy throughout history. If previous ages were defined by materials used to produce implements, whether stone or bronze, the industrial epoch can be defined by its leading-edge fuels: coal, oil, and the stunted atomic era. At about twice the specific energy of wood, high-quality coal was a much more efficient source of energy than burning wood or relying on animal or early wind and water power. At about 46 megajoules per kilogram, oil does even better, with three times the specific energy of wood, as well as being better suited for transportation use. And splitting uranium-235 atoms is off the scale compared to mere molecular rearrangement, yielding 80 million megajoules/kg.

Coal and the Industrial Revolution

The foundations of the Industrial Revolution in England remain a subject of debate. Historians cite factors ranging from the "Protestant work ethic" to the enclosure movement or the establishment of a patent regime in 1624. Whatever the enablers, the effects of industrialization were profound and far-reaching. By the start of the 1800s England and the United States were experiencing rapid urbanization and industrialization, and continental European countries such as Belgium, France, Germany, and Sweden were hard on the heels of the early movers by mid-century.

The Industrial Revolution was very much about coal: its low cost and high energy density made it the key element in a positive feedback loop of technological advances in mining, industrial processes, and transport. The accelerating demand for coal from urbanization and deforestation drove innovations that led to the introduction of the steam engine in coal mining, which led to major advances in industrial mechanization and transport. As manufacturing no longer relied on proximity to running water to run mills or forests to provide charcoal for ironworks, coal allowed industry to be concentrated more efficiently and accelerated urbanization.

In echoes of contemporary concerns about extensive deforestation in the poorest areas of the world today — not to mention the tragic inefficiencies of families spending hours daily gathering firewood for heating and cooking — royal commissions to study the state of forests in England during the reign of Elizabeth I (1558–1603) were distressed to find that England's forests were dwindling rapidly from the clearing of land for sheep grazing and the use of firewood for building, heating, and producing iron. The decline was exacerbated by increasing urbanization and compounded by the bitter cold of the Little Ice Age, the unusually frigid period in Europe from about 1350 to 1850. The most obvious fuel to replace firewood for heating was coal, which was plentiful and cheaper for the common folk, though it would take decades more before the gentry were gradually weaned from the cozy wood fire and took to burning coal.

As early as the 1660s, English botanist John Evelyn described coal fires as "those hellish volcanos, disgorging from the brew-houses, sope and salt-boilers, chandlers, hat-makers, glass-houses, forges, lime-kilns, and other trades, using such quantities of sea-coals, one of whose funnels vomits more smoak than all the culinary and chamber-fires of the whole parish, . . . perniciously infecting the ambient air, with a black melancholy canopy, to the detriment of the most valuable moveables and furniture of the inhabitants, and the whole country about it."[2] It was also during this period that coal began to be charred, in a process analogous to making charcoal out of wood, to produce coke, which reduced its smell and smoke when burned. Coke was initially used for roasting malt to produce pale ale and, by the beginning of the next century, as fuel to produce cast iron, in lieu of charcoal.

Like all natural resources, coal extracted from quarrying and shallow mining — the easy pickings — became increasingly scarce, forcing the mines to go deeper and below the water table. If the accidents that occur with alarming regularity (particularly in China) today make coal mining seem dirty and dangerous, it was even more brutish and nasty during the last millennium. Among the constant and high-probability unpleasantness faced by the miners were tunnel collapse, asphyxiation from carbon dioxide, carbon monoxide poisoning, catastrophic gas explosions, and drowning. Persistent water seepage and flooding were particularly challenging for mine productivity and addressed by digging elaborate drainage tunnels or, if too deep for gravity drainage, human-powered bucket chains or animal-powered pumps. But as the demand for coal grew and mines became ever larger and more complex, a reliable means of conquering the water was sorely needed.

Like other technologies that were applied later in a range of areas beyond their initial provenance, the steam engine was originally used as a means of pumping water out of coal mines much more efficiently than through the use of humans or horses. As coal mines had to be dug ever deeper, an ironmonger and amateur inventor named Thomas Newcomen designed the first practical steam engine to remove water from coal mines efficiently, and his design was first put to work at a coal mine in 1712. Soon hundreds of Newcomen steam engines — still inefficient compared to later designs and therefore sometimes quite massive — were in use at coal mines around England and Scotland, but their use was largely limited to pumping water. Despite allowing massive productivity improvements, steam engines did little to eliminate the dangers of coal mining, as illustrated by the Hartley Pit disaster in 1862, when the beam of the pumping engine fell into the mine, trapping and killing 204 miners. Covered extensively by the burgeoning popular press, the accident prompted the adoption of regulations requiring all coal mines in England to have at least two shafts.

It took the Scottish inventor James Watt, the namesake for the derived unit of power familiar to most of us mainly in the context of electricity (a watt is defined as one joule per second), to turn the steam engine into a more efficient machine suited for all types of industrial applications. Watt improved upon Newcomen's design through the use of a condenser to obviate the wasteful need to repeatedly cool and reheat the steam engine's cylinder, and improved the steam engine's power fourfold. Watt also adopted the term "horsepower"—a quaint reminder now of an era long gone — to compare the output of his steam engines to the power of draft horses. Among his many inventions, Watt developed compound engines and throttle valves for controlling engine power, as well as the "sun and planet" gear to convert the vertical motion produced by steam engines into rotary motion (and bypass a patent already held on the crank). Watt's famous and productive partnership with foundry owner Matthew Boulton spanned from 1775 to 1800, and their developments to refine the steam engine set the stage for the widespread use of coal-fueled steam power in myriad industrial and key transport applications.

By the first half of the 1800s, factories became massive cathedrals of production: the largest coal-powered textile mills of Manchester employed thousands of workers each, performing repetitive, specialized functions. William Murdoch, an employee and later partner at Boulton & Watt, developed coal gas lighting during the last decade of the 1700s, and its widespread adoption for industrial lighting during the first decade of the 1800s allowed factories to work around the clock in shifts. Like the well-documented abuses in coal mining, child labor was used for maximizing production efficiency and lowering labor costs.

By the mid-1800s, more people in England worked in the cities than in the countryside, as advances in agriculture and industrialization made small-scale farming and cottage industries obsolete, and jobs that provided alternative livelihoods were increasingly concentrated in urban centers. The rapid industrialization and urbanization witnessed in England from the late 1700s also brought with it tremendous pollution, urban squalor, and new social problems. Manchester in the mid-1800s was fertile ground for Friedrich Engels, the eldest son of a wealthy German cotton manufacturer sent by his parents to wean him away from his revolutionary tendencies. Unfortunately their designs backfired as he observed the wretched conditions under which the working class toiled, and, with Karl Marx, he honed their theories into their famous socioeconomic worldview — an unattributed Russian saying goes that Marx got everything about capitalism right but everything about communism wrong.

A succession of cities in Scotland and England including Glasgow, Manchester, and London were nicknamed "the Big Smoke" during the Industrial Revolution, owing to the poor air quality caused by burning coal. Perhaps the most famous phenomena caused by coal soot and sulfur dioxide emissions were the London "pea-souper" fogs, described (if not called that specifically) by authors such as Charles Dickens and T. S. Eliot. The descriptions of the atrocious air quality experienced in England at the time are remarkably suggestive of the haze that covers many of China's major cities today. In short, led by England but quickly followed by the other rapidly industrializing nations, it was during the 1800s that humanity began to have a significant impact on the global environment.

Coal was very dirty in the 1800s and remains very dirty today. A 2008 report from the European Environment Agency estimates that power generation in Europe from coal emits about twice the CO_2, three times the nitrogen oxide (not a greenhouse gas per se like nitrous oxide, but, along with sulfur dioxide, a major cause of acid rain), and orders of magnitude larger amounts of sulfur dioxide and particulate matter as does generating the same amount of power from gas.[3] Similarly, the International Panel on Climate Change (IPCC) aggregated the life-cycle estimates for global greenhouse gas (GHG) emissions from various electricity generation technologies and found that the median estimate for coal is 1,001 grams of CO_2 equivalent per kilowatt-hour (CO_2e/kWh), slightly more than 840g CO_2e/kWh for oil and more than twice that of natural gas at 469g CO_2e/kWh.[4] Moreover, ash from burning coal in power plants (fly ash) — mandated since the 1960s in the United States to be largely captured and separated rather than being released through exhaust flues — contains traces of uranium and thorium in addition to toxic substances such as arsenic, mercury, and lead. An Oak Ridge National Laboratory study estimates that the energy content of the nuclear fuel released in coal combustion is more than half the energy content of the coal burned, not to mention the radioactivity released.[5]

Despite progress in scrubbing emissions to reduce the most pernicious particles and pollutants such as mercury, wholesale systematic carbon capture and storage (CCS) technologies that can be applied to the power generation industry to reduce carbon emissions by 80–90 percent have not been widely deployed and will require burning about one-third more coal to produce the same amount of power. Pointing out that governments have announced a total of $24 billion in funding in the past fourteen years but with only one system in commercial operation, the *Financial Times* quips that "few technologies have had so much money thrown at them for so many years by so many governments and companies, with such feeble results."[6] Storage in geological formations or deep in the oceans have been considered as possible methods for sequestration, though the latter has lost luster as it would contribute to ocean acidification. But uncertainty remains about how secure geological storage would be over the long term, and bequeathing an Earth pocked with billions of tons of greenhouse gases to future generations is arguably much less appealing than one in which nuclear waste is stored in a handful of long-term depositories.

Though the latest IPCC reports cite CCS as a technology that will likely be a part of the effort to mitigate carbon emissions, the agency also estimates that capture and geological storage would increase coal electricity costs by up to 100 percent, making renewables, nuclear, and gas much more competitive by comparison.[7] Nor do other ways to reduce emissions from coal come cheap. For example, one technology Japan hopes to tap in order to cap emissions while relying on coal power in the post-Fukushima future is "integrated gasification combined cycle," or IGCC, a process that turns coal into gas-synthesis gas (syngas) to burn, while using the steam and exhaust heat generated during the process to operate a secondary steam turbine. Although more efficient and lower in sulfur dioxide and mercury emissions, IGCC plants are more than twice as expensive as standard coal-fired plants of similar capacity to build and operate when combined with CCS.[8]

If there is one obvious villain in the tale of human-produced greenhouse gas emissions, it is coal. Critics of nuclear power often point to the human and environmental costs of nuclear power, but for coal, the costs are far higher, including the vast number of lives estimated to have been affected by its use. A 2013 study, for example, estimates that the airborne pollution problem in coal-intensive northern China has cut life expectancy by an average of 5.5 years, suggesting 2.5 billion life years, for the five hundred million residents there during the 1990s.[9] Although the U.S. EIA has estimated that the United States alone has enough coal reserves to last two hundred years, burning so much of it that we worry globally about "peak coal" after "peak oil" just seems like a really bad idea.

The Oil Age

As the Industrial Revolution progressed, fossil fuels became increasingly common for transport applications, with coal supplanting wood for railroad engines and also used for powering ships. Early wood-burning steam locomotives had an unfortunate tendency to spit out hot embers and set passengers' garments on fire, and partially open passenger cars were equipped with buckets of sand to deal with such unpleasantness. Coal was much better in this regard, but the soot produced meant that trainmen could no longer wear snazzy white uniforms, and black uniforms became standard. With the development of crude oil and its distillates and their dominance in powering automobiles (although there was a brief period at the beginning of the automotive age when electric cars also were commercially available alongside gasoline-powered vehicles), oil increasingly became the fuel of choice for transport by the turn of the twentieth century.

The ability to use abundant energy for transportation of raw materials and finished goods ever more cheaply meant that distances were decreasingly relevant and allowed tremendous efficiencies in seeking out comparative advantage, though not always to the advantage of colonies, territories, and burgeoning nation-states that produced the raw materials necessary for the industrialized world. And with many major navies making the switch to oil from coal (including the Royal Navy, despite an abundance of domestic coal) and the genesis of mechanized warfare in the Great War, oil was well on its way to become the dominant fuel for transport applications.

Oil defined the twentieth century in much the same way that coal did the nineteenth century. With its association with automobiles and, later, with the jet age, oil was rather more glamorous than sooty, dirty coal. Oil increasingly became the dominant fuel for transport and feedstock for a bewildering variety of petrochemicals and new materials (reminiscent of the famous line in the 1967 movie *The Graduate*, in which the young protagonist is given sage advice about his post-collegiate future: "I just want to say one word to you — just one word . . . plastics"). Much has been written about John D. Rockefeller's Standard Oil Trust, usually in the context of the pantheon of monopolist "robber barons" from America's Gilded Age. But pre-Rockefeller, oil was a superb example of the problems stemming from excessively diffuse ownership, with numerous wildcatters exploiting and often squandering the resource while driving prices down to uneconomic levels. Despite the distaste felt by many regarding his monopolistic practices, Rockefeller's trust rationalized production and saved oil for future use by holding back supply at times to optimize price — a function that, for a while after the Standard Oil breakup, would be performed in the

United States by the Texas Railroad Commission (despite its name), and later internationally by OPEC starting in the early 1960s.

The impact of OPEC withholding supply after the Yom Kippur War in 1973 between Israel and its Arab neighbors was particularly dramatic despite the minimal amounts withheld, as it came shortly after the peaking of conventional crude supply in the United States (before the tapping of Alaskan fields) and the end of the post–World War II Bretton Woods accord and resultant U.S. dollar devaluation. More "mature" readers may remember that crude went from three to twelve dollars per barrel in the United States, spurring gasoline rationing based on odd- and even-number license plates and dramatic calls for energy conservation, including President Jimmy Carter, in a cozy cardigan on national television, calling the energy crisis the "moral equivalent of war." In a fascinating example of the unexpected consequences of energy price shocks, Japanese consumers lined up for hours to hoard toilet paper, as rumors of catastrophic shortages led to that product's rapid disappearance from shop shelves.

A brief look at the concept of peak oil is appropriate at this point. Peak oil can refer to the point beyond which a well or oil field's rate of extraction begins to decline, but is more commonly applied to oil extraction more broadly at the national or global level. Petroleum expert M. King Hubbard is commonly credited with pioneering the concept during the 1950s, when he correctly predicted that U.S. oil production would follow a bell-shaped curve and peak during the late 1960s to early 1970s. Despite a dramatic uptick in domestic production after the opening of the Alaskan pipeline and the repeal by the Reagan administration of Carter-era oil price controls, U.S. oil production has been unable to exceed the peak set in 1970. With technological advances in horizontal drilling and hydraulic fracturing ("fracking") developed during the past decade, we may see a second peak for U.S. crude production yet, though recent low oil and gas prices have dented this prospect. In its annual Statistical Review of World Energy, the oil giant BP points out that U.S. oil output overtook that of Saudi Arabia in 2014 (though some observers criticize BP's inclusion of liquids that come from natural gas wells, which have lower energy content than crude, and if excluded would make Russia number one, followed by Saudi Arabia and the United States).[10] But the challenges of tapping "tight oil"—not to be confused with oil shale, which is closer to coal than oil, requires much more energy to process, and has heavy environmental impacts along the way — dictate that prices must be significantly higher than break-even levels for conventional drilling. Few doubt that one of Saudi Arabia's objectives for refusing to curb production and helping crude prices fall by half during the second half of 2014 was to squeeze high-price producers, like those in the United States, out of business.

Experts have argued for several years about whether oil production is peaking globally, with the debate muddied by Saudi Arabia's long-standing refusal to open up about its reserve figures, but there is increasing acceptance that the peak will occur within the decade or so, if it hasn't already. Demand for oil may peak as well, driven by structural demand declines in the developed world and increasing adoption of alternatives globally. In turn, major projects in deep water or the Arctic that require oil prices to stay above $100 a barrel or so to be economical would be shelved, paring future supply. It is therefore useful to consider a more meaningful dimension to the peak oil debate — extraction cost.

When one considers the energy return on investment (EROI), a key concept we touched on earlier, it becomes apparent that EROI for U.S. oil and gas extraction has been declining since the early 1900s. A study conducted in 2011 by researchers at the State University of New York and Boston University found that the EROI for discoveries in the U.S. oil and gas industry — the ratio of the mean quantity of energy (over a five-year period bracketed around the year in question) discovered from oil and gas activities over the quantity of energy used in that activity — fell dramatically from 1,200:1 in 1919 to 5:1 in 2007. The slow long-term erosion of production EROI — the quantity of energy supplied from gas and oil produced over the quantity of energy used in that activity over a given year — is illustrated by a decline from 20:1 during the period between 1919 to 1972 to about 8:1 in 1982, a bounce to 17:1 between 1986 to 2002, then a fall again to about 11:1 in the mid-to-late 2000s. (The study's authors attribute the apparent bounce during the last two decades of the twentieth century to a lower intensity of drilling.) Although focused on the United States, the study shows how, in general, increasing amounts of energy must be expended to discover and extract a unit of fossil fuel as the easy pickings are exploited, making them increasingly expensive.[11] Increasing reliance on tar sands and shale oil for production threatens to lower North American oil EROI even further.

Total U.S. crude oil demand for 2011 and 2012 was about 6.9 and 6.8 billion barrels per year, respectively, according to the U.S. Energy Information Administration (EIA), down from the peak of 7.6 billion in 2005 before the financial crisis. A $10 increase in the price of crude sustained over the course of one year therefore translates to an extra $68 billion fuel bill for the United States, or about 0.4 percent of 2012 GDP, and studies have shown that every major U.S. recession for the past forty years has been preceded by a spike in oil prices.[12] The price spike in West Texas Intermediate crude oil from about $70 a barrel in 2007 to a high above $140 a barrel in 2008 may have been a major factor (along with subprime mortgage speculation) in causing the global recession that followed.

Extreme oil price volatility can also be harmful to major energy-producing nations. Many oil-producing countries finance much of their government spending from oil exports, so they tend to benefit from higher prices; but many also subsidize domestic fuel use heavily. An extreme example would be Venezuela, which sells gasoline to domestic consumers at only six cents a gallon, but less extreme examples can be found in many Persian Gulf oil states. For example, Saudi Arabia sells gasoline domestically for sixteen cents a liter, which translates into an estimated $80 billion a year in forgone revenue.[13] In Asia, despite its long history as an oil producer since the foundation of Royal Dutch Petroleum (now Royal Dutch Shell) at the end of the nineteenth century, Indonesia became a net importer around 2008, and government finances periodically came under pressure from heavy domestic fuel subsidies, which encouraged energy inefficiency and exacerbated the nation's fiscal plight, especially during periods of global price spikes. The administration of President Joko Widodo finally scrapped gasoline subsidies and capped the subsidy for diesel at the end of 2014, during a period of low oil prices: how domestic consumers and voters will respond to a period of dramatically higher prices remains to be seen.

Although technical divergences between the U.S. West Texas Intermediate crude and the more international Brent crude benchmark have occurred over the past few years, driven by North American pipeline inefficiencies and the forty-year-old U.S. ban on crude exports (lifted at the end of 2015), the price of oil is still set generally by the marginal global supplier or consumer. On the supply side, easily accessible reserves have been tapped steadily, and new reserve discoveries are almost exclusively more expensive to capture or process, from deepwater deposits to shale oil or tar sands. Moreover, the largest oil-exporting nations find themselves situated along the arc of instability stretching from Iran to North Africa. Meanwhile, global crude demand continues to grow — by about 6 percent from 2005 to 2012, according to the EIA, despite a temporary plateau during 2008 and 2009. So even allowing for improvements in efficiency and substitutability, the oil market will remain vulnerable to major supply shocks for some time yet.

There is another element to the "peak oil" debate: as with coal, there are serious questions about whether we can afford to keep burning oil if all the costs, including those of addressing the impact of global warming, are incorporated. It is likely that, regardless of reserves being made increasingly accessible through technological advances, the broader costs of burning the dirtiest fossil fuels will become increasingly prohibitive — in other words, for how much longer can we continue to burn them at anywhere near the current pace as a civilization?

Got Gas?

Natural gas has traditionally been oil's somewhat less glamorous, local cousin. Although scoring high marks on specific energy (a bit higher than oil when measured in terms of megajoules per kilogram) and for half of coal's carbon emissions, gas must be liquefied at about $-162°C$ ($-260°F$) and reduced to about one six-hundredth of its original volume to approach the energy density of oil. There are not that many facilities worldwide for processing liquefied natural gas (LNG), as they cost billions of dollars, and turning natural gas into liquid consumes a lot of energy and so decreases its effective energy density significantly.

Given the properties of natural gas, it is less suited for many transportation applications, such as aviation. But liquid petroleum gas (LPG, propane or butane), widely used for heating in areas that are off electricity and gas grids, has been used as a motor fuel since the 1940s and now powers over twenty-one million vehicles worldwide, with over half concentrated in five countries — Italy, South Korea, Poland, Russia, and Turkey.[14] Aided by policies and incentives to use less polluting and carbon-emitting fuels, compressed natural gas (CNG, methane) use is also growing around the world to power municipal vehicles such as buses, corporate fleets, and small commercial passenger vehicles such as taxis. In Sweden, some municipal buses are fueled by CNG from landfill biogas, a cycle that lowers greenhouse gas emissions significantly.

The market for natural gas historically has been fragmented into many regional markets, often pegged to the price of oil and sometimes wildly disparate in price terms. Natural gas has grabbed the limelight increasingly over the past several years, as the new extraction technologies of hydraulic fracturing, or fracking, promise to ameliorate the impact of peak oil on transport and of dirty coal on power generation, particularly in the United States. But because these techniques require tremendous water use, laced with proprietary chemicals, they also promise to cause major headaches, particularly in areas of water scarcity and significant competing demands from agriculture or industry.

The hydraulic fracking boom sweeping the oil and gas industry in North America has inspired commentators to predict a renaissance in the U.S. energy and manufacturing sectors in the years to come. McKinsey Global Institute estimates that the United States could add 2 to 4 percent ($380 to $690 billion) to annual GDP and create up to 1.7 million jobs by 2020 if the potential is realized.[15] Others are not as sanguine, pointing out that output from tight gas and oil wells declines rapidly, and that these wells have far shorter productive lives than conventional wells, necessitating constant new drilling and investment; but most would agree that the development is nevertheless positive for the U.S. economy. Energy author Richard Heinberg argues, however, that increased production and hype around fracking in the United States is allowing the nation to not invest enough in renewable energy and in low-energy infrastructure to reduce its dependence on fossil fuels.[16] Whether tight oil and gas production can be sustained at high levels for many decades or will be shorter-lived, one can only hope that the United States does not squander any windfall and instead follows a prudent path, similar to that taken by Norway — which pared budget deficits and created a huge sovereign wealth fund during the North Sea oil boom — not easy during times of stubborn underemployment and divisive politics.

Natural gas is also often associated with the use of more than one thermodynamic cycle in power production. The combined-cycle gas turbine (CCGT) uses the hot exhaust from a gas turbine to operate a steam power plant, to turn up to 60 percent of the energy into electricity — a significant improvement from the 35–40 percent efficiency typically found in standard fossil fuel power plants. Although they would run much less efficiently if constantly turned on and off to provide backup, CCGT plants are often cited as one of the ways, along with energy storage, to smooth intermittent power from renewable sources such as wind. With an EROI approaching that of coal-fueled power plants but with less than half the emissions, natural gas CCGT power plants are what advocates of a "N2N" (natural gas to nuclear) strategy such as journalist Robert Bryce have in mind to provide power during a transition to nuclear, particularly for the United States.[17]

The German government's 2011 decision to close all nuclear power plants by 2022 refocused attention not only on these plants' ability to cut carbon emissions (rising 1.6 percent in 2012 and 2 percent in 2013 as coal-fired plants replaced nuclear), but also on the geopolitical aspects of natural gas supplies to Europe: for example, Finland and Sweden get all their gas from Russia, the Czech Republic about 80 percent, and Germany about 40 percent. European dependence on Russian natural gas is also exacerbated by most Western European countries' reluctance to embrace fracking to the extent exhibited by the United States, due, among other factors, to population density and environmental concerns. Russia, eager to maintain the dependence of Central and Eastern Europe on its energy sources, plays a balancing game of using gas (and oil) to apply leverage in Europe: not so easy as to let its customers forget, but not so hard as to drive them to rely significantly less on Russian supply.

Geopolitics drive the pipeline construction projects to supply gas to Europe. For example, the completion of the €15 billion Nord Stream pipeline from Russia to Germany in 2012 allows Russia to bypass Ukraine, the other main route for gas pipelines into Central Europe. During the years after the dissolution of the Soviet Union, Russia supplied Ukraine with cut-rate gas in return for using pipelines passing through its territory to supply Europe. But against the backdrop of economic mismanagement and deteriorating relations with Russia, Ukraine began to fall in arrears on its payments and also diverted significant amounts for itself, leading the Russian gas giant Gazprom to cut the amount of gas flowing through the pipeline on several occasions. The result: major gas shortages in the rest of Europe during the winters of 2008 and 2009, which does not exactly endear you to your major customers. So Nord Stream, combined with the purchase of a major pipeline passing through friendly Commonwealth of Independent States member Belarus, has allowed Russia to reduce considerably its dependence on increasingly hostile Ukraine.

The geopolitics of gas can be seen on the other side of Eurasia as well. As part of Vladimir Putin's "pivot to Asia," Russia and China signed a major agreement in May 2014 for Gazprom to supply China with about a quarter of its current annual natural gas consumption for thirty years, starting in 2018. A long-discussed pipeline from Western Siberia to China, needed to execute the deal estimated to be worth about $400 billion, will finally be constructed at a cost of tens of billions of dollars. Developing natural gas infrastructure, including liquefaction facilities, in its Far East would also enable Russia to supply South Korea and Japan with LNG.

Japan's imports of liquefied natural gas picked up considerably to make up for the loss in electric generation capacity as nuclear power plants were shut down for extensive inspections following the Great Tohoku Earthquake. The cost to Japan of LNG, linked to the price of crude oil, increased from $10 per million Btu (British thermal unit) before Fukushima to $18 per million Btu in 2012, despite the price of natural gas delivered to the Henry Hub in the United States falling slightly to $3.50 per million Btu during the same period.[18] The burden of imported fossil fuels to Japan is estimated to have been 5.3 percent of Japan's GDP in 2013, considerably higher than the 3.1 percent for China and 1.5 percent for the United States,[19] and was one of the main drivers for the record $134 billion trade deficit for the fiscal year.

Busy Burning Fossils

Traditional fossil fuels — coal, oil, gas — will continue to play central roles in the world's primary energy mix for decades to come, according to most estimates. The International Energy Agency (IEA) is widely considered, along with the U.S. Energy Information Agency and BP, to be among the most authoritative sources of aggregated data on world energy production, usage, and projections. The IEA publishes a very handy (and free) data book on aggregated energy statistics every year, in which it slices and dices the data in very useful ways. At the most "macro" level, the IEA breaks down global energy supply by fuel according to the form found naturally before being subjected to conversion or transformation to other forms of energy (e.g., flowing water or coal to electricity), called primary energy. Using this measure, the world total primary energy supply of 13,541 million tons oil-equivalent (Mtoe) in 2013 was, broken down in order of magnitude, 31.1 percent oil, 28.9 percent coal, and 21.4 percent natural gas, with the balance composed of biofuels and waste (10.2 percent), nuclear (4.8 percent), hydro (2.4 percent), and "other" (1.2 percent, covering solar, wind, geothermal, etc). The unit "Mtoe" is probably unfamiliar to most readers unless they are energy enthusiasts, but is about 42 gigajoules (billion joules) and is often used for very big energy numbers, as using units such as giga and terajoules (trillion joules) becomes pretty unwieldy and unintuitive. Coal provided almost half the electricity generated globally in 2013 at 41.3 percent, followed by natural gas (21.7 percent), hydro (16.3 percent), nuclear (10.6 percent), and oil (4.4 percent). Solar, wind, geothermal, biofuels, and waste collectively contributed 5.7 percent, a notable increase from 0.6 percent in 1973 but still a minor part of the mix.[20]

The *BP Energy Outlook 2035* projects that total world primary energy consumption will increase by 37 percent from 2013 to 2035, with 96 percent of this growth coming from non-OECD nations. Power generation — where most coal is used — is expected to grow 51 percent by 2035, representing 58 percent of the total growth in energy consumed during this period, with energy used directly in industry accounting for another 24 percent. Although growth in coal use should slow, BP expects its use for electricity generation to continue to increase by 23 percent from 2013 to 2035. If, as forecast, coal still produces 36 percent of electricity globally in 2035, it will remain the biggest contributor by fuel to carbon emissions.[21] So, two centuries after the Industrial Revolution began with the extensive use of coal for industrial processes and for fuel, we are still relying heavily on that dirtiest of fuels to power our civilization Behind the wishful image of a brave new age of cleaner energy lurks our exceptionally hard-to-kick fossil fuel habit.

Now let's look at the numbers from the perspective of global greenhouse gas (GHG) emissions. According to the Global Carbon Project, out of the net increase in Earth's atmospheric CO_2 concentrations from 228 parts per million (ppm) in 1870 to 395 ppm in 2013, the cumulative contribution from coal, the single biggest, is estimated to be +87 ppm. The use of other fossil fuels contributed significantly as well, with oil and gas accounting for +65 ppm and +27 ppm respectively. Earth's land and oceans act as carbon "sinks" by absorbing more CO_2 than they produce, and are estimated to have soaked up about 145 ppm worth of CO_2. But again on the other side of the ledger, land-use change — human-induced use of land and forestry — contributed about +68 ppm, and cement production, which emits almost as much CO_2 by weight as the cement produced (from heating calcium carbonate and from the fuel used), added another +5 ppm. As can be seen from the Global Carbon Project's analysis, the use of fossil fuels overwhelmed land and ocean carbon sinks during the period and caused the net increase in CO_2.

Total CO_2 emissions from burning fossil fuels and cement production were 36.1 gigatonnes of carbon dioxide equivalent (Gt CO_2e, or billion metric tons in terms of CO_2) in 2013, or 61 percent above the Kyoto baseline year of 1990. (One tonne, called a metric ton in the United States, is equal to 1,000 kilograms, in contrast to the North American ton representing 2,000 pounds or 907 kilograms. Making things even more confusing is the British ton, which is equal to 2,240 pounds or 1,016 kilograms. In this book, I use tonne for the sake of consistency.) In 2013, the top four emitters — China (28 percent), the United States (14 percent), the EU (10 percent), and India (7 percent) — accounted for 58 percent of the global CO_2 emissions from fuel-burning activities. Other major contributors to emissions are land-use change — mainly cutting down forests and increasing agricultural land — and food waste.[22] A 2015 study by the British anti-waste organization Waste and Resources Action Program estimates that, mainly through agricultural processes that account for almost a quarter of global GHG emission, the one-third of food produced for human consumption that is wasted every year accounts for as much as 7 percent of total GHG emissions.[23]

According to the Global Carbon Project's per capita estimates, the United States emits 16.4 tonnes of GHGs per person (t/p), which is well over twice that of the EU (6.8 t/p), but China, at 7.2 t/p, has surpassed the EU and has the highest growth rate for this metric. Coal burning emitted over 15 Gt CO_2e, or 43 percent of all global emissions from fossil fuel use and cement production in 2013, followed by oil at 33 percent, gas at 18 percent, and cement at 6 percent. During the same year, coal accounted for 59 percent of the growth in global fossil fuel and cement emissions (oil was 18 percent, gas 10 percent).[24] In its latest report, the IPCC estimates that total GHG emissions from human activity, a number that incorporates other sources such as land use, must fall 40–70 percent from 2010 levels by 2050, and to near zero or below by 2100, to contain atmospheric concentration levels to within about 450 ppm CO_2e by 2100 — consistent with a likely chance to keep temperatures to within 2°C of preindustrial levels.[25] With fossil fuel use accounting for about two-thirds of all emissions today, these numbers illustrate the importance of minimizing such use.

The world produced a total of about 54 Gt CO_2e greenhouse gases in 2012 (fuel burning as well as direct emissions from agriculture, land-use change such as logging or clearing forests for agriculture, and organic waste), up 45 percent since 1990. The United Nations Environment Programme (UNEP) estimates that global GHG emissions would rise to about 59 Gt CO_2e in 2020, 68 Gt in 2030, and 87 Gt in 2050 under a business-as-usual scenario. Various countries have expressed their intention to reduce GHG emissions — called Intended Nationally Determined Contributions (INDCs) — going into 2014 year-end, which should dampen their growth below business-as-usual levels: if the pledges are kept (a big if), UNEP's median estimate is for emissions to come in around 52–54 Gt instead of 59 Gt in 2020. But global emissions should not be higher than 44 Gt in 2020 to have a likely chance of staying within the +2°C target, so there is still a gap of 8–10 Gt in further emissions reductions required. The UNEP estimates that the emissions gap will be 14–17 Gt in 2030 — more than a quarter to almost a third of all current emissions — the difference between 56–59 Gt if promises are kept versus the need to keep emissions within 42 Gt by 2030. Failure to curb emissions earlier increases the cuts, or even net carbon withdrawals, that need to be made further down the road.[26]

To put the scale of the challenge in perspective, the 14–17 Gt CO_2e gap forecast for 2030 is roughly about how much is emitted from burning coal around the world today, not just for power generation but for heating and industrial processes. As a simplistic exercise, replacing all coal-burning with low-carbon energy, whether renewable or nuclear, would fill the gap. Of course the reality is more complex, but the example highlights the importance of replacing the dirtiest fuels with cleaner alternatives as quickly as possible. It is fairly unlikely that this transition can take place in just fifteen years, but, as the IPCC and others explain, the longer we wait, the more onerous the necessary reductions in CO_2 — even net withdrawals from our atmosphere — will become, so it's time to "get on the bike." The alternatives put forth by those who believe that we can continue to have our coal cake and eat it, too — removing and sequestering mind-boggling amounts of the carbon we emit in geological formations, for example — are a distant second-best (and very expensive) but will increasingly become necessary if we keep on delaying meaningful emissions reductions.

3

SUSTAINABLE, SHUSTAINABLE

In 2007, lenders around the United States were busy originating mortgages by subprime borrowers to sell on to big financial players who were repackaging them into slices of securities that represented different levels of (badly) modeled risk. The well-documented excesses of the market participants, their reliance on flawed models, and provision of huge leverage continued even after the first signs of trouble: Citicorp ex-CEO Chuck Prince famously served up a wince-some morsel when he commented that "as long as the music's playing, you've got to get up and dance." Regulators and noted economists alike also failed to appreciate just how bad it could all become, as ex-Fed chairman Ben Bernanke insisted that Fannie Mae and Freddie Mac would "make it through the storm," two months before they were nationalized in 2008. What does this all have to do with resilience and sustainability? When it comes to complex, nonlinear systems, whether in our financial system or Earth's environment, we have a pretty poor grasp of how seemingly minor factors can cascade into major shifts to less desirable conditions. We also have a habit of ignoring warning signs about impending shifts so long as the going remains good on the surface. In fact, the global financial crisis (GFC) of 2008 offers valuable lessons for understanding the incipient crisis of our environment and civilization.

The first lesson is that we are terrible at making accurate predictions about complex adaptive systems. Economists' predictions regarding economic cycles — timing, length, amplitude, quality, and so on — are so dismal that some have commented that monkeys with dartboards do better. In 2008, Queen Elizabeth, whose portfolio had tanked by 25 percent, famously asked a group of august economists at the London School of Economics why they had not seen the GFC coming: the answer she got from them was that it was a failure of the collective imagination of many bright people. Four years later, an economist at the Bank of England named Sujit Kapadia answered (sort of) the queen's question during a tour of the bank: financial crises were a bit like major earthquakes and flu pandemics, rare and hard to predict, and that many people had gotten complacent.[1] Kapadia's explanation is undermined, however, by the simple observation that unexpected financial crises of varying intensities had been occurring about once every decade or more since the 1970s, quite a bit more frequently than the black death of the fourteenth century or the great influenza pandemic of 1918.

Interestingly, the BOE economist also mentioned earthquakes, which are indeed notoriously difficult to predict with accuracy better than probabilities spanning several decades — a 70 percent chance of a strong earthquake during the next thirty years, for example, is often a bit too imprecise a prediction to affect our behavior today (although earthquake building codes in Japan are strict and changed frequently, which helps account for the abundance of retro-reinforced buildings and relatively short service lives). But we all rely on weather forecasts today to go about our lives, and, despite the grumblings when one is caught without an umbrella in the rain, forecasters have become increasingly adept at predicting the behavior of this most complex of systems. Of course, weather forecasting becomes far trickier as the time horizon lengthens, and when it comes to decadal climate forecasting, there are tremendous uncertainties. But climate scientists are generally quite open about uncertainties and what they do not know, and like to ascribe odds to their predictions over various time frames: their forecasting ability will be better than that of almost all economists, perhaps in inverse proportion to the money typically earned in the respective professions.

Second, the Great Financial Crisis of 2008 also showed that complexity can add a lot of risk, like accumulating tinder in a forest system, till a match sets off a major conflagration. Five years before the GFC, Warren Buffet famously referred to the increasingly complex derivative instruments being cooked up by Wall Street as "financial weapons of mass destruction, carrying dangers that, while now latent, are potentially lethal."[2] The underappreciated leverage and complexity throughout the system, much of it under the radar of most market participants and regulators, allowed the crisis to spread rapidly throughout its many corners once the match was lit. Similarly, societies throughout history that added significant complexity required ever more energy to sustain them, and became increasingly vulnerable to shocks that finally did them in. In ancient societies these shocks were often environmental, and since the Industrial Revolution it appeared that civilization had overcome the limits previously imposed by the energy available to build and sustain complexity. But the urgent need — teed up by two centuries of relentless fossil fuels use — to pay proper heed to our only home has once again recoupled our destiny to that of the broader environment. And it is far from clear that adding even more complexity is the answer.

Having said this, it is likely that, in the absence of catastrophe, our world will continue to become even more complex for some time yet. Although efforts to spread the word about changing practices, such as huge, vulnerable supply chains for food and manufactured goods, are to be commended, many examples of these types of complexity will likely take a while to unwind, depending also on the diffusion of technologies such as advanced hydroponics and 3-D printing. But even technology itself, though it may enhance resilience in some respects, raises the bar for the minimal capabilities needed to sustain its level.

Another important lesson is to always leave plenty of room for error. Capital for many financial institutions evaporated quickly within the rapid, discontinuous narrative of the financial crisis and required extensive taxpayer top-ups. If abundant energy is the bedrock of our current civilization, and we find that there are significant, unforeseen shortfalls, no one is going to bail us out — we are on our own. Moreover, scientists have come up with environmental thresholds for the Earth (more on this later) that we should not violate if we want to minimize the chances that runaway change makes our home a far less hospitable place. But we do not yet understand well how some of the thresholds interact, and how they may lead to unforeseen consequences: better, then, to stay well within them where possible.

A key point highlighted by the Great Financial Crisis of 2008 is that using the right metrics is vital if we are to avoid (or more likely minimize) crises. Very few people, including regulators, understood just how much risk was being introduced in the system, as looking at collateralized debt obligations (CDOs) and other mis-rated securitization in "face-value" terms ($1.1 trillion total issuance in 2006) was meaningless in understanding how much more risk they really represented. Entities that issue short-term debt to finance mortgages and other risks traditionally used to be called banks: these entities were called "special purpose vehicles" during the period leading up to the GFC, and were designed to hide risk and avoid regulations such as those about how much capital to hold. And just as the crisis stemmed from the failure to measure the potential costs of all the risk in the system, as well as those of the moral hazard introduced through the concept of "too big to fail" (perhaps better amended to "too intertwined to fail"), the major costs to our commons that are not reflected in corporate or national accounts — what economist call "negative externalities"— are driving a major market failure for our environment.

The aftermath of the GFC offers interesting insights as well. A 2013 Dallas Federal Reserve Bank study conservatively estimated that the total cost of the crisis to the United States was somewhere between $6 trillion and $14 trillion in 2012 dollars (or between 40 and 90 percent of 2007 output), not including the additional spillover to the rest of the global economy at about the same or even greater scale.[3] By not revamping the financial system entirely in its wake to minimize moral hazard and separate it into "utilities" and "casinos," the crisis also reinforced the primacy of the "too big to fail" rule for systemically and politically important (nominally) private entities: not just in the financial system but, as seen through the GM and Chrysler bailouts, in manufacturing as well. Although the appetite for bailing out financiers remains at an all-time low, the political impetus to preserve jobs in many industries that are seen (often symbolically) as sectors key to national well-being remains high. Moreover, over the coming decades technology threatens to obviate the need for large swaths of jobs across many sectors, straining the ability of governments to support incomes and shore up consumer spending. In a parallel to the eroding resilience of our natural environment, the combination of strained government finances and major disruptive change to employment — first in the advanced nations but eventually around the globe — will not be conducive to shoring up global socioeconomic resilience.

On the monetary front, the governments and central banks of many developed countries embarked on a massive "race to the bottom" during the years following the crisis to see who could print more money in an attempt to kick-start economies and make one's currency cheaper (and exports more competitive) than those of trading partners, against a backdrop of trying to avoid the kind of deflationary spiral seen in Japan during the post-bubble "lost decades." Given the ineffectiveness of tweaking short-term interest rates that were already near zero, massive central bank purchases of assets from financial institutions, known as "quantitative easing" (QE), has become the preferred strategy to stimulate economies and mitigate deflationary pressures.[4] First, central banks buy government bonds, then those of corporations, then exchange-traded funds, and then what, if all fail? And how will these purchases be unwound? If economies are experiencing structural slowdowns, whether caused by the costs of energy or technological change, permanent QE alone, though it buys some time, is not a sustainable way of conducting economic policy.

Perhaps the massive central bank purchases of government obligations we see today are a prelude to eventual debt cancellation (if not in name), giving nations some extra time to throw money at problems. But lots of money, even if not excessively inflationary, given persistent spare labor capacity, can only go so far if jobs disappear, if retraining workers in an increasingly automated economy will be effective only for a handful, and if our fundamental economic model today — of employment driving consumption in a virtuous cycle — is rendered irrelevant.

Planetary Boundaries and Sustainability

The concept of sustainability is not new. An unknown Native American tribe is credited with the proverb that the earth is not inherited from ancestors but borrowed from future generations. Many indigenous peoples of Asia and South America traditionally practiced agriculture through crop rotation and allowing plots to rest for several years before recultivation to ensure soil regeneration. Although Edo (present-day Tokyo) was the largest city in the world during the eighteenth century, it produced remarkably little waste, as many items such as clothing, ceramics, paper, and candle wax were constantly repaired, reused, and recycled. Even wood ash and human excrement were systematically collected for use as fertilizer in the countryside, with the resultant produce feeding the city populace.[5] The common Japanese expression *mottainai*, with its Buddhist roots and roughly translated into "what a waste," gained wider understanding after Kenyan environmentalist and Nobel Prize recipient Wangari Maathai learned of the term in 2005 during a visit to the country and subsequently used it as the best one-word encapsulation of her "Four Rs": reduce, reuse, recycle, and respect. In one of the successful historical examples of systematic forest management (along with that of the German states during the fourteenth century), the Tokugawa Shogunate embarked on a massive reforestation program throughout Japan from the sixteenth century onward. Putting aside arguments about limiting biodiversity, the bad news for the millions of Japanese who suffer from pollen allergies today is that the bulk of the replanted trees were of just two types — the Japanese cedar and Japanese cypress — great for lumber but notorious for their prodigious pollen production.

Perhaps the most-quoted modern encapsulation of the concept of sustainability is found in the 1987 UN World Commission on Environment and Development report titled *Our Common Future*. More commonly known as the Brundtland Report, after the former Norwegian prime minister who chaired the commission, the report defined sustainable development as "development that meets the needs of the present without compromising the ability of future generations to meet their own needs." But the adjective "sustainable," like the prefixes "eco" or "green," has become an integral part of the common vernacular and is increasingly a catchall descriptor for anything that sounds environmentally benign. In addition to genuine individual and collective efforts to reduce the "ecological footprint" of humanity to below the carrying capacity of the planet, the term "sustainable" is also used primarily to bolster corporations' good citizenship credentials, or is found on packaging for any product seeking to appear eco-friendly (e.g., "sustainably caught" bluefin tuna). Or the concept may be used to lampoon how the extremely privileged 0.001 percent of the global population might use "indulgences" for their yacht and private jet emissions, as in "I had to pop over to attend Davos on the G-550, but it's okay, I bought carbon offsets."[6]

In 2009, a group of researchers led by Johan Rockstrom from the Stockholm Resilience Centre and Will Steffen from the Australian National University defined nine "planetary boundaries": climate change, ocean acidification, stratospheric ozone depletion, interference with global phosphorous and nitrogen cycles, rate of biodiversity loss, global freshwater use, land-system change, aerosol loading, and chemical pollution. They proposed the interrelated boundaries as tipping points that, when exceeded, risk triggering dangerous, nonlinear environmental change.[7] Human activity has been the driver in exceeding three of these boundaries so far: climate change, biodiversity loss, and changes to the nitrogen cycle.

The boundaries are, of course, linked through complex feedback loops that are only partially understood. An example would be land deforestation for agricultural use causing biodiversity loss and increasing phosphorous and nitrogen runoffs into oceans causing "dead zones," as well as reducing a key carbon sink and accelerating warming, which in turn accelerates permafrost melting that releases methane (a powerful greenhouse gas) into the atmosphere, further accelerating warming. The study's authors have not determined boundaries for atmospheric aerosol loading and chemical pollution, pending a deeper understanding of the former and better aggregate global research and metrics for the latter. Although some have criticized the approach of setting individual thresholds as too simplistic, the concept has gained increasing acceptance and has been incorporated into the thinking at multilateral institutions such as the European Commission and the UN.

The Frogs in the Pot

The boundary that sets off the most acrimonious debate today is global warming, possibly the mother of all commons tragedies: whether one agrees with the characterization depends on one's view regarding the main cause. The Intergovernmental Panel on Climate Change (IPCC), the UN body established in 1988 and entrusted with gathering research on climate change, produces the massive reports that form the basis for the periodic multilateral negotiations to stem carbon emissions. The IPCC's first report in 1990 projected a range of outcomes, from "business as usual" resulting in a 0.3 degree Celsius increase in global mean temperature per decade to about 0.1°C per decade if major steps are taken to stem greenhouse gas emissions. The observed data during the two decades since the prediction demonstrated that the IPCC's original 1990 projections were somewhat high, and the revised 1995 call for 0.18°C per decade has been more accurate. Since then, the Arctic sea ice has shrunk to the smallest ever recorded by humanity — down from an average 8 million square kilometers during the 1970s to about 3.5 million in 2012 — and huge glaciers have visibly receded.[8]

The IPCC's more recent reports began to be released in stages with the publication of the summary in September 2013 and served as a basis for discussion at the 2015 international Climate Change Conference, COP 21, held in Paris. To make an incredibly long and detailed story short: "Warming of the climate system is unequivocal, and since the 1950s, many of the observed changes are unprecedented over decades to millennia. The atmosphere and ocean have warmed, the amounts of snow and ice have diminished, sea level has risen, and the concentrations of greenhouse gases have increased." The IPCC adds that "it is *extremely likely* that human influence has been the dominant cause of the observed warming since the mid-20th century."[9] When the IPCC says "extremely likely," the odds it ascribes are 95 percent and above, as opposed to the 90 percent for "very likely" and 66 percent for "likely"— so about as close to "change your ways or run for the hills" as we can expect to get from a group representing the voluntary contributions of more than two thousand experts from over 150 countries.

The IPCC, which operates on a small annual budget (less than US$10 million), a dozen full-time staff, and does not pay any of its scientific contributors,[10] has been a lightning rod for criticism following a couple of high-profile scandals. In 2009, e-mails hacked from a University of East Anglia server, where some contributors to the IPCC worked, purportedly showed that a few researchers tried to downplay cooling data that would undermine their arguments. Although the researchers were cleared of serious wrongdoing, "Climategate," as it came to be known, as well as another uproar regarding a false claim that Himalayan glaciers will likely disappear by 2035 making its way into the 2007 IPCC report (called, you guessed it, "Glaciergate"), were widely publicized through the Internet and news services and used as fodder by critics of the theory that climate change is being induced by humans.

Some of the predictions from the original 1990 report, which called for land temperatures to rise faster than ocean temperatures, and for a faster temperature increase in the Arctic, have turned out to be quite accurate. But the rise in global surface temperatures has slowed in the last fifteen years despite ever-increasing introduction of greenhouse gases into the atmosphere. No one knows for sure why — perhaps it has to do with sulfate particles spewed by coal-burning emerging juggernauts like China and India, or volcanic eruptions like Mount Pinatubo in the Philippines, or an unusually quiet period of solar activity — but researchers point out that climate trends can be very noisy. One recent study suggests that the apparent lull in global warming is really a data issue stemming from not enough observations in the places where the changes are most dramatic: at the poles.[11]

The apparent slowdown has provided further ammunition for skeptics of anthropogenic warming, many of whom characterize scientists involved in the IPCC and similar efforts as part of a "warming establishment" and accuse them of selling out to funding. A group of sixteen scientists who signed an opinion column in the Wall Street Journal claimed that "alarmism over climate is of great benefit to many, providing government funding for academic research and a reason for government bureaucracies to grow. Alarmism also offers an excuse for governments to raise taxes, taxpayer-funded subsidies for businesses that understand how to work the political system, and a lure for big donations to charitable foundations promising to save the planet."[12] Somehow, the structure of the IPCC and the process involved in gathering contributed chapters for the periodic updates do not give the impression that legions of researchers are "living large" off the IPCC's generosity. And the argument that subsidies exist for businesses that know how to work the system is perfectly valid, but the coal, oil, and gas industries spent over $174 million in 2012 lobbying for favorable treatment in the United States alone, while the alternative-energy sector spent $24 million during the same year.[13] The 7:1 ratio for lobbying in the United States is a bit higher than the IEA's estimate of $523 billion of subsidies fossil fuels received globally in 2011 (up 30 percent from 2010) versus $88 billion in subsidies to renewables.[14]

Although much criticism is heaped on the IPCC process for distilling theories and observations into a consensus view, there appear to be no serious scientific disagreements with the basic theory that as the aggregate volumes of greenhouse gases increase, global temperatures would tend to increase. The fixation on CO_2 as *the* greenhouse gas invites criticism from some quarters, as water vapor and clouds are estimated to account for 66 to 85 percent of the greenhouse effect that makes the Earth suitable for human habitation. Here, again, there is no real argument about how the atmosphere holds more water at higher temperatures, and that water remains in the atmosphere for a relatively short time — about ten days as opposed to an estimated half-life of over three decades for CO_2. One key implication from these general observations is that the level of atmospheric CO_2 (and other long-lived greenhouse gases to a lesser degree), whatever its source, is a major factor that influences the balance of energy entering and leaving the atmosphere and is likely to be a primary driver of the feedback loop.[15] But some argue that we still do not understand enough about carbon sources and sinks to conclude that man-made emissions provide the tipping point for dramatic, nonlinear change.

Paleo-climatologist Robert M. Carter, in *Climate: The Counter Consensus*, points out that CO_2 generated from human activity is substantially less than the combined error of the estimated CO_2 production from all other sources, and that IPCC models have selectively incorporated positive feedback loops and neglected negative feedback loops into their projections for anthropogenic warming. Moreover, he argues that the relationship between additional atmospheric CO_2 and warming is not linear, but is generally understood to diminish logarithmically, calling into question the extensive focus on CO_2 from human activity. Carter contends that the real risk to humanity is natural climate change — actually more likely cooling rather than warming — and attention is better focused on mitigation of these climate change effects rather than curbing greenhouse gases at the expense of economic growth and development.[16]

The prediction that the climate will actually cool rather than get warmer is, in part, based on observations — pointed out by Carter and echoed by scientists who study solar cycles — that the current cycle of sunspot activity has been unusually quiet and may precede a period of cooling similar to the Maunder Minimum, which occurred between 1645 and 1715 and coincided with the middle part of the Little Ice Age. At the end of 2013, one leading space physicist, Mike Lockwood at Reading University, put the odds of another minimum like Maunder at 25 percent, but did not expect a new "grand minimum" to bring on a new little ice age, given anthropogenic global warming.[17] The low level of solar activity may also slow the jet stream, making it more likely that cold Arctic air pushes south, causing weather volatility and bringing particularly bitter winter conditions. If, as researchers suggest, the effects of low solar activity are offsetting greenhouse warming, it is sobering to consider what could occur when the episode of low activity ends.

Other criticism of the developing broad agreement about man-made global warming are not quite as fundamentally at odds with the IPCC predictions as Carter's but have much to do with the process of achieving the IPCC consensus view. A prominent scientist who contributed previously to IPCC output but no longer does, Judith Curry, chair of the School of Earth and Atmospheric Sciences at the Georgia Institute of Technology, noted recently that the IPCC process focuses too narrowly on the human impact on climate, essentially neglects natural climate variability, and requires consensus that can lead to groupthink. In an interview with the *Financial Times*, she added, "Defending the consensus creates temptations to make illegitimate attacks on scientists whose views do not align with the consensus and to dismiss any disagreement as politically motivated 'denialism.'"[18] In a recent paper in the journal *Climate Dynamics*, coauthored with independent scientist Marcia Wyatt, Curry hypothesizes that the Atlantic multidecadal oscillation (AMO) and the Eurasian Arctic ice shelf seas work to propagate a signal that is akin to the human wave cheer at sporting events. The AMO sets the tempo, while the sea ice conducts the oscillating signal between the ocean and the atmosphere, resulting in multidecade intervals of warming and cooling, each characterized by four stages. The paper neither supports nor refutes anthropogenic warming directly, but states: "How changes in external forcing might affect the Eurasian Arctic sea ice in context of an apparent quasi-oscillatory ocean-ice-atmosphere system is a burning question." According to the study, the "stadium wave" hypothesis explains the current lull in warming, concurrent with sea ice decline, and suggests that the current pause will likely continue into the 2030s.[19]

Regardless of whether climate change is anthropogenic or primarily part of large-scale terrestrial cycles in which human activity plays a small role, the balance of evidence so far suggest that the Earth, particularly the oceans and at the poles, is indeed getting warmer at a varying pace. Just as important, the occurrence of extreme weather events is clearly on the rise globally. A 2014 study published in the journal *Nature Climate Change* concludes that, based on running twenty different climate models, extreme El Niño events (typically higher rainfall in South America and lower rainfall in Southeast Asia and Australia) are likely to double in frequency over the coming decades because of greenhouse warming.[20]

The industrial civilization we live in today developed during a relatively benign climatic period, even during the Little Ice Age, and preparing for further, possibly runaway, climate change is a risk-management exercise. Even allowing for some regional differences (e.g., growing wheat in the far north), the net risks are asymmetrical, as things either stay tolerably cozy or get worse, but are very unlikely to get much better at the aggregate global level. The IPCC states in its 2014 assessment that without additional measures to mitigate greenhouse gas emissions, atmospheric concentrations will exceed 1,000 ppm CO_2 equivalent by 2100 and will likely lead to global warming of 3°C relative to 1850–1900.[21] In addition to cutting fossil fuel use, newer techniques, such as the use of (the right types of) bioenergy and carbon capture and storage or sequestration (CCS) would be needed to reduce net emissions on a large scale. Moreover, the IPCC stresses that much of the impact of climate change will continue for centuries even if human GHG emissions are stopped, and will be irreversible unless there is removal of

GHG from the atmosphere over a sustained period, an untested and potentially expensive proposition. Even if the odds of global surface warming of 3°C by the end of the century were "up to 33 percent" instead of the "66 percent and above" implied by the "likely" characterization in the latest IPCC report, it is exceedingly difficult to predict how gradual warming may turn into rapid runaway warming that feeds on itself through the massive release of naturally captured greenhouse gases, such as those found in jungles or the tundra. Better, then, to err on the side of caution.

The Earth has experienced very rapid climate change before: researchers examining ice core samples from several locations in Greenland found obvious changes in the ice from the last years of the Younger Dryas (a cold period between 12,800 and 11,500 years ago) that indicated that the area had sometimes warmed as much as 7°C in less than fifty years, with large variations occurring within several years.[22] A world undergoing rapid climate change would experience major food shortages, dislocation, and migration that may make the genocides in Rwanda or Darfur look mild in comparison, and major powers aggressively vying for resources. So even if the odds of significant warming were smaller than the IPCC estimates, the potential consequences of hundreds of millions (billions?) of deaths and a rapid decline in our collective civilization would suggest that we invest now, or even forgo some growth, so as to help ensure against such a suboptimal outcome.

Despite the dire warnings, multilateral efforts to agree to binding emissions targets are stymied by differing views on fairness. Developing nations argue that because economically advanced countries, during their own development, spewed most of the greenhouse gases currently causing headaches, they should take the lead and bear the costs of mitigation. For example, although China spewed 28 percent of all fossil fuel emissions in 2013, more than the United States and the EU combined, the country's cumulative contribution since 1870 is estimated to be about 11 percent, compared to 26 percent for the United States and 23 percent for Europe.[23] Although arguing about relative cumulative responsibility might seem somewhat less relevant when the house is burning, nations and regions that are less developed than China have even more gripes about bearing the costs of mitigation. So sharing the remaining available capacity for con-

tinuing GHG emissions, consistent with the goal of keeping global temperature increases below a given target, becomes a highly contentious issue in
negotiating any global agreement.

Then there are the economic costs of continuing on the current emissions path. Although noting its estimates' incompleteness and high dependence on assumptions, the IPCC calculates that global annual economic
losses from additional temperature increases of up to 2°C from current
levels[24] (or close to 3°C from preindustrial levels) will be between 0.2 percent and 2.0 percent of income, with losses more likely to be greater than
smaller. Moreover, it notes that losses accelerate with more warming, and
that the economic costs of a 3°C warming relative to current levels are
largely unknown. The IPCC passes the buck on the complex task of evalu-
ating the costs and benefits of mitigation, though it notes that the benefits
of mitigation may be underestimated because of the possibility of tipping
points and high-consequence, low-probability events.[25]

In the same report, the IPCC estimates that mitigation measures to maintain atmospheric concentrations of greenhouse gases to within 450 ppm
CO_2e by 2100 would knock global annualized consumption back by only
0.04 percent to 0.14 percent (median 0.06 percent) versus baseline growth
per year, through the balance of the century. Although the IPCC estimates
of slowed growth in consumption are not directly comparable with the
costs of insufficient action, they provide relative numbers behind the
thinking that the costs of inaction are significantly higher than the costs of
mitigation.[26] A group of British scientists proposed at the G-7 summit in
June 2015 that nations join a global Apollo-type R&D program for climate
change mitigation to spend about $150 billion over a decade, or 0.02 percent
of world GDP annually — even less than the lower end of IPCC estimates,
but nevertheless in the same ballpark.[27]

The frog in a pot of slowly warming water is too often used as a metaphor
for lethal complacency in the face of gradual adverse change (it apparently
does notice and tries to jump out if it can). But in the global warming debate, many frogs, particularly American, are too busy arguing past each
other to take meaningful steps to avoid becoming soup stock, or at least
slow the cooking time. The issue of global warming divides people across
many dimensions: both libertarian and state capitalists against those con-

cerned about the environment, between the developed and developing worlds, and in the context of shifting geopolitical and economic fortunes between economic powers such as China and the United States. There are regional differences in the debate as well, with Europe, Japan, vulnerable developing nations, and, increasingly, China mostly discussing what steps should be taken, while the United States is still at the stage of (often partisan) debate between those concerned and skeptics. Aside from the United States, the world has generally come to accept that there is less uncertainty about the trajectory of the global climate, and has moved on to how to address the problem.

Perhaps the opposition among a portion of the U.S. electorate to taking steps to curb carbon emissions is rooted in the history of ever-expanding frontiers and the traditional view that the government's function is mainly to protect the right of people to pursue individual goals, rather than to bind people together to take collective action. But the polemics of the political debate (as opposed to the scientific debate, though sometimes it can be pretty nasty as well on both sides) can be alarmingly amusing, as Iowa congressman Steve King — the same gent who described children of illegal immigrants as having calves the size of cantaloupes because they haul marijuana across the desert — described global warming in 2013 as "more of a religion than a science . . . and if sea levels go up by 4 or 6 inches, I don't know if we'd know that."[28] Some critics of climate change theory compare how they and their heroic efforts are treated to the suppression of Galileo and heliocentricity by the Church to preserve its dogma. But instead of being remembered for their struggle against scientific tyranny, hard-core deniers of climate change may well need to share office space with the Flat Earth Society someday.

After decades of severe environmental degradation and rapidly deteriorating air quality, China, which overtook the United States as the biggest producer nation of greenhouse gas emissions several years ago, appears to be focusing on the problem to an unprecedented degree. Readers may recall that, going into the 2008 Beijing Olympics, China's leadership ordered many industrial activities in the region to be halted, to head off threats by some athletes to boycott the games because of poor air quality. With polls showing that pollution has become a top issue for its citizens, the Chinese government, like other governments in the West and Japan before it, has come to realize that citizens now care about the quality of life beyond GDP and industrial production. In August 2013, the State Council decreed that environmental protection would be elevated to a "pillar industry," a significant policy announcement that follows on the heels of steps already announced to curb pollution and stem carbon emissions.[29]

Meanwhile, many citizens who are spectators of the debate over anthropogenic climate change feel powerless to affect the climate's broad trajectory, even if they "do their bit" individually by endeavoring to live less wastefully. For example, many of us in developed nations now separate garbage for recycling, or drive fuel-efficient cars (often while taking long-distance vacations by plane that may increase our carbon footprint more than the savings), and it makes us feel good, not only individually but as role models for our children. But the problem is that the sum of these daily individual actions is just a small fraction of the problems of industrial waste — almost 80 percent of all waste produced — or emissions from coal power generation. This realization is not particularly encouraging and may be one of the reasons some of us (mea culpa) slip in and out of acting as concerned citizens and lapse into environmentally unfriendly behavior. The feel-good factor is even less relevant in the emerging world, where many denizens must feel better about the quality of their lives before worrying about the environment.

When the Kyoto Protocol to the United Nations Framework Convention on Climate Change (UNFCCC) was adopted by the parties to the convention in 1997, there was a cautiously hopeful atmosphere to the process of addressing climate change: that even if targets were not binding yet for all members, multilateral progress had been initiated. The New York Times reported at the time that "despite the uncertainties, some environmentalists hailed the agreement as a remarkable political and economic innovation, in that it would establish a global system for dealing with what many scientists believe is the overarching environmental concern."[30] A decade and a half later, with the United States still not a ratified signatory, Canada dropping out, Japan not renewing binding targets, and China and India adopting the treaty but without binding targets, even the most ardent champions of the accord would probably concede that the Kyoto era has met an ignominious end.

Many hope that the most recent 2015 Paris climate conference will usher in a more promising era of multilateral cooperation to stem climate change. The initial post-conference feel-good level has been somewhat high, given the stated goals to keep warming well within 2°C and to pursue efforts to limit it to 1.5°C. But a sober look indicates that the results fall short of what is needed to achieve the stated goals for the latter half of the twenty-first century, unless major emitters keep their promises and take increasingly stringent actions when they review and update their goals — which must be at least as ambitious as those for the previous period — every five years. Moreover, the conference conceded that, in order to meet the +2°C-or-less objective during the latter half of the century, we need to develop and deploy scalable ways to take carbon out of the atmosphere — the techniques for which are currently very expensive or unproven (more on this later).

An increase of 2°C from preindustrial levels is often cited as a boundary that the Earth should not breach, and was also articulated as a goal by the Conference to the Parties (COP 15) to the UNFCCC held in Copenhagen in 2009. The conference is generally seen as a major failure, as the parties could not agree to emissions-reduction targets in an effort to prevent a breach of 2°C. The Stockholm Resilience Centre defines one of the boundaries for climate change as atmospheric CO_2 concentration of 350 parts per million by volume (other researchers cite 450 ppm as the threshold for a fifty-fifty shot at not exceeding 2°C), and daily measurements breached 400 ppm in 2013, according to the Mauna Loa Observatory in Hawaii.[31]

More recently, at the Asia-Pacific Economic Cooperation meeting in November 2014, the United States and China jointly announced measures to curb their emissions: Beijing promised that its GHG emissions will peak by 2030, and the United States plans to emit 26 to 28 percent less in 2025 versus 2005. To put the first promise in context, China added roughly two 600-megawatt coal plants (with typical service lives of forty years) a week between 2005 and 2011, and will still likely add the equivalent of the entire U.S. fleet of coal-fired plants over the next ten years.[32] U.S. emissions have fallen about 10 percent already since 2005, and the Obama administration hopes that the remainder will be met by tighter auto emissions standards and reduced emissions from coal — hence the strong indignation from the Republican Senate majority leader from the coal state of Kentucky, Mitch

McConnell. Though far from enough to tackle global warming meaning-fully, that the two biggest GHG emitters look to join with the EU, which has already set its own target of reducing emissions by 40 percent from 1990 levels by 2030 (the three together are responsible for over half the total an-nual global GHG emissions) is undeniably positive.

Hopes for a meaningful deal at the December 2015 COP 21 in Paris were elevated further as India, the third-largest national emitter, declared, ahead of the conference, its goals on reducing GHG emissions. Although some of the details regarding how to meet the goals are sketchy, India's targets include lowering the emissions intensity of GDP — not emissions in absolute terms — by 33 to 35 percent below 2005 levels by 2030, and deriving 40 percent of electricity from non-fossil sources by 2030. The Climate Action Tracker, which consolidates analyses on global efforts to check global warming from four research organizations, characterizes India's goals as "not consistent with limiting warming to below 2°C, unless other countries make much deeper reductions and comparatively greater effort."[33] Although the government's efforts are generally good news for those who live in India, the health impact will likely be minimal for those in rural communities who still rely heavily on burning kerosene for light-ing or firewood for cooking. In a recent *New York Times* article, Professor Michael Greenstone of the University of Chicago (an author of the China emissions report cited earlier) points out that bringing the regions of India that violate their own air-pollution standards back into compliance would increase life expectancy for the 660 million people affected by an average of 3.2 years, or about 2 billion life-years.[34]

Unfortunately, whatever boundary is considered for CO_2 as a likely tip-ping point, human GHG emissions broadly look set to keep increasing for the foreseeable future in the absence of adherence to an international re-gime with binding targets. In aggregate, the pledges made by the major CO_2 emitters going into COP 21 are not enough to reach the 2°C target, though they may help hold global temperatures to within 3°C above preindus-trial levels, according to the Climate Action Tracker,[35] but only if they are kept — and we all know that there has been a yawning gap between what countries have promised and delivered to date. Despite growing hopes for overcoming political hurdles — arguably the most important first step in addressing climate change — to produce meaningful follow-on agreements from future COP meetings, ambitious promises mean little if they are not enforceable, not kept because of political contingencies, or cannot be kept given near-term technologies (which we will review). In contrast to the U.S. Acid Rain Act and Montreal Protocol, which met all the above criteria, with the COP process it is not pragmatic to assume that the required results will be delivered in time. And given its long life in the atmosphere, CO_2 would likely remain at high levels for centuries even if *all* human CO_2 emissions were immediately curbed — an unlikely event.

Climate engineering (or "geo-engineering") is emerging as a field with increasing backing from governments, private enterprises, and even the UN, as a "least bad option" if emissions cannot be sufficiently curbed. The ideas range from the simple but potentially effective, like former U.S. energy secretary Steven Chu's suggestion to paint all building roofs white, to the fantastical, such as putting numerous mirror satellites in low Earth orbit. Estimated at several trillion dollars, the cost of the mirror proposal is reminiscent of the line from the screen adaptation of Tom Wolfe's *The Right Stuff*: "no bucks, no Buck Rogers"— not to mention that the bucks, and significantly fewer of them, are better spent to help head off the problem than to complicate it.[36] Somewhere in between are ideas to make clouds whiter and more reflective by delivering the right-size water droplets into them. Even more controversial are proposed techniques to replicate the cooling effects of major volcanic eruptions by introducing massive amounts of sulfate particles into the atmosphere.

Other ideas focus on tackling the primary cause of warming by removing and sequestering the carbon from the atmosphere. Proposals have included dumping iron into the oceans to encourage phytoplankton blooms (but which would also worsen acidification); developing a new generation of carbon scrubbers to remove carbon directly from the atmosphere; planting a whole bunch of trees to sequester carbon; or injecting carbon into disused oil and gas wells. Some of the approaches require large amounts of energy, which could potentially be provided by safer nuclear or power from renewable sources if cheap enough. All these approaches face considerable challenges: ecosystem disruption, ocean acidification, long lead times, high cost, lower societal EROI, or sheer scale and subsequent stability. In the absence (for now) of sufficient computing power and knowledge to simulate the Earth's little-understood feedback loops realistically, emerging large-scale climate engineering and carbon capture technologies sound like cool, high-tech solutions to global warming, but the more untestable and ambitious are really "break glass in emergency" mitigations with possible unintended, global consequences. But research into them must continue in case the glass really needs to be broken, as the recent Paris Agreement suggests.

Violating Thresholds

Biodiversity loss is the second major threshold humanity has breached, according to the planetary boundaries approach. Mass extinctions are not a new phenomenon. Earth has witnessed five prior episodes of major biodiversity loss to date. Up to 96 percent of all species were lost in a particularly nasty episode about 250 million years ago called the Permian-Triassic extinction. The most recent (66 million years ago) major event, called the Cretaceous-Paleogene extinction, is believed to have been triggered by a massive comet or asteroid impact and did away with an estimated 75 percent of all species, including all non-avian dinosaurs. Earth is currently losing over one hundred species per million annually, versus a preindustrial background loss of between one and five per million, and a suggested boundary of ten per million. The current rate of loss, caused overwhelmingly by human activity, may sound a bit less dramatic than the major "Hollywood blockbuster" mass extinctions that have taken place in epochs past, but is nevertheless a huge problem with little-understood but potentially major consequences.

There are many benefits of biological diversity and major costs from its loss. Diversity is key to maintaining nature's (and by extension, humanity's) resilience and ability to adapt to change. We all learn about the disaster that struck Ireland during the nineteenth century from monoculture reliance on the Irish Lumper potato variety when it was decimated by blight. Or we react to the epic folly of ancient Easter Islanders cutting down the last large tree with an incredulous "what were they thinking?" But broad public reaction to an unusual global plunge in the number of honeybee colonies (called colony collapse disorder) globally since the beginning of the twenty-first century has been very muted to date, despite the pivotal pollination services these bees provide to the environment and agriculture — many modern beekeepers can earn more money from renting out mobile colonies for crop pollination than from honey production. Or there is limited understanding that replacing indigenous livestock varieties in Africa with the few varieties that are the most productive under Western industrialized husbandry, while ignoring how indigenous varieties originally developed to adapt to local conditions, would degrade resilience significantly.

Some of the most dramatic examples of overexploitation and diversity loss can be seen in the world's oceans. The phenomenon most directly caused by human CO_2 emissions, ocean acidification — the result of carbon capture increasing the amount of carbonic acid in the sea — has decimated coral reefs around the world and disrupted ecosystems. While some species do not seem to be affected by increased acidity, many calcifying organisms such as coral and mollusks suffer. Overharvesting of fish stocks and indiscriminate collateral destruction of many marine organisms through increasingly efficient fishing techniques have also had a major impact on biological diversity, with many stocks such as Atlantic cod around Newfoundland and orange roughy off Australia having crashed and never recovered. Fish farming has become increasingly prevalent around the world as wild stocks decline, although the use of antibiotics and copious quantities of smaller fish for feed has raised additional concerns. With developments in sequestering much of the negative environmental impact, such as the use of plant proteins for feed and waste recycling, fish farming, which requires far less feed to produce a unit of protein than animal husbandry (one-seventh of that needed by beef to produce the same weight of salmon, for example), may play a vital role in addressing the need to feed the world's growing billions while helping preserve biodiversity.

Deep inside a mountain on a remote Norwegian island in the Arctic Ocean, the Svalbard Seed Vault is a secure depository with the capacity to hold 4.5 million distinct seed samples. Its mission is to function as a backup for seed banks around the world to ensure against loss of diversity through seed bank mismanagement, accidents, wars, or natural disasters. A handful of institutions, many of them zoos, have also established facilities for storing genetic material from animals at very low temperatures optimized for long-term storage, but a backup facility for these depositories currently does not exist. Re-creating Noah's Ark is an invaluable safety net against loss of biological diversity, but stemming the pace of biodiversity loss in the first place remains the primary goal for those who raise alarm over the problem. Unfortunately, destruction of tropical forests, encroachment of development on wildlife habitats, wetlands/ocean degradation, and massive overfishing will likely continue to accelerate diversity destruction. If stemming diversity losses through outright changes in economic activity (i.e., business practices) is very difficult, a "distant second-best" system of "biodiversity offsets," such as compensating conservation activities, may ameliorate the losses caused by private and public sector development. But the lack of widely agreed standards and metrics for biodiversity offsets currently presents challenges far greater than those for the more established but still very problematic markets for pricing carbon.

Accounting for 78 percent of Earth's atmosphere, nitrogen, as we learn in school, is as handy as it is plentiful: along with carbon and oxygen, it cycles through ecosystems; it is essential for photosynthesis and is a component of amino and nucleic acids (RNA and DNA). Put simply, plants depend on atmospheric nitrogen that is processed into nitrates via ammonia, or "fixed," largely by bacteria, for photosynthesis and growth. When plants and animals die, other bacteria and fungi once again convert the organic nitrogen left over from assimilation into plant life into largely inert nitrogen gas, completing the cycle. Many of us have seen unsightly, bright green rivers, or toxic algal blooms in the sea called "red tide." These phenomena are often associated with significant, human-caused transfer of nitrogen into ecosystems through the use of chemical fertilizers, mass meat production, and industrial activity.

During the nineteenth century, developed countries used guano and saltpeter from Peru and Chile extensively as sources of natural fertilizer, as well as for making gunpowder. But with the realization that "peak guano" was on the horizon, and exacerbated by supply disruptions during the War of the Pacific — fought over these resources by Chile and an alliance between Bolivia and Peru between 1879 and 1883 (and a superb trivia question for non–South Americans) — a new source of fixed nitrogen had to be found, and fast. To the rescue came Fritz Haber, a German chemist who worked out a method to synthesize ammonia from the nitrogen in air by using hydrogen gas and a catalyst. Haber and his colleague Carl Bosch were awarded the Nobel Prize in 1918 for perhaps the single most important innovation for preventing Malthusian stagnation, which has helped feed billions of people and is estimated to account for about half of the nitrogen atoms in the body of an average person living in a developed country today.[37] The darker flip side is that their innovation allowed Germany to continue manufacturing munitions (recall that terrorists routinely buy lots of fertilizer to make bombs) during World War I despite its significantly degraded access to saltpeter, and Haber played a key role in the development of chemical weapons used to horrifying effect during the war.

Although the Haber-Bosch process has enabled dramatic increases in agricultural productivity, it is a dirty energy hog that requires temperatures of 400–550°C and pressures of two hundred or more atmospheres. Even using the most efficient techniques available, every kilogram of fixed nitrogen produces 3.6 kilograms of CO_2-equivalent emissions.[38] Between 3 to 5 percent of global natural gas production is used for industrial ammonia synthesis, and China also uses coal for the process: together, they add materially to global emissions of the gases we want to curb.[39] One study estimates that fertilizer production accounts for about 5 percent of the total emissions from the entire global food system (deforestation, agricultural production, fertilizer production, refrigeration, etc.), which comprise about one-third of all human-caused greenhouse gas emissions.[40]

To use electrolysis of water instead to separate out the hydrogen that is typically introduced from natural gas in the Haber-Bosch process, one needs to burn economically and environmentally prohibitive amounts of dirty fossil fuels, and using electricity produced from solar panels or wind turbines is still far too inefficient to power the process at scale (though there are laudable efforts to develop efficient and cleaner small-scale versions of the Haber-Bosch process, as well as an emerging technique, called N-fix, which covers seeds with a bacteria that would allow nitrogen fixation with far less fertilizer). But modern nuclear power remains the best clean alternative for producing the copious amounts of heat needed to produce hydrogen for ammonia synthesis or fuel, or for any other process that is so energy intensive, such as water desalination.

Despite its huge contribution to human welfare, industrial nitrogen fixation has contributed significantly to ecosystem disruption. In lakes, rivers, and oceans, excess nitrogen (along with phosphorous, another key crop nutrient) from agriculture, industrial activity, and untreated sewage can cause excessive plant growth and decay, resulting in oxygen depletion and severe ecosystem disruption. Called eutrophication, the phenomenon is most often due to human activity and becomes apparent in river and lake algal blooms as well as ocean dead zones around major runoffs. The effects of the excess transfer also include undesirable increases in nitrous oxide (N_2O) and ammonia (NH_3) levels in the atmosphere, contributing to global warming and acid rain. Of the boundaries for the nitrogen and phosphorous cycles, the Stockholm Resilience Centre argues that, at over 120 million tonnes annually, the current pace of nitrogen removal from the atmosphere for human use far exceeds the proposed boundary of 35 million tonnes, while the 8.5–9.5 million tonnes of phosphorous introduced into the oceans annually is approaching its threshold of 11 million tonnes.

Although the numbers are large in absolute terms, and continued advances in agricultural productivity are vital to our continued well-being, some researchers contend that, as the share of greenhouse gases from agriculture will fall to 10 percent of the global total or less by 2050, the main issue is not agriculture as a source of greenhouse emissions, but rather to protect agriculture from the effects of climate change.[41] Nevertheless, industrial nitrogen production is an important part of the interrelated challenges — energy, food, climate — in building a sustainable future.

Dangerous Waters

Although not one of the thresholds already exceeded under the planetary boundaries framework, clean freshwater availability has been one of the biggest obstacles to improving the quality of life for billions of people throughout history. Millions die from waterborne diseases in the developing world every year, and water-related diseases are a major contributor to child mortality in areas without access to safe water. Parents in the affected areas are driven to bear many children to offset losses, thereby increasing the net population burden. The good news is that the first part of one of the 2000 United Nations Millennium Development Goals — to halve, by 2015, the proportion of the population without sustainable access to safe drinking water and basic sanitation — was met by 2010, leaving about 600 million who still lack access to safe water. With 2.5 billion people still without access to adequate sanitation facilities, the second half of the goal has proved more challenging, though progress may be accelerating with the support of organizations like the Bill and Melinda Gates Foundation, which has funded a project to significantly upgrade toilet technology to re-cycle waste and even produce electricity cheaply — recharge while you dis-charge. Proponents of an abundant future often point to progress in these areas as a "poster child" of ameliorating population stress and improving the lives of billions of people toward the bottom of the global quality-of-life pyramid, and the progress being made by a confluence of tech entrepre-neurs and nongovernmental organizations is encouraging and inspiring. But how soon these developments can significantly reduce aggregate global water stress is still an open question.

Although 70 percent of the planet is covered with water, less than 3 percent is freshwater, of which about two-thirds (and falling) is trapped in polar ice caps and glaciers. According to the UN Food and Agriculture Organization, about 109,000 cubic kilometers (km^3) of water falls on the land areas of the Earth annually as precipitation, of which about 43,000 km^3 remains in lakes and rivers as runoff or feeds aquifers.[42] The Stockholm Resilience Center proposes a human freshwater consumption boundary of 4,000 km^3 per year, against 2,600 km^3 in 2009 and 415 km^3 before industri-alization. These figures, combined with the renewable nature of freshwater, suggest that there is still "wriggle room," but several factors make it difficult to be complacent.

We often associate the need for freshwater with drinking, bathing, and using the toilet, but agriculture and animal husbandry account for 70 per-cent of global use (industry uses 19 percent), overwhelming the 11 percent that is needed at the level of personal health and hygiene. Animal husbandry is far more freshwater intensive than crop production, with a kilogram of beef requiring about 13,600 liters to produce, over three times more than pork or chicken, eight times more than soybeans, and almost seventeen times more than corn.[43] Dietary patterns in developing nations are shifting rapidly to consuming more animal proteins, increasing direct and indirect (through feedstock) water consumption, even in the face of more efficient water use for crop production. Total Chinese meat consumption has quadrupled in the last three decades, to the point that the country now consumes two times more meat than the United States (along with Argentina, the country best known for serving silly portions of meat), and still has a long way to catch up when measured per person.[44] Moreover, rapid growth in water demand has outstripped the capacity of groundwater supplies to replenish themselves in many parts of the world (the top four irrigators in the world — the United States, China, India, and Pakistan — all pump out more groundwater than can be replenished), and mismatches between where freshwater is abundant and major population pockets mean that water scarcity will remain a serious, growing global problem. A 2009 study from McKinsey & Company[45] points out that the shortfall between human water withdrawals and existing accessible water supply would reach 40 percent by 2030 assuming no efficiency gains, and a 2012 OECD study projects that over 40 percent of the world's population will likely be living in areas of severe water stress by 2050.[46] Changes in precipitation patterns related to warming will also exacerbate water stress at an aggregate level (though there will be some lucky localized winners), as existing agriculture and water infrastructure have been based largely on patterns and cycles observed over the past century.

Although interrelated through the hydrological cycle, efforts to address water scarcity can be broadly categorized under demand or supply management. Hydroponics, drip irrigation, and conservation are vital to minimize profligate water use, but these may remain more mitigations than true long-term solutions for securing adequate supply. On the supply side, additional locations where the classic methods of tapping aquifers and rerouting rivers would work have become increasingly scarce, and those currently being developed, like China's construction of huge canals to channel water from the Yangtze River to the industrialized north, are beset with environmental concerns. Every so often we get good news, such as the discovery of a new major aquifer, like one discovered recently under Kenya that could make a significant difference if managed properly, but that is the exception rather than the rule.[47]

There is tremendous need and potential for wastewater treatment and desalination to address water availability in much of the world. However, traditional treatment and desalination techniques are very energy intensive, while water purification techniques incorporating emerging nanotechnologies such as graphene (ultrathin carbon) are promising, but uncertainties about the timing of widespread adoption remain. This is a key area in which a cheap source of abundant, clean, 24/7 energy like modern nuclear power can make a huge difference in enhancing resilience and sustainability.

Freshwater availability draws headlines in the United States when we read that California, which produces nearly half of the vegetables, fruits, and nuts grown in the United States, is facing a severe water crisis due to changing weather and overuse. The ruins of pueblos and large adobe structures built by the Chacoans in present-day New Mexico attest to the importance of water in enabling complex societies in dry regions and the terrible consequences of prolonged drought. Numerous water-related lawsuits between states, such as those pitting Texas against Oklahoma or New Mexico, or Georgia against Alabama and Florida, suggest that massive engineering solutions to U.S. regional water scarcity have largely run their course. Very heavy water demand for hydraulic fracking has caused severe water shortages in dry areas of the United States where it is practiced. And the accelerating drawdown of the Ogallala Aquifer stretching across eight states in the Great Plains, exacerbated by changing rainfall patterns, threatens to turn these areas back into the dust bowls they became during the worst periods of the 1930s (recall the haunting Farm Security Administration photographs of displaced farm families from that era).

But the problems of U.S. water availability are dwarfed by the problems in other parts of the rapidly developing world. Though its population growth has begun to plateau rapidly because of development and its one-child policy, China has 1.34 billion people (2012 census) or about 20 percent of the world's population, but only 7 percent of its freshwater. The situation is even more serious next door, where India has 1.22 billion people (2013 estimate) or about 18 percent of the world's population (and is projected to overtake China as the most populous nation by about 2025) but just 4 percent of the world's freshwater. India is the largest user of groundwater in the world and has been depleting its aquifers at an alarming rate. Conservation can play an important role in addressing scarcity but can only go so far when surging population growth means that India must double its water generation capacity by 2030. In the absence of innovations that greatly reduce the energy needed for freshwater production or water recycling, or the means to provide enough energy to use today's techniques efficiently, India's water problems and associated regional instabilities are set to worsen. Here again, modern nuclear power can provide the means to address this impending crisis by providing the energy needed to provide enough water for all.

Beyond Conventional Metrics and Worldviews

When examining the sustainability of our civilization, it is essential to focus not only on the state of our environment but also on the conventions and metrics that we use to measure our economic well-being. Concepts of resilience and sustainability rarely play central roles in our collective worldview because of the most common metrics we use to measure performance and conventions that govern our behavior. During the prelude to the 2008 financial crisis, credit ratings (paid for by investment bank packagers) were widely accepted as proof that highly rated CDOs were extremely safe, creating pockets of poorly understood risk throughout the system. The giant insurer AIG required a total bailout of $182 billion, and the fact that the U.S. government nominally made money out of it makes Washington look like a lucky investor in distressed assets, when in fact the bailout was very costly for taxpayers when adjusted for risk and the true cost of capital. For the wider economy, GDP is accepted shorthand for economic welfare but woefully unsuited for measuring depletion of stock, whether private, public, or the environmental commons. Corporations have also been slow to incorporate negative externalities into their standard reports (unless something goes terribly wrong, like the Deepwater Horizon spill), and the bodies that govern corporate reporting are in no hurry to change the rules.

Modern corporate capitalism has long operated under the convention that most effects of resource use and waste are hard to measure and therefore treated as "externalities" when measuring enterprise performance. Similarly, national economic performance has been largely based on measurements of gross domestic product (or gross national product, its predecessor in the United States until 1990) for about eighty years. These measures are neither complete reflections of reality, nor were they meant to be: because GDP measures flows rather than assets, a country that borrows to pay (far too much) for imported energy, for example, can record nominal growth even while running down physical assets that detract from the ability to maintain future growth. Moreover, many of the most pressing global problems stem from the market's propensity to ignore or harm the resources that are shared and do not have market prices incorporated into GDP. On the positive side of the ledger, like the value of labor at home that is not reflected in national accounts, technological optimists contend that GDP ignores much of the growing and pervasive impact of digital innovations that increase utility and well-being but have very low market prices or are free to consumers (e.g., Internet search, e-mail, Wikipedia, YouTube, etc.). It is, however, pretty hard to expect (for most of us) that having access to all these digital innovations will help pay the bills.

In an effort to define some of the natural "shared resources" category of factors largely ignored in GDP, the 2005 UN Millennial Ecosystem Assessment divided ecosystem services into four broad sectors: provisioning services of products such as food, fuel, and freshwater; regulating services that effect climate, disease, wastes, and water quality; supporting services that are necessary for all other eco-service provision such as soil formation or oxygen production; and cultural services for human recreation and spiritual enrichment.[48] Assigning hard numbers to these ecosystem services is obviously tricky and extremely difficult to aggregate, though one attempt in 1997 to value the world's ecosystem services and natural capital came up with a "drive a Mack truck through it" range of between US$16 trillion and $54 trillion per year.[49] By comparison, nominal gross world product for 1997 in purchasing power parity (PPP) U.S. dollars was estimated at $38 trillion, according the CIA's *World Factbook*, so even the low-end estimate is pretty significant.

In 1972, the king of Bhutan made an informal remark that "Gross National Happiness" was more important than gross national product in measuring his nation's performance. Although obviously hard to quantify, the statement took on a life of its own and even serves as a guide to Bhutan's periodic national planning process. Although attempts have been made to develop GNH into a more uniform metric, it has (understandably) had a hard time gaining mainstream acceptance. Perhaps that mantle has been assumed by the "genuine progress indicator" (GPI). The familiar GDP, used by most as a shorthand measure of output and progress, aims to measure the total monetary value of all goods and services produced in a nation in a given amount of time. GPI adjusts personal consumption expenditure, a key component of GDP, for income inequality, and goes on to incorporate twenty-four other factors, both positive and negative. The factors are broadly categorized into economic, environmental, and social. For example, net capital investment or the value of housework would be incorporated, while negatives would include environmental costs or the costs of crime. GPI better reflects whether the economic activity of a nation has improved or degraded its ability to produce goods and services in the future: that is, its sustainability.[50]

Criticisms of GPI point to its subjective choice of components or the methods to estimate some items. But despite its shortcomings, GPI represents a fuller picture of economic welfare than GDP, and one 2012 study suggests that global GPI per capita peaked in 1978 and that globally, GPI/capita does not increase beyond a GDP/capita of around $6,500.[51] Canada and Finland have begun to incorporate variants of GPI into their national accounts, and the EU is actively pursuing ways to incorporate GPI into regional accounts as a key metric. In North America, the state of Maryland and the province of Alberta have incorporated GPI into official accounts, with other states considering the use of GPI. The governments of Ecuador and Bolivia have gone even further, rewriting their constitutions to incorporate the rights of nature and empowering citizens to defend its interests through legal means.

The use of income inequality in the GPI formulation and the increasing attention paid to the "Gini index" (developed by the social statistician Corrado Gini) as a measure of relative income distribution — with zero representing perfect income equality and 100 meaning that one person receives all income — bring up an important issue. Over the last decade, the re-concentration of wealth and income growth in the very top tier of many advanced economies has become a controversial socioeconomic issue.[52] Though often couched in social justice terms, extreme income inequality can undermine growth and aggregate human economic welfare. A recent IMF study finds that lower net inequality — after taxes and transfers — is highly correlated with faster and more durable economic growth and that, except in extreme cases, redistribution does not have negative effects on growth.[53] However, if many of the 99 percent (to borrow from the Occupy Wall Street movement) engage in frenzied consumerism in an effort to mimic the 1 percent and narrow the gap, the Earth can hardly support the next 10 percent living like the 1 percent, much less the remainder, when transposed on a global scale. But moralizing about it is not going to be particularly meaningful, as many of the six billion people in the developing world aspire to vastly more comfortable lives and are far from the point of material wealth enjoyed by some of the one billion in the developed world beyond which their happiness perhaps plateaus and even declines.

Persistent budget deficits in much of the developed world — driven by ballooning entitlement spending to curry favor among an aging population — also threaten economic resilience and sustainability. One of the most dramatic examples can be seen in the United States, where the budget deficit, exacerbated by the costs of fighting two recent wars and ballooning entitlement spending, is systematically underreported, crowding out much-needed investment in infrastructure, research, and public education. But just because Japan and southern Europe, for example, have some enviable infrastructure like speedy trains does not mean all is rosy for them, either, since they have made massive investments (often wastefully) while also meeting the demands of aging populations, to the detriment of their national debt levels.

Many readers with young children will be familiar with the phenomenon known as Kidzania, a global chain of theme parks where kids get to play grown-up in a variety of jobs. Although occasionally criticized for its tie-ins with famous brands that may encourage materialistic tendencies and identification with "big business," the concept is a huge hit with kids, who receive Kidzania money for "working" and can deposit the money in a bank in exchange for an ATM card or spend their spoils on goods and services. We recently took our daughter to Kidzania Tokyo, where she took part in a runway fashion show and also packed bananas. The pay for being a model was eight units, the same as working as a retail securities salesperson, while packing bananas, like other food-related jobs, yielded five units of pay. That the pay for certain service jobs was higher than that for food-related or basic manufacturing jobs is somewhat true to reality, but ask those who really pack bananas for a living and they will tell you that they would much rather work in the world of Kidzania. Kidzania represents a kinder, gentler, storybook version of capitalist society, without the extremes and pervasive income inequality. But in the increasingly winner-take-all societies of the world today, few would imagine that a low-level job in food services or basic manufacturing would translate into middle-class comfort or even any semblance of security, much less a life of prosperity.

The pervasive application of technology across almost all sectors of the economy today is bringing back many of the concerns, notably pointed out by Karl Marx during the Industrial Revolution, about capital supplanting labor. More recently, technology author Martin Ford made a powerful case that accelerating automation will increasingly replace many human jobs permanently across many sectors. And, with personal consumption accounting for almost 70 percent of GDP in the United States, for example, massive structural unemployment and underemployment threaten the very model of mass consumer capitalism that has driven exponential economic growth for so long. After all (as a thought experiment), the top 10 percent of the economic pyramid will not want the nine more cars that may become unaffordable to the remaining 90 percent as their incomes fall, and the value to the overall economy — not just the price but materials, supply chains, employment, etc. — of the car, or two or three, that the 10 percent purchase will be less than that of the nine forgone.[54]

The flip side to the continuing destruction of traditional full-time jobs, particularly in the developed world, is the growing diffusion of freelancing and the sharing economy. Uber, the car service founded in 2009, is arguably the best-known model for the systems-matching tasks and labor in a rapidly growing range of on-demand services, from housecleaning to coding computers. It may turn out that some tasks, such as housecleaning or dog-sitting, require more consistency and trust than can be delivered under on-demand freelancing, but others, such as coding or car services, appear well suited for the model. While on-demand services may improve the chances of younger people to find some form of work, particularly in countries with high levels of youth unemployment, they will have fewer benefits and rights (overtime, sick days, parental leave) compared to traditional full-time employees.

Meanwhile, the sharing economy, from crowd-sourcing through Kickstarter to car-sharing services such as Zipcar, continues to make inroads throughout the world. Despite the warm and fuzzy connotations of the term and the general "goodness" of sharing resources more efficiently, ranging from cars or preowned goods (eBay, Craigslist) to data and knowledge (Wikipedia, Open Data), this sector is not without its dark side. Those who own the successful platforms in the for-profit portions of the sharing economy may do very well, but the benefits may not trickle down nearly as widely as one might suppose. Moreover, the sharing economy has prospered as the more traditional sectors of the economy have languished or shown lackluster growth, raising the question of whether this emerging sector is the cause or the effect of the phenomenon — probably both. The "creative destruction" unleashed by digital technology promises to increase convenience and utility for consumers, but without creating enough of the jobs and income needed to drive continued growth in consumer-led economies. To the extent that this would appear to be the wave of the future, there is no sense in merely bemoaning the process; rather it behooves us to find ways to adjust to this new world. But inadequate understanding of the transition taking place, due to current conventions or not paying heed to the appropriate metrics, will result in clearly suboptimal ways to cope and adjust.

In pricing the Model T so that his employees could afford it, Henry Ford understood that workers were not just costs but a vital part of a thriving, sustainable consumer "ecosystem." That ecosystem, however, is becoming more difficult to replicate today, given the accelerating shift to automated manufacturing and services in many countries, with simply fewer jobs. Perhaps the current ascendancy of capital over labor is just a phase, after which labor will again reap major benefits; but it is more likely that the current wave of technological change, by wiping out large swaths of employment concurrently and permanently across a wide range of manufacturing and service industries, will bring on significant social dislocation and upheaval, which democracies (or any political system, for that matter) that evolved over the past two centuries will be ill-equipped to manage. The corrosion of resilience in our socioeconomic realm mirrors the erosion that is taking place in our civilization's ability to secure the energy needed to maintain its complexity without doing irreversible damage to our environment.

In the United States, northern Europe, and Japan, real wages have stagnated during the last two decades despite improvements in productivity and corporate profitability. Japan has suffered a long cycle of lower wages and deflation during the "lost decades" since the bursting of its real estate bubble at the beginning of the 1990s, and the Abe government is only now, after imposing its will on the Bank of Japan, engaged in an effort to engineer demand-led inflation to help kick-start the economy. At times stymied by a resilient euro currency, Germany has made painful adjustments to increase productivity and competitiveness since reunification, but wages have remained stagnant, and its economy remains very dependent on exports. And wage stagnation among the middle class has become an increasingly central political issue in the United States, with American liberals focusing on insufficient redistribution and conservatives fixated on excess government intervention choking growth. Whatever the cause — and it is probably a confluence of several, including technology — the fact remains that median American incomes have stagnated despite higher productivity and record corporate profits.

Within most developed countries, significant declines in labor share (the ratio of labor compensation to domestic output) have occurred concurrently with rising market income inequality. And although correlation is not necessarily causation, a number of studies, including one published by, of all places, the Organisation for Economic Co-operation and Development (OECD) — a club of rich countries committed to market economies — have suggested that globalized competition and weakened labor bargaining power have contributed to both phenomena.[55] The degree to which concerns about inequality have become increasingly mainstream is reflected in the enormous success of economist Thomas Piketty's

2014 tome, *Capital in the Twenty-First Century*. In it, Piketty argues that capital will continue to accumulate faster than income from labor as long as the return on capital is much faster than the rate of economic growth — an observation that resonates with many when looking at today's economy.[56]

Despite continued improvements in productivity over many decades, the apparent slowdown in improvements over the past several years often emerges in discourse about the state of economies in the developed world. In economics, productivity is often defined as a measure of output per unit of input, typically capital and labor. There are different measures of productivity, such as the commonly used GDP per hour worked, each suited to a specific purpose. Princeton economics professor and former Federal Reserve vice chairman Alan Blinder observes that growth in U.S. nonfarm labor productivity has slowed from about an average of 2.6 percent between 1995 and 2010 to only about 0.4 percent since. And while he points out that only a few years is too short a period to draw conclusions about its causes, Blinder contends that we need to be concerned about whether technological innovations to improve productivity have slowed or the benefits of technology are still to come.[57] But all the talk about the trajectory of labor productivity, while important, is separate from the potentially very disruptive issue of whether technology, no matter how it may enhance labor productivity, may be displacing human workers extensively and, as Martin Ford stresses, the consumers who form the bedrock of market economies.

Companies looking to remain competitive in the context of global competition, and technological advances that reduce the need for human labor, are two among the most significant factors contributing to the phenomenon of fewer jobs and the stagnation of average wages. Moving manufacturing and basic service jobs offshore to lower-cost countries is, by now, a familiar exercise, but hopes of replacing them with jobs in the sectors most commonly associated with the competitive advantage of the developed nations — pockets of high-value manufacturing and information technology — runs into the reality that far fewer employees are needed than in traditional secondary or tertiary industries. As one rough illustration, GE and Facebook had comparable market capitalizations as of May 2015, but GE employed over thirty times as many people (305,000 versus 9,000). Or Apple, the icon of U.S. outperformance in consumer technology but also at the forefront of outsourced manufacturing, recorded net income of $39.5 billion in fiscal year 2014, over 2.5 times that of GE, with fewer than one-third the employees.

There are serious shortcomings as well in (and insufficient broad understanding about) other important measurements of broad economic health that are commonly used as primary performance metrics — an even bigger-picture version of markets using insufficient metrics going into the 2008 financial crisis. Like the Federal Reserve using a "core CPI" (consumer price index) *excluding* food and energy prices to help make rate decisions, the U.S. government has attracted criticism over the years, particularly from those affected by cost-of-living adjustments for salaries or Social Security, regarding the way it uses inflation statistics. For example, the use of "chained" CPI — which assumes that consumers will choose less-costly substitutes in an inflationary environment and thereby understate inflation — to index benefits is good for the bloated federal budget but bad news for retirees who depend on Social Security to subsist.

In terms of U.S. employment, the official numbers published by the Bureau of Labor Statistics (BLS) serve as benchmarks to gauge the health of the U.S. economy, as well as targets for the Federal Reserve in fulfilling its non-complementary dual mandate of checking inflation and maximizing employment. But the headline unemployment rate mentioned most often by the Fed for setting policy, and by extension the object of market fixation, is fraught with problems. This measure, one of several released by the BLS, is called U-3 and does not include those who are discouraged and have effectively stopped looking very actively for work. When the Fed proclaims, as it did in 2012 as part of its effort to provide "forward guidance," that it will not contemplate any short-term rate increases until the unemployment rate is at or below 6.5 percent, it is referring to U-3. For financial market participants who operate under the mantra of "never fight the Fed" and, by unfortunate inference, the broader economy that gets wagged by the tail, U-3 is the number everyone looks at as holy writ. But a broader measure of unemployment covering those who are broadly underutilized, including those who are employed part time for economic reasons (U-6), reveals a far gloomier picture of about twice the U-3 unemployment rate, one in which

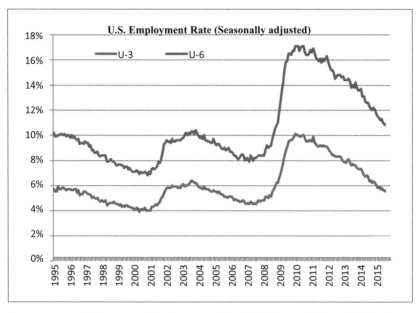

Two measures of labor underutilization: U-3 and U-6 (U.S. Bureau of Labor Statistics).

many of the discouraged threaten to join the ranks of the "structurally unemployed."

Commentators often speak optimistically of a manufacturing renaissance in the United States, powered by plentiful domestic energy supplies through extensive fracking and the development of advanced manufacturing technologies. Some even argue that the answer to so many college graduates facing bleak employment prospects is to shift more young people to vocational training or a tweaked and expanded *meister* system like one found in German manufacturing. But the hoped-for gains in employment may well fall far short of expectations. For example, increased design and production automation, such as 3-D printing for prototyping, making high-value components, and even constructing housing, will erode the demand for manufacturing jobs and likely reduce demand for global logistics. And in the new field of self-driving vehicles — where the impact may vary according to regulatory jurisdiction and ability to insure, and where applying the technology to large vehicles will probably take much longer —

automated cars promise to eventually eliminate almost all the jobs involving driving small passenger vehicles. Moreover, technology is steadily eroding traditional service-sector jobs that involve well-defined routines — from retail services to clerical functions — and is precipitating an intensifying squeeze on middle-class employment.

Accelerating advances in machine intelligence promise to broaden this trend even further to jobs traditionally thought to be immune to automation, as illustrated by the development and growing adoption of software that replaces junior corporate lawyers or radiologists. Some of these jobs are steadily being moved to locations with lower labor costs, allowing many to believe that a vibrant, middle-class consumer society will rise in those societies to offset the losses in the advanced world. But if, as in many broad technologies, the costs of automation continue to fall with gathering momentum, it may only be a matter of time before the current beneficiaries of off-shoring also see their jobs disappear — this time forever as tasks commonly performed by humans.

There is yet another factor gnawing away at the foundations of sustained economic growth in many nations and regions: infrastructure. The observation that decent infrastructure is vital for sustained economic development and improving quality of life is fairly uncontroversial, though there are vociferous ideological arguments about what should be funded by the state or by the private sector. Many readers have probably come across news reports about the sorry state of U.S. infrastructure: the American Society of Civil Engineers, in its annual report card on U.S. infrastructure, gives the nation a cumulative grade of D+ in 2013, just three notches above F for failing. The letter grades range from a high of B– for solid waste to a low of D– for inland waterways and levees, and the ASCE estimates that about $3.6 trillion in investment would be needed to improve the U.S. infrastructure GPA to B by 2020.

At the global level, the McKinsey Global Institute estimates that about $57 trillion worldwide in infrastructure spending through 2030 — 60 percent higher than the previous eighteen years and 3.5 percent of anticipated GDP — would be required just to keep up with expected global growth, not including renewal backlogs and current infrastructure deficiencies.[58] Infrastructure is vital to building and maintaining socioeconomic complexity, but how will so much investment be funded when many countries need to devote more resources to secure cleaner energy while still recovering from financial strain?

Why do we focus on the current state of economies and the measurements used in our discussion of sustainability? Because, like the extensive use of flawed metrics going into the Great Financial Crisis, we need to understand that major problems such as persistent budget deficits, income inequality, and structural unemployment, which simmer in the background even as economies seem to be recovering cosmetically, quietly erode the resilience of the current socioeconomic regime.

In another example of the need to look beyond the numbers most often used: Since the 1960s, U.S. government accounting has been on a cash basis, cash in versus cash out, without accruals for funds that are owed in the future, such as Social Security. But by applying generally accepted accounting principles (GAAP) — which the U.S. companies must use for financial reporting (but the government doesn't) — the U.S. federal budget deficit was a whopping $6.6 trillion in 2012 instead of the $1.1 trillion most often cited, according to economist John Williams on his Shadow Government Statistics website.[59] The huge budget deficits run by many developed nations today and massive use of the printing press by many central banks will undermine the ability to address another crisis effectively if one were to occur before these nations have had a chance to unwind persistent excesses.

The world is also increasingly interconnected and synchronized. The origins of the Great War continue to be debated a century after its outbreak, with some commentators (and even Japan's Prime Minister Abe) making comparisons between the rise of Germany before the war and that of China today. Princeton historian Harold James argues that, in a parallel to U.S. policies today, the global financial fragility highlighted by the Panic of 1907 inspired Great Britain to use its central position in international finance to shore up its role as global hegemon, helping sour relations between the major powers going into the Great War.[60] With the stage set by punitive World War I reparations and, as author Liaquat Ahamed argues in *Lords of Finance*, the folly of central bankers and their policies, the Great Depression fostered militarism and totalitarianism, teeing up the second worldwide conflagration in half a century. In the Cold War order following World

War II, Western recessions had little impact on the USSR, China, and other states outside or with only minor stakes in the global capitalist system. But the fall or co-option of communist systems, the rise of the developing world, and globalization have again made the world a much more synchronized place, much like the system of the Mayan city-states.

Today, very few corners of the globe are unaffected by economic turbulence and the ebb and flow of liquidity originating in one of the larger centers, as we saw during the Great Financial Crisis. And despite some recovery experienced since 2009, growth remains sluggish, budget deficits remain persistently high across much of the developed world, and the biggest potential engines of global growth, such as China, India, and Brazil, all have their challenges — more consumption, less bureaucracy, and more investment, respectively — to sustain balanced growth. The drive to shore up national economies through expansionist monetary policies and resulting currency devaluations has sparked comparisons to previous episodes of beggar-thy-neighbor policies such as those between the world wars. The huge accumulation of debt and the reliance by much of the world upon taking on even more debt to kick-start growth is simply not sustainable. Against this backdrop, the last thing the world needs is an energy crisis — one not triggered merely by temporary supply shocks but a more enduring condition caused by structural changes to fossil fuel extraction, the urgent need to pay better heed to our environment, and the insufficient energy return on investment (EROI) of many alternatives.

Internalizing Externalities

Like measures of national performance, negative externalities are slowly being introduced into corporate reporting, though so far mainly through style rather than the substance of meaningful, common metrics when considered as a whole. Internalizing negative externalities is further hampered by how far the corporate person as a legal construct has evolved beyond its original intent, and how this development has encouraged irresponsible societal behavior. Externalities reporting at most large firms has traditionally been relegated to sections on corporate social responsibility or through sustainability reports such as those outlined by the Global Reporting Initiative.

One of the more comprehensive efforts to broaden corporate reporting is spearheaded by the International Integrated Reporting Council, whose framework seeks to incorporate human, social, and natural capital in addition to financial, manufactured, and intellectual capital. The approach also requires disclosure of material external factors such as economic conditions, technological change, and environmental issues. Although the council is promising as a framework, a glance at the participants in its pilot program is telling: of the almost one hundred participants, thirty-four are financial institutions, while eight are from the oil and gas industry (all non-U.S.). It should come as no surprise that financial companies, which as a group favor increased corporate disclosure of potentially material factors, would be the biggest group of participants in the initiative.[61] The integrated reporting approach no doubt appeals to the financial community in much the same way that the Securities and Exchange Commission, in conjunction with the Sustainability Accounting Standards Board, has been at the forefront of pushing for disclosure of material externalities reporting in the United States. Since the 1980s, the SEC has required disclosure of the costs of compliance with environmental regulations and potential costs from environmental legal liabilities when material, but the potential costs of major mishaps such as the Deepwater Horizon accident remain grossly underreported.

A true sea change in the way externalities are incorporated into corporate performance and reporting is difficult to achieve without the elephants in the room: the U.S. Fair Accounting Standards Board (FASB) and the International Accounting Standards Board (IASB). These bodies set the most commonly used standards for financial reporting globally, and it is difficult to effect a wholesale shift by corporations to incorporate externalities into performance measurements and reporting without them. Although FASB's generally accepted accounting standard (GAAP) and the IASB's international financial reporting standards (IFRS) are currently being merged into a single standard, the convergence process does not address negative externalities. Perhaps the person who drives incorporation of externalities into broad industry standards someday will find himself or herself inducted into the Accounting Hall of Fame (yes, at Ohio State University), but likely not in time to have a material positive impact on our commons.

In both national and corporate reporting, practices that systematically overstate our cosmetic well-being reduce our ability to grasp the nature and scope of the many problems that face us today, as well as delay positive changes in socioeconomic conventions. In the run-up to the Great Financial Crisis, risks were masked by the extensive use of special-purpose vehicles outside the regulated banking system, abetted by rating agencies that slapped high ratings on complex securities to the satisfaction of their sell-side paymasters. Similarly, without understanding the problems adequately, much less the possible solutions, it will be easy for nations — particularly those in which powerful constituents successfully pursue their particular interests, with tacit consent by electorates and without regard for pragmatism at a broader level — to sleepwalk toward decline. But the broad diffusion of new metrics and adoption of conventions rarely take place overnight, so waiting for a Bob Marley-esque moment of sudden clarity — a new worldview, broadly shared with sufficient urgency, and leading to concerted, dramatic actions to address the pressing issues of our time — is likely to end in disappointment.

Desperately Seeking Resilience

In May 2007, Fed chairman Ben Bernanke told Congress that he expected no significant spillovers from the subprime mortgage market to the rest of the economy: perhaps a case of needing to sound confident, but, fast forward sixteen months, Lehman Brothers declared bankruptcy and a global economic implosion ensued. We know from repeated failures among experts to predict and prevent catastrophe that, whether the Great Tohoku Earthquake or the Global Economic Crisis, complex adaptive systems such as those found in nature or in economies are actually very hard to predict, much less do anything about. Even where massive data sets and increasingly accurate predictive models exist, such as in weather forecasting, experts can disagree a lot when horizons become multi-decadal. There are approaches much better suited for thinking about the equilibriums and cycles of complex adaptive systems, and which help explain the rise and fall of civilizations, but they are still far from mainstream. These approaches would suggest that, in a globalized and increasingly synchronized world, we are far less resilient to adverse shocks — environmental, resource scarcity, financial — than we would like to believe.

During the early 1920s, Soviet economist Nikolai Kondratiev, a proponent of small free-market enterprises in the Soviet Union under Lenin's New Economic Policy, posited that capitalist systems experienced successive cycles of expansion and contraction lasting for about fifty years: these have come to be known as Kondratiev waves. Although ideas about the existence and duration of economic cycles had been around for centuries, and Kondratiev's theories have been criticized for being subjective and unscientific, his work strongly influenced, among others, Joseph Schumpeter, the Harvard professor well-known for his theories of business cycles. With Kondratiev's influence waning as Stalin replaced Lenin as Soviet leader, the Soviet economist was stripped of the directorship of his institute in 1928 and arrested in 1930 on charges of being sympathetic to "kulak" farmers, who were being brutally starved and collectivized during the period. Kondratiev was rearrested and executed in 1938 during the Great Purge, a sad but unsurprising end for a renowned student of capitalism in Stalin's Soviet Union.

In a well-known theory of more recent vintage, the late economist Hyman Minsky argued in his "financial instability hypothesis" that recurring cycles of financial system robustness and fragility, and of boom and bust, were the norm. The point at which a credit cycle turns abruptly and asset values plummet suddenly after a debt-fueled run has come to be popularized as the "Minsky moment."

Modern industrialized society has engendered a strong belief in optimization: that consumers maximize utility while companies maximize profit, or that inputs and processes, as in supply chains or manufacturing, can be adjusted so as to generate the most desirable outcomes. This belief is closely linked to confidence that, with enough data and quantitative discipline, both natural and socioeconomic phenomena can be forecast, and suboptimal outcomes avoided, through tweaking inputs and variables. The optimization approach traditionally assumes that the way to gain maximum sustainable benefit is to nudge a system into a particular optimal state and hold it there, based on linear responses to inputs. An example would be the much-touted "just in time" inventory techniques associated with long supply chains and component outsourcing pioneered by Toyota and emulated across the world today in many industries. This optimized system works very well most of the time, but shocks such as the Tohoku earthquake and flooding of areas with many industrial parks in Thailand in 2011 placed tremendous stress on supply chains and reduced the output of many companies and industries materially.[62]

Ignoring links between scales of systems and externalities makes eminent sense when players' short-term payoff structures are designed to maximize immediate utility without incorporating non-mandated, hard-to-measure, potential long-term system-wide costs of "business as usual." But multiple players optimizing without regard to system-wide consequences makes the whole system more vulnerable to shocks and erodes resilience, defined by Brian Walker and David Salt in *Resilience Thinking* as "the ability of a system to absorb disturbance and still retain its basic function and structure."[63] In this context, sustainability can be defined as meeting current needs so as not to undermine the ability of desirable or beneficial systems regimes to meet future needs.

Instead of a single equilibrium, complex ecological and social systems have many potential equilibrium regimes, much like depressions or basins on a three-dimensional plane. Walker and Salt suggest picturing a ball moving in and among basins on a plane. The contours of the basins change constantly as conditions change, and as a basin representing the current regime becomes smaller and less shallow, the current state of the system, represented by the ball, can cross over more easily into other regimes that are undesirable to those who are dependent upon the old state. One example that Walker and Salt provide is the massive coral die-off witnessed over the past three decades in the Caribbean, a region that draws billions of tourist dollars from its pristine beaches and coral reefs. In a reef ecosystem with less biological diversity than others, and with many small island nations conducting environmental policies with little coordination, a confluence of factors — ocean acidification from absorbing increasing amounts of atmospheric CO_2; nutrient runoff favoring fleshy seaweed growth; overfishing of species that graze on fleshy seaweed; an outbreak of disease that decimated the population of seaweed-eating sea urchins; and coral bleaching caused by ocean warming — changed the shape of the indentation it occupied and allowed the region to slip into a new, less-desirable regime.

Another dramatic example is the large-scale shift in ecological regimes from semiarid land to desert globally due to unsustainable farming practices, overgrazing, and other human activity. According to the International Fund for Agricultural Development, about 25 percent, or 3.6 billion hectares of Earth's land area, is desertified, about 12 million hectares (a 1 percent increase in three years) — an area about the size of the state of Pennsylvania — is lost to land degradation annually, and the pace is accelerating.[64] Despite efforts to reclaim degraded land in China, a bulletin published by China's State Forestry Bureau in 2011 put the percentage of desertified land at 27 percent (2.6 billion square kilometers) of the national territory as of 2009,[65] and a senior Chinese official was quoted by the BBC in 2011 as saying that, at current treatment rates, it would take three hundred years to reclaim 530,000 square kilometers that could be recovered.[66]

Scholars from a number of different disciples have identified four phases of the recurrent cycles seen in most complex ecosystems: rapid growth (r), conservation (K), release (omega), and renewal (alpha). The vertical axis of the cycle represents the system's potential, and the horizontal axis represents "connectedness" among the controlling variables: the system is dominated by external factors when connections are loose, while strong connections mediate or control external factors.

The third phase, often associated with Joseph Schumpeter's theory of "creative destruction" in describing innovation and economic cycles, underscores the concept's utility in describing other complex adaptive systems, such as markets and economies.[67] The rapid growth and conservation phases of the adaptive cycle under the framework comprise the "front loop," characterized by slow, stable accumulation of capital or potential, while the "back loop" of release and renewal takes place rapidly and has the greatest potential for destructive or creative change. The cycles of complex adaptive systems are nested hierarchically in space and time, and many levels synchronized at the same point in the conservation phase would tend to make a major release correspondingly larger.

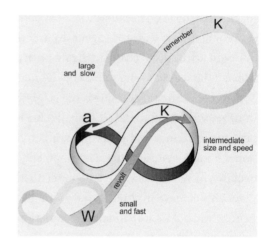

Panarchical connections (figure 3.10 from *Panarchy: Understanding Transformations in Human and Natural Systems*, edited by Lance Gunderson and C. S. Holling; copyright © 2002 Island Press, reproduced by permission of Island Press, Washington, DC).

A release that occurs during a cycle can sometimes cascade up to a higher, slower level, such as a small fire spreading upward to a system-wide forest fire when enough flammable capital has been accumulated. A familiar example in the socioeconomic realm is how U.S. subprime mortgages, a relatively small corner of the vast global financial system, through significant leverage throughout the system, cascaded upward to a vast systemic crisis in 2007 and 2008. Perhaps another example in the future will be another economic crisis growing to dismember the current U.S. dollar-dominated global economic order and give rise to a new, more volatile, system.

During its conservation phase, how a higher-level cycle looks can provide the context for reorganization in a similar form at a lower level undergoing renewal, such as the reconstruction of socioeconomic systems ravaged by warfare or natural disasters. Examples include the reconstruction of Europe's economies and institutions after two devastating wars. After the Great War, there was enough socioeconomic structure at a pan-European and global level (mostly the United States) to rebuild along somewhat similar lines, though the ruinous reparation terms dictated by the Allies helped set the stage for the Second World War. Following World War II, the developed world west of the Iron Curtain recovered economically thanks to the Marshall Plan and the reconstruction of Japan, both led by the United States as a model to emulate.

The interrelated adaptive cycles at different levels in socioeconomic and environmental systems described above are represented by the term in the title and articulated in the book *Panarchy: Understanding Transformations in Human and Natural Systems* (2001).[68] The adaptive cycle framework presented by ecologist C. S. Holling and the proponents of panarchy (panarchists?) is useful in analyzing how, after decades or centuries of seeming stability and glory, complex civilizations can become vulnerable to shocks and collapse, sometimes rapidly, as anthropologist Joseph Tainter described. Resilience is the capacity of socioeconomic or ecological systems to absorb disturbances or shocks while maintaining their overall structure and functions. Sufficient energy surplus that does not displace much of the energy for other economic activity — EROI comfortably above the "net energy cliff"— is vital to enhancing resilience in the mature, conservation phase of our collective global civilization.

Populations packing up and leaving en masse when the going just gets too tough was a regularly occurring phenomenon throughout history, from ancient Mesoamerica to the Khmer kingdom. Even direr outcomes were experienced when populations simply couldn't leave, such as the ancient Easter Islanders, and the parallel with humanity and the Earth is hard to miss. For this to happen in our highly complex, increasingly synchronized, and, by historical standards, very densely populated world, seems like the stuff of dystopian science fiction, but this cognitive dissonance does not make it impossible. In fact, advanced and complex socioeconomic systems may well prove to be more rather than less fragile, as various scholars have theorized. We have already seen examples of mass human migrations in sub-Saharan and Central Africa over the past several decades, driven by populations unable to feed themselves.

The U.S. Department of Defense, generally not associated with tree-hugging and sustainability (but, as proven risk-management experts, actually at the forefront of exploring alternative energy such as biofuels), articulated in its Quadrennial Defense Review in 2010 that "assessments conducted by the intelligence community indicate that climate change could have significant geopolitical impacts around the world, contributing to poverty, environmental degradation, and the further weakening of fragile governments. Climate change will contribute to food and water scarcity, will increase the spread of disease, and may spur or exacerbate mass migration."[69] In 2014, the Pentagon took the "could" out of its view and called climate change a threat multiplier that "will have real impacts on our military and how it conducts its missions."[70]

Perhaps it is not impossible to gradually and peacefully decrease the tightly woven complexity of the global system and stave off or cushion decline. By minimizing waste, maximizing recycling, emphasizing local food production, reducing reliance on long supply chains and transport, and even sometimes introducing local community currencies, the Transition Towns movement looks to build resilient local communities that could thrive in a future without extensive fossil fuel use. Some key technological developments such as 3-D printing, by reducing the need for energy-intensive, high carbon footprint logistics in all but the most large-scale industries, may also help foster resilience (though what this means for employment is another, probably less rosy, story).

Parts of the emerging world may be able to leapfrog some of the phases of development observed in the "advanced" nations, in areas such as telecommunications and energy. In many developing countries, the mobile phone has surpassed landlines as the primary mode of communication, trade settlement (through payment services), and information access. According to the United Nations Development Programme, about 1.4 billion people in the world do not have access to grid electricity, and another 1 billion only have access to unreliable electricity networks. Moreover, about 3 billion people globally rely on burning dirty biomass and coal to meet basic energy needs. But looking at India as an example, where about 300 million people have no access to reliable electricity, technologies for renewable energy, distributed power, and smart grids would enable these and other underdeveloped areas around the world to build efficient, resilient power networks to begin with, without having to go through a build-out of vulnerable, centralized grids.

On the other side of the ledger, urbanization continues at a torrid pace: about half the world's population lives in cities today, up from 2 percent in 1800, with 1.5 million joining the urban dwellers, through migration and births, every week.[71] The UN expects virtually all the growth in the global population over the next several decades — another two billion by 2050 —

to be concentrated in the urban areas of the less developed regions.[72] Research indicates that, though urbanization in highly developed regions can ameliorate emissions, urbanization in lower-income countries aggravates them:[73] for many this makes intuitive sense, as one would expect that residents of cities in the developing world are much more worried about improving their own lot and that of their family than worrying about their contribution to global sustainability. But admonitions to the people of the developing world, those who increasingly look to the cities for a brighter future, that moving to the cities will degrade sustainability are unlikely be very effective.

The effort to build more sustainable cities is not without its bright spots. Stockholm is frequently cited as a major city that leads the world in urban planning that minimizes sprawl and maximizes resource use. In the developing world, Curitiba, Brazil, home to over 1.7 million residents, has become an exemplar of urban planning and environmental policy since its master plan was adopted in the 1960s, when its population was still under half a million. But it would take a pretty big optimist to believe that the bulk of the most rapidly growing cities of the developing world — Karachi, Lagos, Kinshasa — can replicate the achievement.

As a general rule of thumb, the carbon intensity of economic activity (annual emissions divided by GDP at national or global levels) tends to fall more rapidly than GDP growth as economies become more advanced, but GDP growth tends to outpace improvements in carbon intensity in lower-income countries. So the hope is that low-income countries' carbon intensities will fall much more quickly than income growth as they develop further, but the process is in a race against the energy needs of rapid population growth and urbanization. A recent PricewaterhouseCoopers report points out that although global carbon intensity fell by 1.2 percent in 2013, the global economy would have to cut carbon intensity by 6.2 percent every year from now until 2100 in order to meet a cumulative carbon budget consistent with the goal of keeping warming within 2°C.[74] But much of the developing world will likely continue to increase its emissions, and broad paradigm shifts to follow alternative, cleaner paths to development could take generations to take place — time we do not have.

So it is far from certain that we can materially enhance global resilience by grand design, or that our civilization's complexity could be preempted or unwound without tremendous, probably violent, dislocation. At the socioeconomic level, we face profound changes to how economies have been driven by consumers who depend on employment to drive the economic engine, and many societies have ever-fewer resources (both fiscal and monetary) to cope with the transition. Meanwhile, the deterioration of our global commons continues, and the eventual costs of inaction — costs we are loath to bear because of the pressing problems in our respective economies — will soar. This sounds disturbingly like a broad trend that, through lack of will or capacity, is cascading up to a bigger environmental cycle to the detriment of our future ability to cope with change and feeding back into our socioeconomic realm. For every successful international agreement such as the Montreal Protocol (very specific and enforceable), there are many more failures like the Kyoto Accord (extremely broad without real enforcement), and betting exclusively that treaties that cap greenhouse gas emissions can be hammered out and implemented effectively is quite risky. But against this backdrop, the single most important factor to enhance resilience and increase the odds that our highly complex socioeconomic system will not unravel sordidly will be the availability of cheap, abundant, and clean energy.

Don't get me wrong: I love nuclear
energy! It's just that I prefer fusion to
fission. And it just so happens that there's
an enormous fusion reactor
safely banked a few million miles away
from us. And it delivers more than
we could ever use in just about eight
minutes.
—**William McDonough (1951–)**

For a successful technology, reality must
take precedence over public relations,
for nature cannot be fooled.
—**Richard P. Feynman (1918–1988)**

4

RENEWABLES REALITY CHECK

Renewable energy — energy that is continually replenished through natural processes — is commonly touted as the broad panacea for achieving sustainable, long-term energy security while moderating humanity's ecological footprint. People around the world see wind turbines dotting the countryside and solar panels popping up on roofs in their communities and perhaps get a warm and fuzzy feeling about an impending era of decentralized, nonpolluting energy. The growth numbers are indeed impressive, especially in countries that have subsidized them extensively like "sunny" Germany and pollution-ridden China. In the ten years leading to 2014, cumulative global installed capacity for solar has increased by almost seventy times, and wind by almost eight times. But predictions of powering civilization soon exclusively through renewable resources is often laced with hype and wishful thinking. Now, hype isn't always bad for kickstarting progress, but wishful thinking is suboptimal if it leads to adding too much power with an energy return on energy investment lower than what is needed to maintain complexity. In this chapter I will show why it may be premature to extrapolate from the past half decade's furious pace that growth in renewable energies will be able to largely replace fossil fuels over the coming ten to twenty years without expending inordinate energy and resources — resources that could be better deployed to build a more supple power mix, including nuclear.

As we discussed earlier, EROI estimates for various energy sources can differ considerably, depending on scope of costs and outputs incorporated, as well as the favored fuels of the persons doing the calculating. A recent article by EROI pioneer Charles Hall and colleagues provides useful mean EROI values for electricity produced by various sources, based on meta-analysis of peer-reviewed studies, including typical plant efficiencies but not including energy storage. I will refer to their EROI numbers, along with figures found in the other studies where available, for comparing various forms of power generation.[1] It is also worth pointing out that, like other sources of energy that must be extracted, processed, and transported, the mean EROI from various studies for electricity from coal is below 20, despite its nominally high 80 EROI at the "mine mouth," due mainly to transportation energy costs and the efficiency (about one unit of electricity produced for every three units of thermal energy) for a typical coal-fired plant.

A 2013 study by a group of scientists at the Institute for Solid-State Nuclear Physics in Berlin (for the purposes of full disclosure, they are developing a new-generation nuclear reactor so have skin in the game) standardizes the energy output as much as possible between, and compares EROI for, typical power plants generating wind, solar PV (photovoltaic cells that convert sunlight directly to electricity), solar thermal, hydro, natural gas, biogas, coal, and nuclear power. Importantly, the study also offers extended EROI figures for various power technologies adjusted for providing energy storage through pumped hydroelectricity storage, which uses off-peak electricity to pump water to a higher elevation to store the potential energy and accounts for almost all the bulk storage capacity today (though it is unlikely that so much capacity would be geographically available), to address intermittencies, which they call buffered EROI. For example, the authors find that wind power in Germany has a headline EROI of 16 but a buffered EROI of only 4 after the energy costs of storing its output are incorporated.

The study differentiates between EROI and a measure the authors call "energy money returned on [money] invested," or EMROI. EMROI incorporates the phenomenon that fossil-fueled power plants typically use three units of thermal energy to produce one unit of electricity, which is more usable for most applications, since all you have to do is plug them in. EMROI is typically higher than EROI, as the output (the numerator) is electricity, which is given a weighting of three times, while many of the inputs (the denominator) are not. Although EMROI excludes capital and labor costs, which are typically very significant for power production, it is a step closer to measuring the return on monetary investment. The authors point out that the EROI numbers often presented for renewable energy, by giving higher weights to their electrical energy output, are actually EMROI. Looking at the United States, the authors find that a kilowatt-hour of energy costing ten cents produces seventy cents of GDP for about 7 EROI (similar to Hall's earlier observations and around where the "net energy cliff" falls off), or about 16 EMROI. The ratios are similar for Germany, leading them to conclude that countries with OECD-like energy consumption technology probably have similar thresholds: adding too much of an energy technology below the threshold would shrink GDP.[2]

So, in a nutshell, the study finds that both the buffered EROI and buffered EMROI of solar PV and wind power — the most commonly deployed renewable energy technologies today — are below the threshold for sustaining economic production. It also derives a very high EROI of 75 for nuclear power using second-generation (1970s vintage) pressurized water reactors, a finding that diehard foes of nuclear power find difficult to swallow. Despite the controversy the study has garnered, the findings from making an apples-to-apples comparison between the most common power sources in use today, incorporating the cost of addressing intermittencies, provide valuable insights as we look across the energy landscape.

In 2014, renewables including hydroelectricity accounted for 9.2 percent of total worldwide consumption of primary energy (energy found in nature that has not been converted or transformed), up from 8.9 percent in 2013. But stripping out hydro left just a 2.5 percent share for 2014, mainly from bioenergy, solar, and wind. The consumption of energy from non-hydro renewables more than doubled (+130 percent) between 2009 and 2014, but

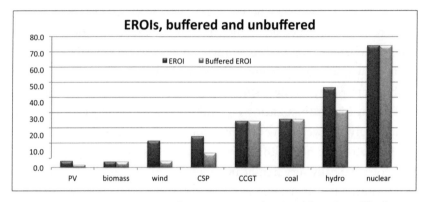

Energy return on energy investment for power sources (reprinted from D. Weißbach et al., "Energy Intensities, EROIs [Energy Returned on Invested], and Energy Payback Times of Electricity Generating Power Plants," *Energy* 52 [April 2013]: 210–221; copyright 2013, with permission from Elsevier).

looking at the absolute numbers reveals that the increase of 179.5 million tons oil equivalent (Mtoe) between 2009 and 2014 was overwhelmed by the growth of fossil fuel consumption, by 1,285 Mtoe during the same period.[3]

Every year, the International Energy Agency publishes a detailed tome called the *World Energy Outlook*. The 2014 edition outlines a "New Policies Scenario" for projecting global energy trends out to 2040. The scenario lies between a continuation of current policies and a challenging but plausible way to enact policies compatible with a 50 percent chance of keeping the average global temperature increase to 2°C or less versus preindustrial levels in the long term (called the 450 Scenario, for the 450 parts per million threshold for atmospheric carbon articulated by many climate experts). The IEA's New Policies Scenario calls for a 37 percent increase in total world primary energy demand (all unconverted energy for human use) from 2012 to 2040, but for electricity generation to grow by a much larger 76 percent over the same period. Coal is forecast to account for 31 percent of global electric power generation in 2040, down from 41 percent in 2012 but an outright increase of 33 percent, which would enable it to retain the largest share of electricity generation by fuel.

The projections for faster growth in power generation over the next several decades are important because of the major roles played by dirty coal and natural gas in producing electricity. Forms of oil will continue to play an ever-minor (about 5 percent now, probably about 1 percent in 2040) role in electricity generation but will likely remain the dominant fuels for most airborne or marine propulsion applications because of their high energy density (the U.S. Air Force toyed with the idea of nuclear-powered aircraft during the 1950s as the navy was getting all the cool nuclear-powered toys, and thankfully abandoned the idea, but drove the initial research into molten fuel reactors). In the developed world and, increasingly, in the developing world, most of the busiest passenger rail lines are electrified, and even lines that use diesel fuel are more energy-efficient than other forms of transport, particularly for freight. Land transport is slowly moving toward a mix of fuels, with natural gas and electricity (including hybrids) increasingly popular, particularly among commercial fleets and for relatively short distances. But the increasing use of electricity for land transport will further broaden demands for grid-scale electricity, adding to the pressure to continue large-scale coal use in the absence of cheap alternatives for base-load power.

Base load refers to the power needed to meet the minimum level of demand on an electrical grid during a day, and is typically supplied by coal or nuclear, as they provide electricity constantly but do not ramp up or wind down very efficiently. Renewable sources that do not fluctuate, such as geothermal, biomass, biogas, and hydro, can also be used to provide base-load power. In theory, fairly predictable wind power from dispersed sources can also be used for base load but will sometimes be unavailable because of unexpectedly poor conditions. Intermediate-load plants ramp up and down to follow demand during a day, and utilities often use older plants that were once base-load plants or gas combined-cycle plants. Peak-load plants must increase their output quickly to meet demand when it is highest, so utilities commonly rely on gas turbines or pumped hydro storage. Although solar PV capacity does not respond rapidly to demand, it coincides with summer demand peaks from air conditioning use in some regions, making it useful. But solar PV and wind power that utilities must take under feed-in schemes from diverse sources are the trickiest to manage, particularly as their contribution to the grid grows. An electricity grid must use the various different sources of power at its disposal to meet fluctuating demand without "dropping the ball" and causing brownouts or blackouts.

The IEA New Policies Scenario projects total power generation from renewable sources (excluding hydroelectricity and bioenergy)[4] in 2040 to increase almost eightfold from 2012, but still less than the amount by which electricity from coal alone actually grew in the period between 1990 and 2012 and representing only 13.5 percent of total power generation in 2040 (up from 3 percent in 2012).[5] Now let's compare the IEA's scenarios to a far more ambitious set of scenarios about our energy future.

If anyone has an interest in painting rosy pictures for the future of non-hydro renewables, industry bodies representing renewable energy and the organization Greenpeace must be at the top of the list. In conjunction with the European Renewable Energy Council and SolarPowerEurope, Greenpeace released an update of its *Energy Revolution: A Sustainable World Energy Outlook* in 2015. The report builds its scenarios based on population and economic growth assumptions used in the IEA World Energy Outlook 2014, extrapolated an additional ten years to 2050. For its central Energy Revolution (ER) scenario, the report further assumes that a carbon emissions trading system will be established in all regions and nuclear will be phased out globally, and forecasts that falling costs for capturing renewable energy, combined with greater energy efficiencies, will drive a near 51 percent fall in energy intensity (final energy demand per unit of GDP) between 2012 and 2050. Based on these and other assumptions, Greenpeace's ER scenario diverges most dramatically from those of the IEA in projecting that, instead of increasing by 37 percent in the IEA New Policies or 17 percent in the 450 Scenario to 2040, primary energy demand increases only slightly until 2020 before easing back to 2012 levels.[6]

Against this backdrop of significantly throttled-back global energy demand, the ER scenario would see a massive increase in installed capacity for wind, solar, and geothermal by over fifteenfold, about sixtyfold, and almost thirtyfold respectively by 2040 compared to 2012. By 2040, all renewables would comprise 80 percent of total installed electric power generation capacity: 60 percent from fluctuating power sources (solar PV, wind, and ocean), a significant share increase from 7 percent today (3 percent by electricity actually generated as opposed to capacity). For transport applications, electricity, biofuels, and hydrogen generated from renewable electricity would largely replace the fuels in use today. Greenpeace estimates that achieving the ER scenario will require around US$48 trillion, or $23.5 trillion in investments beyond the "business as usual" scenario through 2050, but that fuel cost savings of $39 trillion from implementing the strategy would more than cover the incremental cost. In contrast, the IEA puts the cumulative bill through 2035 (so fifteen years shorter) for its optimistic 450 Scenario, which may be enough to place us on a +2°C pathway, at $53 trillion — with $40 trillion on energy supply and the remainder on energy efficiency. More than half of the $40 trillion investment in energy supply is required to offset declining production from existing oil and gas fields (lower EROI) and to replace aging power plants and other infrastructure.

Greenpeace expects fuel cost savings under its Energy Revolution scenario to more than make up for the incremental cost of building renewable energy capacity, but it provides very little about the costs of addressing the fluctuations associated with 66 percent of the installed electricity capacity envisaged by 2050, except to note that they "require implicitly the implementation of smart grids and a fast expansion of transmission grids, storage, and other load balancing capabilities." And for other infrastructure needs to achieve the Energy Revolution scenario, such as hydrogen or synthetic fuel production, "it is therefore implicitly assumed that such infrastructural projects will be implemented in all regions without societal, economic and political barriers."[7] This not a trivial issue, as the reliability and resilience of a power mix can be reduced significantly by an overreliance on intermittent renewable sources, even given improved storage technologies or the ameliorating effects of advanced grid technology. As for the scale of the envisaged role for renewable energy, environmentalist Mark Lynas notes that, according to his calculations, the wind farm build-out in the previous 2012 Greenpeace Energy Revolution scenario (along similar lines to the 2015 edition) would require about one million square kilometers, or twice the area of Spain, with an additional fifty thousand or so square kilometers for solar power, and characterizes the Greenpeace outlook as "enormous renewables investments, which surely must be at the absolute upper end of what can be considered realistic."[8]

As a major objective of the Energy Revolution scenario, Greenpeace projects that about 17 gigatonnes of carbon emissions from power generation, transport, and industry (but not land-use change or waste) would be saved annually by 2030 from the "business as usual" scenario of 39 Gt, based on assumptions of reduced or more efficient transport use, widespread improvement in energy efficiency, and general adoption of other technologies leading to significantly moderated overall energy use. About 8 Gt in emissions savings by 2030 would be derived directly from power generation, where much of the dirtiest energy sources are used: emissions from coal for power generation (including combined heat and power plants) are projected to fall 34 percent from 2012 to 2030, but they will still account for 26 percent of *all* CO_2 emissions (excluding land-use change and waste) versus 29 percent in 2012.[9]

The Greenpeace ER scenario calls for the phasing out of nuclear energy, substantially by 2030 and completely by 2050. But shutting down nuclear plants almost completely by 2030 in a world without proper carbon pricing would mean that they would likely be replaced with coal as the cheapest fuel for providing 24/7 power (as in Germany today), canceling out or even exceeding the savings from renewables adoption. Using the IEA's 2010 carbon emissions data for coal power generation of about 1.04 million tons per terawatt hour (a trillion watts of power sustained for one hour), replacing 4,016 terawatt hours of nuclear power in the IEA's central New Policies Scenario with coal generation by 2030 would translate into an additional 4 billion tonnes (gigatonnes) of carbon emissions per year. To put this in context, replacing nuclear with coal would increase the IEA's New Policies projection for total annual emissions from energy use in 2030 from 36 Gt to 40 Gt, or almost back to the "business as usual" projection of 41 Gt. The additional emissions from replacing the 24/7 power provided by nuclear would be ameliorated somewhat if natural gas were used instead of coal. But a call for eliminating nuclear power altogether when so many promising reactor technologies are under development sounds excessive and appears to be motivated by sheer ideological opposition.

Phasing out nuclear power and replacing it with coal would have a significant impact on human health as well. James E. Hansen, the former NASA scientist who is well known for his Senate testimony in 1988 that raised public awareness about global warming, coauthored a 2013 article in which he estimates that between 1971 and 2009, nuclear power prevented an average of 64 gigatonnes of CO_2 equivalent (Gt CO_2e) greenhouse gas emissions globally that would have resulted from fossil fuel burning. The study projects that nuclear power, if assumed to be in lieu of coal use, would prevent an average of 150 to 240 Gt CO_2e cumulative global emissions between 2010 and 2050, based on low- and high-end International Atomic Energy Agency projections for nuclear power. The study also provides a mean estimate that 1.84 million deaths have been prevented globally by nuclear power production from 1971 to 2009, with an average of seventy-six thousand annually from 2000 to 2009, and nuclear power would prevent millions of more deaths by 2050 if used in lieu of coal.[10]

Antinuclear environmentalists assume that both fossil-fueled and nuclear power plants, which provide 79 percent of the electricity generated today, will be replaced by renewable energy over the next three decades or so. Greenpeace rightly points out that, aided by declining costs and supportive government policies (mostly subsidies and favorable feed-in tariffs), their past scenarios for the growth of renewable capacity over the past decade or so have been far more reflective of the actual trajectory than those of agencies such as the International Energy Agency and the U.S. Energy Information Administration.[11] But to successfully supplant, instead of merely supplement, the fuels that meet the bulk of today's massive power needs, the most scalable renewable sources must have EROI that are high enough to support our civilization's complexity. So let's review the various means of capturing renewable energy, their EROI, and their roles in the broad energy mix of our civilization, with particular emphasis on the two that are likely to grow most dramatically: solar and wind power.

Hydroelectric Power

Early industrial factories were built next to rivers to use waterwheels for mechanical power, one of the oldest means of tapping energy. Since the first commercial hydroelectric power plants commenced operations in the United States during the 1880s, modern dams for water management and generating electricity have become among the biggest infrastructure programs in the world for their respective eras, ranging from the Hoover Dam in the 1930s to the massive Three Gorges project in China today. The obvious advantages of hydropower are that, once the projects are built, the EROI is very site-specific but high over the long term — a mean of 84, though Hall and colleagues point out that the best sites in the developed world have already been tapped. And while wind and solar power do not produce much electricity when the air is calm or the skies are heavily overcast, hydroelectric power can be produced so long as there is enough water behind a dam or running through a river, with little time needed for ramping up power to help meet peak demand.

The major problems with dammed hydroelectricity have to do with silting, damage to ecosystems, and methane emissions from reservoirs built over uncleared forests in tropical regions. Dam construction can also become a source of conflict in areas of water scarcity, as those upstream have the ability to turn the tap off at will and harm those living downstream. Run-of-the-river hydro, which uses the flow of a river to generate electricity with little or no reservoir capacity, has the potential to provide additional energy globally with much less environmental and water resource impact than conventional dams. In their comparative study, Weißbach and colleagues derive an EROI of 49 (buffered EROI of 35, accounting for seasonal flows) for a medium-size run-of-river hydro plant: less than many hydroelectric plants with big dams but still well above the net energy cliff (around 8).[12] So the good news about hydroelectric power plants is that they have high EROI; the bad news is that there are limits on good places to situate them, as even run-of-river sites need to have steep enough drops. The IEA expects that growth in hydro overall will almost manage to keep up with total global electrical capacity, from 1,033 billion watts (gigawatts, or GW) in 2010 (20 percent of total capacity) to 1,583 GW in 2030 (18.4 percent). But hydro projects are far from a panacea for the world's energy challenges, as there are simply too few good places to put them to replace the 24/7 power provided by fossil fuels or nuclear power, especially against a backdrop of environmental concerns, water scarcity, and changing precipitation patterns.

Solar Power

Broadly defined, much of the energy that civilization can capture can be called solar power, from the winds generated by convection of sun-warmed air to fossil fuels derived from ancient organic matter. But for classifying renewable energy, solar generally refers to photovoltaic cells, which convert light directly into electricity, and concentrated solar, in which sunlight is focused to heat working fluids (typically water but also molten salts) to power turbines. Defined in this way, global solar power consumption has grown almost eight times to about 253 trillion watt-hours (terawatt-hours, or TWh) over the past five years, supported by government policies and improving costs. Surprisingly, Germany has the second-largest national installed capacity, at about 40 GW as of 2015, which has grown fourfold over six years. Solar has seen particularly robust growth in Asia during the same period, from 0.8 GW to 43 GW in China, and from 2.6 GW to 35 GW in Japan.[13] During the 1970s, a key goal of photovoltaic technology was to convert more than 20 percent of the total solar energy captured into electricity — the United States, in the name of national security, even used the Invention Secrecy Act of 1951 and a subsequent 1971 list of applicable technologies to screen any patents for processes that promised to be more efficient.[14] Today, many commercially installed crystalline silicon solar cells range from 14 percent to 20 percent efficiency and are sufficiently cheap so that solar in some locations is now said to be approaching "grid parity" with fossil fuels. Moreover, emerging technologies offer efficiencies of over 40 percent at ever-lower cost, and techniques for concentrating large amounts of sunlight into a small area and generating electricity directly (concentrated photovoltaic) or through heat (concentrated solar thermal) are increasingly being developed and applied.

The point at which a renewable energy source can produce electricity at a cost equal to or below the cost of buying electricity from the grid is called "grid parity." Grid parity is often seen as a tipping point for renewable technologies, beyond which it is expected that adoption should broaden and accelerate, driving a virtuous circle of lower costs and even more adoption. Grid parity is often used simply as shorthand for the point at which it becomes as cheap for a consumer to use power from renewable sources as those from fossil fuels, but it is a slipperier concept than meets the eye.

First, the levelized cost of electricity (LCOE) represents the financial cost of building and operating an electric generation facility over its assumed operational life, and is often used as the measure of comparative competitiveness for various power generation technologies in determining grid parity.[15] LCOE typically incorporates installed capital cost, operating expenses, cost of financing, and energy production. Although the LCOE of renewables incorporates capacity factors lower than those for technologies that can dispatch power on demand, it does not incorporate the costs of addressing intermittencies, thereby understating its true costs and making direct comparisons with technologies that can provide power constantly or on demand difficult. This is key since, after all, the overriding priority for grid electricity is to have power on demand, day or night, rather than, say, very cheap power from solar just during sunny days.

LCOE also does not incorporate the very real but "external" costs of the environmental and health damage associated with the production and consumption of power from these sources. Although technologies to capture renewable energy have negative environmental impacts as well (e.g., chemicals used in the production of PV cells), the total external costs of fossil fuels are generally higher, thus favoring renewables if these costs were incorporated. But incorporating the environmental and health costs into one number for comparing power sources is fiendishly difficult: suffice it to say that, because of the potential immeasurably high costs to our commons, fossil fuel use must be curtailed dramatically, and leave it at that for the time being.

For power users, grid parity is also a function of where one is on the power generation and transmission chain. For example, a local power distribution company may buy an agreed amount of power at fixed cost, but also buy power at peak times at much higher cost, with pricing changing according to the time of day. Or a large manufacturing facility will typically buy power from the grid at commercial rates significantly below those charged to retail customers, lowering the break-even for incorporating renewable energy sources. A residential retail customer will be charged the most, representing the least onerous hurdle for solar power as the most realistic alternative to the grid for individuals and small businesses, particularly when tax incentives are incorporated. But retail customers also typically still pay flat rates, which do not reflect the varying price of electricity depending on time of day, so do not receive price signals about, say, the value of using solar PV during summer peak demand hours when it would be most efficient. In a study outlining grid parity as a potentially misleading concept, a trio of Australian researchers recently pointed out as well that deployment of renewable energy technologies may not necessarily take off quickly beyond the point of parity, owing to various factors such as the need for utilities to recoup additional infrastructure costs through higher retail tariffs, access to finance, or regulatory risk.[16]

We also need to be disciplined about thinking about the impact on the net energy contribution and net carbon emissions from deploying renewable energy sources, particularly solar PV, on a massive scale. Solar PV units emit no greenhouse gases from their operation, but they do require a lot of energy from fossil fuels in their manufacture and installation, resulting in greenhouse gases. A 2015 article in Resilience.org points out that researchers who do not have a positive bias toward solar PV think the industry has increased net energy use and emissions and that its plunging costs are due not so much to massive improvements in productive efficiency but more to manufacturing moving to low-cost Asia (from almost all being made in Europe, Japan, and the United States a decade ago to 87 percent made in Asia in 2015, mostly in China), where the electric grid is much less energy efficient and twice as carbon intensive. Moreover, by emitting a lot of CO_2 during production and installation, building too much solar PV capacity too quickly overwhelms the savings from its use, particularly if it is installed in locations that are not well suited (think Germany). The article estimates that the maximum nonpolluting growth rates of solar PV made in Asia is around 16 percent (depending a lot on where units are deployed) and, though very recent research is not available, significantly lower than the close to 60 percent average annual growth observed from 2008 to 2014.[17]

Don't get me wrong: adding PV or any other renewable energy capacity can be a very good thing, so long as it is done right. Even if renewables achieve grid parity for some users, replacing the nastiest fossil fuels with fluctuating renewable energy efficiently will require major investments in power distribution infrastructure and energy storage to ensure 24/7 availability. Moreover, using favorable feed-in tariffs and tax subsidies to add capacity as quickly as possible, even if the technologies are not yet mature enough to provide sufficient energy return on (energy) investment, does little to enhance a society's long-term energy resilience.

Although very site-specific, the mean EROI of photovoltaic calculated by Hall and colleagues in their meta-analysis is roughly 10.[18] However, Charles Hall and Pedro A. Pieto recently published a very detailed study of real historical data on solar PV in Spain, where massive subsidies to existing technologies encouraged massive capacity buildup, particularly before the 2008 financial crisis. The study's 2.45 extended EROI figure for Spanish PV is very sobering, even allowing for technological improvements since Spain's massive build-out.[19] Similarly, Weißbach et al. derive a 3.9 EROI (1.6 buffered) for solar PV in Germany, though a theoretical concentrated solar power (CSP) plant in the Moroccan desert is calculated to have EROI of 17–21 (8.2 to 9.6 buffered), depending on the technology used.[20] CSP plants focus a lot of sunlight onto a small area through mirror arrays that track the sun or parabolic mirrors to achieve very high temperatures, producing steam to operate turbines. Although their EROI numbers look better than solar photovoltaic, as they can usually store their heat to generate power on cloudy days or at night, CSP plants are more complicated to build and particularly dependent on deployment in consistently sunny locations. For Europe, placing them in North Africa or the Sahara just puts them in the same "arc of instability" as the source of much of their oil and some of their natural gas, to say nothing of the additional energy demands and losses from power transmission over great distances.

In October 2014, the green blogosphere was abuzz with talk of a report by Deutsche Bank showing that the cost of residential solar electricity would be at or below that of power from the grid (grid parity) by 2016 in forty-seven U.S. states, assuming that the 30 percent solar investment federal tax credit is maintained when up for renewal in 2016, and in thirty-six states even if the credit is reduced to 10 percent. If true, this is good news for U.S. power consumers who can deploy solar PV to save money, particularly if they could be paired eventually with cost-efficient energy storage. Indeed, given rapidly falling costs (systems prices fell to a third, and module prices to one-fifth, in six years), the IEA also revised its "PV Roadmap" in September 2014 to estimate that solar PV's share of global electricity capacity could rise to 16 percent by 2050, instead of 11 percent by 2050 in its 2010 projection. But just because solar reaches grid parity for some, it is still way too early to break out the champagne. After all, as an example, solar PV in Australia is said to have reached grid parity in 2011 but still provides only about 2 percent of that nation's electricity today.[21]

Some of the technologies currently under development could see fixed solar PV becoming ever more efficient, and PV cells even being printed on various surfaces such as vehicles and appliances, increasing their diffusion throughout society—all good news. The IEA adds, however, that measures to address the variability of solar energy, such as interconnections, flexible generation, and storage, need to be developed successfully for the PV Roadmap to be realized.[22] And measures to substitute PV and wind for base-load power add substantial costs: though many of the technologies are improving rapidly, they are doing so much more slowly for energy storage. Moreover, the IEA's Energy Technology Perspectives scenarios, the basis for its PV projection, consist of three scenarios that parallel those used in its annual World Energy Outlook, based on the number of degrees by which average global temperatures would be expected to rise as the result: 6°C or business-as-usual (Reference); 4°C, which takes into account recent pledges to limit emissions and improved energy efficiencies (New Policies); and 2°C (450 Scenario), which would cut emissions by more than half by 2050, consistent with a 50 percent chance of keeping the temperature increase to within 2°C. The revised IEA PV Roadmap is based on the ambitious 2°C scenario: in other words, the IEA's PV Roadmap is an aspirational goal, and there is simply no assurance that the renewable capacity that is built will replace the dirtiest of fossil fuels in the absence of concerted and enforceable international action or the availability of clean, abundant base-load power.

Wind Power

Windmills have come a long way since Cervantes's hero Don Quixote battled them in the 1600s. Windmills have been used for a couple of thousand years to mill grain, saw lumber, and pump water, but since the end of the nineteenth century they have also been used to generate electricity. Although modern wind turbines come in a variety of shapes and configurations, the vast majority used for grid-scale power generation today have three blades that rotate in front of a turbine housing. The amount of kinetic energy flowing through the turbine that can theoretically be captured is 59 percent (Betz's Law),[23] and sets the ceiling against which turbine designs seek to maximize efficiency. Because wind speeds vary, wind turbines produce only a proportion of the nameplate maximum: this is called the "capacity factor" (used to estimate actual instead of rated power production, so applicable to other energy sources as well) and ranges between 18 percent and 50 percent (median 38 percent) for onshore wind generation.[24]

Global wind power consumption more than doubled between 2009 and 2014, from 278 to 706 trillion watt-hours. As of 2015, China led the world in total installed capacity at 145 billion watts (GW), followed by the United States with 75 GW and Germany at 45 GW. Utility-scale wind turbines have power ratings of over 100 kilowatts, with some as high as 8 million watts (megawatts, or MW) and are typically clustered in "wind farms" comprising as many as several hundred units. Although the land below and between them can be used for agriculture or grazing, wind turbines must be spaced sufficiently apart to minimize the effects of their wakes (putting a turbine too close behind another means capturing less wind), dictating the amount of land needed to accommodate wind farms. The extensive land area required by large wind farms, their aesthetic impact on landscapes, the hazards they pose to flying animals, and the noise the turbine blades produce have made wind power among the most prone among renewable energy sources to "not in my backyard" (NIMBY) opposition. Clustering turbines offshore overcomes these problems and also benefits from higher capacity factors (offshore winds tend to have higher speeds and can be more consistent), but the cost of building offshore wind turbines can be significantly higher (two times or more) than onshore.[25] Nevertheless, the IEA and Greenpeace both expect offshore wind to play a greater role in total wind generation over the next several decades.[26]

Although very site-specific, Hall and colleagues' mean EROI estimate for wind of 20, based on meta-analysis of various studies, puts it in the same "above the net energy cliff" ballpark as plentiful, cheap, and dirty coal. But Weißbach and colleagues examine EROI for a reference turbine — the Enercon E-66 with 1.5 MW nameplate capacity, two thousand full-load hours annually, and twenty-year lifetime — located on flat land in Germany and come up with 16 EROI and, more tellingly, 4 when the energy costs of buffering intermittencies are incorporated.[27]

The Others

Although promising because of better predictability, lower intermittency, and potentially fewer NIMBY issues, methods to capture energy from the oceans are still in their early stages of commercial development. Although a form of hydropower, tidal and current turbine generation can be considered wind's submerged cousin. One of the most high-profile tidal power projects is a licensed plan to build a series of thirty turbines, with total capacity of 1 MW, at the bottom of the East River in New York City. Since water is eight hundred times denser than air, underwater turbines can capture far more energy for a given diameter than their surface counterparts. Studies have suggested that there is tremendous potential for using current and tidal energy as base-load power, but technological hurdles such as cost, maintenance, and corrosion resistance remain. In addition to turbines to capture kinetic energy, technologies for capturing the ocean's thermal energy through temperature differences at various depths and energy from salinity differences at river mouths (osmotic power) have been developed and applied, though not yet on a large scale. More intermittent than the other marine technologies, wave energy is an emerging marine renewable energy application, with commercial wave farms of 1–3 MW nameplate capacity deployed in Portugal, the UK, and perhaps soon the United States, but still not significant enough to make a noticeable contribution to total electricity generation.

Geothermal heating has a long history, with the ancient Romans using hot springs for under-floor heating in addition to bathing, so it is fitting that the first commercial geothermal electric power station was built in Italy in 1911. Like nuclear power, geothermal power captures the Earth's energy, but through convective heat from radioactive decay instead of splitting those elements. Most geothermal plants today either directly use the steam drawn from underground (dry steam) or separate out the steam generated by hot water flowing up through wells (flash steam) to turn turbines. A more recent technology, binary cycle steam plants use water at lower temperatures (so widening the range of sites that can be used) to boil a working fluid with a low boiling point to produce vapor to turn turbines. Modern geothermal power plants offer the advantage of operating stably at near full capacity for most of their service lives, making them very suitable for providing base-load power. Their main disadvantages are that capital costs (drilling costs, with risks of failure) are high, and you cannot just build them anywhere. Although geothermal plants typically emit some carbon dioxide from the fluids that are drawn from the holes drilled deep underground, the amount is very small compared to fossil fuel CO_2 generation (about one-eighth that of coal, for example).[28] EROI estimates for geothermal power vary greatly, between 5 and 39, depending on location, type of technology used, and the boundaries for including the energy inputs in the denominator.[29]

Total global installed capacity for geothermal generation worldwide stood at 13 GW in 2015, with another 12 GW or so of planned additional capacity. Some nations and regions where underground temperatures are higher at a given depth than in other areas are well-suited for geothermal generation; the United States has the largest installed capacity at about 3.6 GW, followed by the Philippines with 1.9 GW and Indonesia with 1.4 GW. Volcanic Iceland, with 665 MW of installed capacity, derives almost all its heating and about a quarter of its electricity from geothermal (the remainder from hydro)[30] and is now exploring construction of an undersea cable to export electricity to the UK.[31]

As one of the most volcanic countries in the world, Japan is particularly suited for geothermal generation, but installed capacity stood at only 544 MW in 2015. The Earth Policy Institute has suggested that the country has potential geothermal generation capacity of about 80 GW using conventional technologies, or half of Japan's electricity demand — a curiously ambitious claim, given that total installed generation capacity across all types of power was not 160 GW (as the analysis would suggest) but 286 GW in 2011.[32] Japan has experienced its own peculiar form of NIMBY-ism, as communities relying on *onsen* hot springs for tourism, concerned about possible overuse, have united to oppose geothermal development, although attitudes and regulations are changing gradually since the Great Tohoku Earthquake and Fukushima disaster.[33] Moreover, many prime sites for capturing geothermal energy are located in national parks and other protected areas, which would have to be opened up for geothermal exploitation. Japan's environment ministry has a somewhat less ambitious take on geothermal potential: about 34 GW total, and about 10 GW if development were prohibited in parks, conservation areas, national heritage sites, and other protected areas.[34] But even at the lower end of estimates, geothermal could provide, as base-load power (aside from district heating and other applications), over 10 percent of the electricity needed by Japan if its potential can be tapped fully.

Bioenergy, the energy captured from biological sources such as wood, manure, and agricultural by-products, is the single largest renewable source of energy today, providing about 10 percent of the world's primary (unconverted) energy supply, so also worth examining. Modern bioenergy encompasses a very wide range of fuels and applications: pellets produced from trees are used to generate electricity, biogas from organic waste is burned to provide district heating, and bioethanol from corn, sugarcane, jatropha, trees, and grasses can power vehicles. Researchers are also developing techniques to use microalgae to produce large quantities of biofuels. In much of the developing world, burning biomass still provides basic energy for cooking and heating, much as it did in Europe before the Industrial Revolution, often with unfortunate health and environmental effects. But technologies that use bioenergy much more efficiently and cleanly, such as advanced biomass cooking stoves, heaters, and generators, promise to improve the quality of life for many residents of areas that are not serviced by grid electricity.

Bioenergy produced about 2 percent of the world's electricity in 2012, so quite a bit lower than its share of primary energy supply, and the IEA's New Policies Scenario projects that its share will increase only slightly to 4 percent by 2040. While bioenergy is plentiful where there are crops and forests for fuel, and also encompasses burnable waste that would otherwise end up as debris or emit greenhouse gases through decay, there are massive uncertainties about its contribution to carbon emissions. In theory, many forms of bioenergy emit little or no net greenhouse gases: for example, forests and crops that absorb carbon from the atmosphere are replanted to (eventually in the case of forests) compensate for emissions from their use. In practice, however, the use of plant biomass for energy tends to encourage deforestation and changes in land use that increase net emissions or are otherwise detrimental to the environment. In some instances, such as subsidized corn ethanol, bioenergy use raises questions about whether it displaces food production and drives prices up. So these and other major challenges make it difficult for truly sustainable bioenergy to provide large-scale base-load electricity, a position taken by Greenpeace and other environmental organizations. In one of the notable areas in which its central scenario forecasts are similar to those of the IEA, Greenpeace looks for bioenergy to meet 12 percent of global final energy demand and produce 6 percent of the world's electricity in 2040.

Resource Impediments to Renewable Energy?

A potential problem that affects solar PV, wind power, and battery technologies is the availability and cost of rare metals, which occasionally makes the news because of the world's current dependence on China as the near-monopoly supplier for many of these materials. The U.S. Department of Energy published a report in 2011 on potential supply risks for a number of rare metals that are important for clean energy technologies, using lower- and upper-end projections produced in the IEA's 2010 *World Energy Outlook* and *Energy Technology Perspectives*. The list of rare metals sounds like Lex Luthor's favorite elements: dysprosium and neodymium, used in permanent magnets for wind turbines and electric vehicle motors, and supplies of which are classified as "critical"; yttrium, europium, and terbium, used as phosphors for lighting; and tellurium, used in newer thin-film photovoltaic technology and considered "near-critical." Among other elements, lithium, used in high-performance batteries, may also become near-critical over the medium term (2015–2025).[35] Quicker adoption of many major "green" technologies will increase the chances of shortages in key materials over the medium term. In addition to securing new supplies of rare earths and encouraging recycling, manufacturers have, for example, sought to replace permanent magnet motors in electric or hybrid drive vehicles with induction motors, or reduce the rare earth content of wind turbines through complex gearing. Research into using more abundant materials to replace rare elements and applying nanotechnology to materials development is currently under way as well and may ameliorate many of these issues, perhaps even significantly, but the potential impact is difficult to quantify. Finally, mining for rare metals, particularly the extraction of the rock monzanite, often produces thorium and uranium oxide as by-products, which must currently be handled, at great expense, as low-level radioactive waste in some jurisdictions and disposed of accordingly. The demand for rare metals, driven by the increasing share of power generated from renewable sources, therefore dovetails elegantly with stockpiling and using some of the waste materials to support a modern nuclear energy infrastructure as the backbone of very low carbon emission, base-load power.

Energy Storage

Energy is stored in many ways, from the potential mechanical energy in a windup toy to the chemical energy in our food and fuel. For our purposes, we want to examine the outlook for energy storage technologies that may compensate for the fluctuations of renewable energy, particularly those of wind and solar.

Pumped hydropower — moving water uphill to reservoirs, from which it can be released as needed to produce electricity — is the only mature technology for large-scale energy storage today. According to the Department of Energy, the United States currently has about 24.6 GW of grid storage, representing 2.3 percent of total electric production capacity, 95 percent of which is pumped hydro.[36] Although it can operate at high efficiency, at large scale, and for many hours, the technology is limited largely by the availability of mountainous terrain (underground and ocean applications are exceptions but not very developed), and building more dams often causes environmental harm. Compressed-air energy storage in geological formations can also potentially store energy on a grid scale, and although such projects have been run in Europe and the United States since the late 1970s, the technology has not been deployed widely to date. Flywheels, in which low-friction disks are accelerated to rotate at high speeds and the energy released as needed to produce electricity, have been used mainly in applications that require bursts of power (such as high-power lasers) or to provide uninterrupted power to vital functions such as data centers during the brief interval required for alternative means of power to take over in the event of a main power outage. In the latest versions using magnetic instead of mechanical bearings, flywheels are capable of high efficiencies (storing and releasing up to about 80 percent of the energy input) but are not the most suited for providing sustained power to the grid.

Several other energy storage technologies are also worth mentioning. Adiabatic compressed-air storage is designed to capture and use the heat of compressed air to improve efficiencies to around 70 percent, but a demonstration plant has yet to be completed.[37] Superconductive magnetic energy storage is designed to store energy in a magnetic coil cooled to superconducting temperatures so that electricity flows without energy loss. Although very efficient, such systems are very costly to manufacture and maintain. Electrochemical capacitors (EC, also called supercapacitors), which store electricity directly in materials and can discharge and recharge very efficiently, are a promising technology but are still too expensive to use for large-scale grid storage.[38] In addition to hydrogen storage (which we will cover later), the technologies listed above represent the main means of storing grid electricity today, apart from traditional electric batteries.

There are broadly three types of batteries in use today for grid power storage: lead acid, sodium sulfur, and lithium ion. Lead acid is a mature technology with low costs but is constrained by low energy density (energy output per unit of mass). Sodium sulfur batteries offer high energy density and are suited for discharges of up to about eight hours but require high operating temperatures of 250–300 degrees Celsius. Lithium ion batteries have energy densities almost seven times greater than those of lead acid, and provide good power quality, but are still expensive. Lithium ion batteries have also been known to rupture or even combust if overheated or overcharged, sometimes despite having safety circuits, as demonstrated in several incidents on Boeing 787s equipped with them.

There is a great deal of buzz around two developments in lithium ion batteries. The first is a recently announced process for producing batteries being developed by MIT researchers and a spin-off startup that would use suspended particles instead of coated slabs[39] as electrodes to halve manufacturing costs, as well as making the batteries more flexible and resilient.[40] The other is the announcement that Tesla Motors (partnering with Panasonic), led by the charismatic Elon Musk, plans to build a "gigafactory" in Nevada the size of the Pentagon to produce about half a million lithium ion battery packs annually by 2020 — or about the world's current total production — for its cars. The facility would also complement Musk's solar panel company, SolarCity, to provide batteries for distributed energy storage, and the company estimates that the factory will drive down the cost of its lithium ion batteries by 30 percent in its first year of production, scheduled for 2017.

But remember the Department of Energy comments about the potential supply risk for lithium over the medium term? A "back of the envelope" analysis performed on Greentech Media, a website devoted to providing information about the major changes occurring in the electricity sector today, suggests that if one hundred Tesla-size lithium ion battery factories were built around the world by the year 2040, eight hundred thousand tonnes of lithium would be needed annually for batteries alone, excluding other uses such as ceramics. Given 13.5 million tonnes of known world reserves, based on U.S. Geological Survey estimates, this represents only a seventeen-year supply of lithium, while 39.5 million tonnes of "resources" — supplies that can perhaps be extracted economically at some point in the future — will last fifty years.[41] So while manufacturing efficiencies may help stretch the supply, and recycling, which is currently uneconomical compared to the most common method of extracting lithium from brine pools and deposits, may also help, we cannot take for granted that lithium ion alone will be the solution to the world's energy storage challenges.

We also come across chatter nowadays about the bright prospects for lithium air batteries, that their very high energy densities — potentially comparable to fossil fuels — make them well suited for transport applications rather than grid energy storage, particularly at first, as they will likely cost significantly more than conventional batteries. It will, however, take at least a decade or more for lithium air batteries to become available commercially.

Improvements in battery technologies have lagged developments in other areas, which we sense when our smart phone runs out of juice more quickly than our old flip phone (though the new phone's processing power rivals that of early supercomputers,). Perhaps it is because big leaps in battery capabilities usually come from using new materials, and there are limits to the number of elements out there; or we are in a relatively slow period for improvement because the benefits of the next big leap, through the development and diffusion of nanomaterials and designs concocted by advanced AI, won't kick in for another couple of decades. Maybe grid-scale battery technology has lagged efficiency improvements in other energy areas because there was no urgent need to develop large-scale energy storage until recently, given the long-held view, before awareness of the dangers posed by climate change, that fossil fuels could be used with abandon for much longer. But because of the comparatively slow development of battery storage technology, one must be very cautious about projecting a bright future for clean energy over the next twenty years or so on the basis of renewable energy efficiencies alone — for intermittent renewable energy, power generation and storage are two sides of the same coin. However, a 2105 report by Deutsche Bank predicts that lithium ion batteries will begin to be deployed widely by commercial users in the United States within the next five years if their costs can fall from about $500 per kilowatt-hour (at the end of 2014) to about $150/kWh.[42] If there is one area that, by compensating for the intermittencies of solar PV and wind, can be a major game-changer for renewable power, it is cheap, plentiful, and highly efficient battery technology, so it behooves careful watching.

We often hear about the wonders of a future powered by hydrogen, which would be produced through the use of renewable energy. Fuel cells, for example, would combine hydrogen with oxygen from the air to generate electricity, heat, and leave just water as a waste product. Although it sounds ideal, using hydrogen as fuel presents several major problems. Although it has high energy density by weight, hydrogen's very low energy density by volume calls for significant compression (and the energy required for compression) in transport functions. Liquefaction requires even more energy for cooling, as the boiling point for hydrogen is around −253°C. More important, the energy required to isolate hydrogen from natural compounds — such as natural gas, biomass, or water — and deliver it in usable form is several times the energy value of the hydrogen produced, given current technologies. For example, electrolysis of water to isolate hydrogen and compress it for use in a fuel cell would yield only about a quarter of the energy used to produce it. Moreover, isolating hydrogen from natural gas for use as a substitute for gasoline emits more CO_2 than the fuel it was meant to replace. So although Toyota and Hyundai have introduced fuel cell vehicles for leasing and limited sales, and other are poised to follow, whether hydrogen fuel call cars — without much more efficient ways to provide their fuel — will ever be able to make a significant contribution to building a low-emissions, high EROI world remains a big question mark.

Producing and storing hydrogen produced from renewable energy so that it can be used during periods when conditions are not favorable for capturing renewable energy is another method of storing energy on a grid scale. Although the process eats up energy to compress the hydrogen to about 200 bar (close to 200 atmospheres), the requirement is much less onerous than in transport applications for which the gas must be compressed to between 350 and 700 bar, so it is easier to apply less expensive technologies. A major drawback is that it is inefficient, giving back only 30–40 percent of the original energy input (versus 80 percent for pumped hydro) as useful electrical energy. One technique is to store hydrogen produced from electrolysis in underground salt caverns or tubes, which would then be used to produce electricity through fuel cells or combined-cycle gas power plants when needed. The main advantage is that very large amounts could be stored underground, allowing for extended periods of use when wind and PV energy production levels are low. To date, two large-scale hydrogen caverns are in operation in Texas, with a third under construction, and the UK has three older caverns operating, helping demonstrate the feasibility of long-term storage.[43]

The HyUnder project, a consortium of twelve companies and research institutes undertaking a study of large-scale geological hydrogen storage in Europe, released some preliminary conclusions in 2014: based on assumptions about the likely percentages of intermittent sources providing renewable power in various countries by 2050 (e.g., 62 percent in the UK, 80 percent in the Netherlands), and that 100 percent of surplus electricity would be converted to hydrogen, Europe would need to develop well over one hundred cavern fields.[44] Even if we were to accept that the lack of alternative storage technologies with comparable capacity will justify its inefficiency, whether the European public will accept such a scale of implementation — check the box if you are willing to live near a huge cavern filled with highly flammable hydrogen — remains a big question mark.

Many of us have probably witnessed the familiar science experiment of producing hydrogen and oxygen through the electrolysis of water. Though much cleaner, electrolysis currently cannot compete economically with separating out hydrogen from fossil fuels at high temperatures. But as conducting electrolysis at high temperatures (above 800°C) makes the process much more efficient and competitive, high-temperature nuclear reactors would be among the best sources (the others are concentrated solar and geothermal, but they are constrained by site availability) for the heat to be used during electrolysis, without efficiency losses from conversion to electricity. Although more work would have to be done to increase the purity of the hydrogen produced by the process so that it could be used in fuel cells, hydrogen produced with the high temperatures that can be achieved from next-generation nuclear reactors would be competitive with hydrogen produced from natural gas, but without the emissions. If we are serious about moving in the foreseeable future to an energy system that uses a lot of hydrogen, both for storage and for transportation, it would need to use nuclear power to achieve the necessary efficiency.

So for now, given the limits to places to put pumped hydro storage, and pending developments in other technologies, lowering the costs and increasing the efficiencies of batteries dramatically appears to be the single best bet for providing the large-scale storage necessary to compensate for the intermittencies of wind and solar PV. Producing hydrogen on a large scale may also help, with the added bonus that it can also be used for transportation through fuel cells, but the process must become much more efficient to make a real dent.

Many visions of powering our world exclusively through renewable energy envisage the massive build-out of advanced electricity grids and transmission networks that can balance the variable demand for electricity against fluctuating supply to ensure uninterrupted, 24/7 power. But let's take a look at what this will require in terms of actually building electrical generation capacity.

In a study published in 2012 in the *Journal of Power Sources*, researchers modeled the least costly mix of wind, solar, and storage to meet electricity demand for the PJM Interconnection, a regional transmission system spanning part of the Eastern United States. They found that, in order for renewable generation and energy storage to provide all power 90 percent or 99.9 percent of the time in the region would require, respectively, about twice or three times the generating capacity of the electricity required by the grid during times of peak demand.[45] The authors contend that by 2030, renewable energy can provide electricity 90 percent of the time at costs below those of 2012 grid electricity if the power mix is optimized and assuming incremental advances in technology and efficiency: for example, capital costs for wind and solar fall by half, and storage follows a similar path. The study has come under criticism for understating the costs associated with the uncertainties of wind and solar power, by assuming that adding more capacity from fluctuating sources will keep on adding proportionately more real capacity when it is needed most.[46] But the main takeaway is that even a study that makes some optimistic assumptions about intermittent renewable energy finds that you need to build a lot of extra capacity to provide 24/7 power.

The storage technologies examined in the PJM Interconnection study are central lithium batteries, grid-integrated vehicles (GIVs), and central hydrogen storage. The last two are interesting choices to use for simulating energy storage (one of the authors is a leading expert on GIVs): hydrogen storage is not yet widely deployed, and the study counts 100 percent of the projected registered electric and plug-in hybrid vehicles in the area studied to define vehicle storage availability. By recharging when demand is low and sending power back to the grid when demand is very high, electric vehicles that are incorporated into the grid could provide a lot of storage capacity to meet peak electricity demand, enhancing resilience through broad distribution and even reducing the need for base-load power. But GIVs require the right policies, bidirectional chargers, and work best with advanced grids that have yet to be introduced widely (and the costs of which might have to be absorbed by ratepayers). Consumers around the world are increasingly accepting hybrid and electric vehicles, as a means not only of lowering their fuel bill (though in the case of the Tesla S, it seems to be more about the cachet than economics), but also of doing something positive for the environment. But does the electric car really help the environment?

A 2013 study that compares the environmental impacts over the life cycles of electric vehicles and internal-combustion-engine vehicles published in the *Journal of Industrial Ecology* helps answer the question. In it, the authors point out that producing electric vehicles is dirtier for people, water, and the Earth than producing vehicles that burn fossil fuels. As for emissions, the greenhouse gas footprints of electric vehicles — assuming 150,000 km (93,200 miles) service lives and incorporating production and disposal — depend heavily on the power sources for the grid. Electric vehicles produce 20–24 percent less emissions than gasoline-powered vehicles (10–14 percent less versus diesel) under an average European energy mix (about 60 percent from oil and gas, and the remainder from coal, nuclear, and renewables). When the electricity is derived entirely from natural gas, the reduction in emissions falls to about 12 percent compared to gasoline vehicles and breaks even with diesel vehicles. But when electric vehicles are powered by electricity from coal, they emit 27 percent more greenhouse gases than gasoline vehicles, and 17 percent more than diesel vehicles.[47]

So it appears that driving electric cars, though seemingly helpful in the developed world, is not a slam-dunk way of being environmentally friendly everywhere: in fact, switching to them in places where the electricity is produced from the dirtiest fossil fuels is downright harmful. Now consider that two-thirds of China's electricity, and about 60 percent of India's, is produced from coal, and the need to supplant these with cleaner sources of base-load power in the developing world — especially if the developing world adopts electric vehicles in a big way — becomes very apparent.

As we have seen, moving to an all-renewable energy economy, though theoretically possible, would likely require building a great deal more capacity than a grid requires to meet peak demand, as well as advances and cost improvements in energy storage and grid management technologies to make the system both highly reliable and economically feasible. The challenges would suggest that, though an increasingly vital part of the overall power mix, renewable energy and storage are not the exclusive answer for building a cleaner, more resilient power mix over the next one to two decades.

Energy Efficiency

Although not a renewable energy source per se, improvements in efficiency are an important part of moving toward a world that burns less fossil fuel. The topic is embedded in the development of alternative and renewable power for electricity, but also encompasses a broad set of technologies such as materials, building design and construction, and distributed power and smart grids.

Buildings today account for one-third of global fuel and energy consumption and are responsible for about 8 Gt CO_2e in emissions annually, or about one-sixth of total emissions (including those from agriculture, deforestation, and organic waste). With energy demand from buildings rising steadily, and because buildings are long-lived assets, the sector appears to provide a slam-dunk way to reduce emissions through efficiency gains. But in advanced nations, the efficiency gains are mostly from retrofitting existing buildings, with typical retrofit rates at about a leisurely 1–2 percent per year. And in the developing world, meaningful improvements in efficiency are up against the urgent need — driven by population growth and urbanization — for constructing residential and commercial buildings as quickly and cheaply as possible.[48] So, although promising in concept — and regulations and incentives can be effective in some places — dramatically increasing building efficiencies to more than make up for the global growth in housing or commercial stock has thus far proved elusive.

During the 1970s, environmental scientist Emory Lovins called for the decentralization of power generation through wind, solar, and geothermal at scales suited to specific local applications. He called for using these sources of "soft energy" to replace the centralized "hard energy" produced through fossil fuels and nuclear. Lovins's normative "small is beautiful" approach has not been adopted sufficiently to make a meaningful dent in U.S. power production, and almost all of the growing energy needs of rapidly urbanizing developing countries have been met by centralized, large-scale power. But Lovins's contention that advances in material and design technologies will make electricity and fossil fuel use much more efficient has turned out to be a pretty good prediction.

The energy efficiencies of many of the trappings of our modern lives have improved significantly over the past several decades, and even over several years. In Japan, for example, the Energy Conservation Center of Japan has run a highly successful program for monitoring and labeling the energy efficiency of a wide range of consumer goods. Between 1997 and 2004 under the "Top Runner" program, room air conditioners improved their average efficiency by about 68 percent, and refrigerators by 55 percent.[49] Even in the United States, traditionally the land of big, gas-guzzling SUVs, the Environmental Protection Agency's fleet-wide adjusted fuel economy for the 2013 model year was about 24 miles per gallon, about double that of 1975 (fuel economy shot up from 1975 to 1981, leveled off and backtracked from 1985 to 2004, and has accelerated again since).[50] A 2010 McKinsey Global Institute report estimates that, if effective measures can overcome inertia and obstacles to implementation, the gains from raising energy efficiency in developing countries could slow growth in their energy demand from 3.4 percent a year to 1.4 percent, or 25 percent lower in 2020 than it would be otherwise — a reduction greater than China's total annual 2005 energy consumption.[51]

But there's one little hitch: increasing energy efficiency does not automatically mean less energy used. In 1865, an Englishman named William Jevons published a book in which he argued that efficiency improvements would not delay the depletion of Britain's coal, as goods that become cheaper through coal's more efficient use would stimulate yet more demand. The idea that increased efficiency in using a resource tends to increase rather than decrease its consumption has come to be called the Jevons Paradox. When I was a boy during the 1960s, air conditioners were still a novelty, and I remember taking refuge in the only room equipped with a window model during the hot, humid Japanese summers — the alternative of opening the refrigerator and sticking my head in for a while risked provoking the ire of local authorities, namely Grandma. Nowadays, it is hard to find indoor spaces for human use in much of the developed world without air conditioning. This phenomenon is currently being rerun around the emerging world, where five billion (and rising) of the Earth's people live, across a range of energy-consuming products. So while there is nothing bad about improving efficiency — it will allow us to use energy more productively and will raise the quality of life for many in the developing world — efficiency alone can increase energy use and is no panacea.

The World Energy Organization notes that progress in energy efficiency has not matched expectations, despite its frequent citation as a key solution for world energy problems. The organization points out that, owing to the rapid growth of electricity demand (particularly in developing countries), about 20 percent of energy productivity gains at the consumer level globally have been offset by increasing losses inherent in power generation, with its typical 60–70 percent conversion losses.[52]

So despite past and promising prospective developments, efficiency improvements alone, particularly at the consumer level, are very unlikely to decrease the aggregate demand for energy in the developing world, particularly in the form of grid electricity. Because meeting energy demand through renewable sources alone will be extremely difficult given current policies in the most dynamic developing nations, efficiency gains alone will not be enough to significantly slow the growth of, much less reduce meaningfully, total global use of the most pernicious fossil fuels. While in much of the high-income world, the electricity consumed per capita has begun to plateau or even decline slightly from around 9,000 kilowatt-hours (kWh) annually since the Great Financial Crisis (and whether this will be sustained remains to be seen), five billion people in the developing world today, who produce over half the world's output, are living the Jevons Paradox in their quest to achieve the living standards of advanced nations. Low- and middle-income countries consumed about 1,600 kilowatt-hours per person in 2011, almost double that in 2001, and China's per capita consumption almost tripled to 3,300 kWh during the same ten years. Obviously, the people of the developing world still have a lot more catching up to do.[53] Perhaps someday their electricity and other energy use will also plateau as their living standards increase along with dramatic advances in energy technologies, but we are still far from getting to that point.

Energy Portfolio

As the source of roughly two-thirds of all man-made greenhouse gas emissions today, the energy sector is the central battleground to curb global warming. Reliable 24/7 electricity that defines the quality of our "just plug it in" lives in the developed world is spreading to the rest of humanity. In the densely populated regions of the high-income world, there has also been an inexorable trend toward using electricity for transport applications, typically starting with passenger and freight trains in areas where the benefits — less noise and emissions, lower costs of building and maintaining rolling stock, and better efficiencies than diesel-powered trains — outweigh the higher costs of building electrified infrastructure. But this trend is spreading at an accelerating pace to buses and cars as well, increasing our reliance on electricity to power much of our transportation.

In thinking about the future of energy, it is worth reviewing the objectives of any envisaged portfolio of sources and architecture before arriving at any conclusions about the inherent superiority of one set of technologies or solutions. Electricity is a key enabler to build and maintain our civilization and needs to be reliable, cheap, and cleanly produced, stored, and distributed. Grid electricity with 24/7 availability has been at the heart of dramatic productivity and quality-of-life improvements in much of the world for the past century. The challenge is to now make it significantly cleaner while keeping it reliable and cheap. A related but separate requirement is to make the whole mix as resilient to various shocks and disruptions as possible.

For electricity generation, capital costs for renewable power are generally high, while operating costs are low, but wind and solar provide power only part of the time. Conversely, capital costs for fossil fuel power, which can operate around the clock, are lower, but operating costs for fuel are higher and subject to supply and price increases. Capital costs for nuclear power are high, but nuclear power can operate much of the time with fuel costs that are lower than those of fossil fuels. And the cost to society from continuing to rely heavily on dirty fossil fuels, particularly coal, is large and will continue to grow if unchecked.

Subsidies for renewable energy, such as favorable feed-in tariffs, government-funded research, or favorable loans, are reviled by fans of laissez-faire capitalism, many of whom usually ignore the sixfold larger subsidies to the fossil fuel industry. Conversely, environmentalists often vilify subsidies to develop advanced nuclear energy, although it is far cleaner than fossil fuels. Both are examples of starting from a prior opinion and effectively wanting the government to play favorites.

For power generation, which most generally agree will continue to increase outright and as a proportion of total energy consumed, the broad objectives should be to achieve favorable EROI with comfortable potential surplus capacity as cleanly and as safely as possible, while building a diverse set of energy sources, some distributed and some centralized, to enhance resilience. And to meet these objectives while creating substantial jobs, as Greenpeace and the renewable-energy industry suggest, would be gravy.

The point about resilience is not moot: complex civilizations that do not build resilience will find themselves increasingly vulnerable to shocks that reverberate throughout an interdependent system, with potentially grave consequences. Resilience and redundant systems are important to engineers and designers of complex systems but anathema to businesses and financially strapped governments. The argument that some measures to build redundancy or enhance resilience — a public good — in areas with few natural sponsors are executed better by governments than by the private sector remains valid, despite the mad rush to privatize many governmental functions during the last several decades. But simply not building for enhanced resilience betrays a dangerous lack of imagination about less likely events that may have huge consequences.

In the economic sphere, very few envisaged the far-reaching global impact of U.S. subprime risk going into the Great Financial Crisis. At the broader level of the Earth, the gas and debris spewed from the eruption of the Laki volcano in Iceland in 1783 caused temperatures to plummet around the world for several years, decimating agriculture and causing millions of deaths from starvation. We know that episodes of major volcanic activity that reduce significantly the amount of energy that can be captured from the sun occur regularly, but it so happens that a huge one has not occurred since the Industrial Revolution: today's highly complex world, in which billions more need to be fed and where we derive a significant and growing amount of energy directly from the sun, would be far more vulnerable. As the cleanest of the major energy sources, and to the extent that their EROI keep improving and intermittency issues are increasingly addressed, renewables will play a central role in meeting mankind's future

Median life-cycle assessments of emissions by source (g CO_2e/kWh)

Bio	PV	CSP	Geo	Hydro	Ocean	Wind	Nuclear	Gas	Oil	Coal
18	46	22	45	4	8	12	16	469	840	1001

SOURCE: Adapted from Intergovernmental Panel on Climate Change, *Renewable Energy Sources and Climate Change Mitigation*, 2012.

energy needs. But how quickly can they replace the cheapest but dirtiest fossil fuels, in ways that enhance instead of degrade our resilience, before boundaries that increase the odds of significant long-term global climate change are breached?

At this point, it would also be helpful to compare GHG emissions, that relatively recent but now key requirement for the power mix, from various sources of electric power generation. Researchers like to estimate the total emissions over the entire life-cycles of various power technologies — from extraction, construction, operation, and decommissioning — to conduct apples-to-apples comparisons. In 2012, the IPCC compiled life-cycle assessments (LCAs) of greenhouse gas emissions for various power sources, based on meta-analysis of almost a thousand research estimates, screened for quality. The median estimates provide useful comparisons of the emissions from the most common power technologies.[54]

The estimates illustrate that clean is a relative term: all the fossil fuels are as dirty as one would expect (gas emits 469 grams CO_2 equivalent per kilowatt-hour, oil 840 grams, and coal 1,001 grams), but solar PV and geothermal produce material emissions as well (46 grams and 45 grams CO_2 equivalent per kilowatt-hour respectively), the former through panel manufacturing and the latter through heat extraction. In some cases, the median estimates are derived from fairly wide ranges. For example, solar PV ranges from 5 to 217 grams CO_2 equivalent per kilowatt-hour (g CO_2e/kWh), and estimates for nuclear power, with a median of 16g CO_2e/kWh, span from 1 to 220.

The pace at which renewable energy is being developed and adopted worldwide is encouraging, at least on the surface. Although it is at the optimistic end of the spectrum, most would agree that Greenpeace's Energy Revolution goal of raising the share of renewable energy substantially is laudable. The measures that Greenpeace recommends to encourage growth of renewables include phasing out all subsidies to fossil fuels and nuclear energy (limited basic government-sponsored research should continue for all non-fossil energy sources, in my view); internalizing emissions costs through cap-and-trade mechanisms; and establishing preferential renewable energy access to grids, feed-in tariffs, and strict efficiency standards for all energy-consuming vehicles, buildings, and appliances. (Preferential access and feed-in tariffs have to be handled very carefully, however, as they may well lead to the rapid adoption of technologies that lower overall societal EROI, as seen in Germany and Spain.)

Many of the measures advocated by Greenpeace make sense, though they would be extremely difficult to implement. Into this category falls the single most effective way to reduce carbon emissions: for governments to agree to binding emissions goals, set a legal limit on how much each nation or region can emit (though ideally done at the global level), and then establish mechanisms to price emissions — either auction off the right to emit greenhouse gases, gradually reducing the amount auctioned, or levy taxes on carbon emissions, gradually increasing the rate. The important thing is to then let the markets establish prices, trade the negative externality (for example, a cement plant may buy the right to emit carbon from a gas-fired power plant that has replaced some of its capacity with cogeneration and is left with surplus emissions), and allow emitters to reduce emissions in the ways that make the most sense to them. One caveat is that any scheme to price carbon must incorporate measures to discourage the effective export of emissions through trade in goods from regions with looser emissions standards and pricing. But tariffs on imports from countries with loose emissions standards may be prone to abuse as a front for protectionist tariffs if not administered carefully, as well as raising questions of fairness in imposing costs to low-income countries that have not contributed much to cumulative emissions.

In 2015, several major European energy companies called for governments to establish a global system of carbon pricing — perhaps mainly an effort to stay on the right side of public opinion on the issue — but nevertheless significant. Meanwhile, U.S. energy giants continue to contend that consumers do not want to pay the cost of pricing carbon. Perhaps they have a point, especially regarding consumers in the developing world who are generally much more concerned with improving their quality of life than worrying about the environmental commons.

According the World Bank, about forty nations and twenty cities or regions put a price on carbon today, representing about 7 Gt CO_2e, or 12 percent of global emissions. Though the price varies greatly among schemes, from one U.S. dollar (Poland, Mexico) to $130 (Sweden), 85 percent of the emissions covered are priced below $10, so significantly below the price range that many economic models indicate is needed to stay within the 2°C limit.[55] Finding the right price for carbon is, of course, fraught with controversy and depends on the jurisdiction. The electorates of rich countries with access to low-carbon energy sources will tend to be amenable to putting a (higher) price on carbon, while developing countries that are eager to raise living standards will be constrained in how aggressive they can be. This dilemma makes it extremely difficult to introduce international carbon price regimes other than those that gravitate toward lower prices and do little to help alleviate global warming. Perhaps the best that can eventually be achieved is a patchwork of national or regional carbon price schemes with prices set high enough in the aggregate to make a difference.

Europe has had a carbon cap-and-trade system in place for about a decade, covering about 2 Gt CO_2e of emissions and still the single largest carbon pricing regime globally. Named the Emissions Trading System (ETS), Europe's ambitious emissions scheme established a phased approach to cap-and-trade starting in 2005. But the initial oversupply of permits that were allocated for free by the European Commission to participating members in the first phase from 2005 to 2007, coupled with the subsequent global economic crisis, led to a dramatic crash in prices from a high of €30 to €0.10 per tonne. During the second phase, from 2008 to 2012, prices once again started at about €22/t, but were close to €5/t by 2012 (the failure of the 2009 Copenhagen round of climate talks did not help) — way too low for many firms to care about using them against their emissions. The scheme suffered from the flaw that allowances were initially over-allocated: a series of auctions following more limited allocations would have generated price signals to decrease planned supply. The IEA estimates that carbon pricing of about €50/t is needed to get European utilities to switch from coal to natural gas in the short run (perhaps €25 in the long run),[56] but an attempt by the European Commission in 2013 to reduce the number of future-dated allowances was shot down by the European Parliament and inspired another crash in prices to less than €3/t. Phase 3, which finally introduced a partial auction mechanism, started in 2013, but prices continue to languish a bit above €5 ($6.65) per tonne on average. In May 2015, the EU finally agreed to a scheme whereby it could withdraw allowances during periods of surplus, but it is not scheduled to be implemented until 2019.

Another significant cause for lackluster allowance prices is Europe's generous subsidies to renewable energy in its effort to reach an EU target to derive 27 percent of its energy from renewable sources by 2030. For example, the *Economist* points out that the largest source of renewable energy in Europe is wood, which receives subsidies equivalent to €150–200 ($200–266) per tonne in Germany. With electricity generators cutting emissions through heavy taxpayer subsidies to renewable energy, they do not need all the allowances issued under the European Trading System, depressing prices.[57] The failure of ETS illustrates how top-down bureaucratic rationing processes that do not incorporate market signals to allow the market to set prices are particularly unsuitable for achieving the primary objective of lowering emissions, and represent a superb example of how not to institute an emissions scheme (or subsidies to renewables).

As a successful contrast to the European emissions trading scheme, in 2008 British Columbia became the first jurisdiction in North America to institute a carbon tax across its entire economy. Initially set at ten Canadian dollars per tonne, applied to all emissions from fossil fuel burning, the tax was increased in $5-per-tonne increments annually till reaching $30/t in 2012, at which level it was frozen for five years. The tax is revenue neutral, which means that other taxes are reduced to compensate for it. From its introduction up until 2013, fuel use in British Columbia has fallen, while it has increased in the rest of Canada, and energy-related emissions have fallen 5–15 percent.[58] Meanwhile, the province's GDP has outperformed that of Canada during the six years from 2009 to 2014, although isolating the impact of the carbon tax alone is tricky. Other jurisdictions in North America, such at the State of Washington, are looking to replicate British Columbia's success, but it is generally far easier to establish meaningful carbon price regimes in places that are rich and environmentally aware than in developing nations that are still looking to improve substantially the quality of life for their citizens. As a prime example of the latter, China currently operates pilot carbon-trading schemes in several regions, which, when combined, make them the second-largest in the world after the European Trading System. Here again, prices are not high enough to drive wholesale change in energy investments. China plans to introduce a national carbon market by 2020: let us hope it does a significantly better job than Europe has.

In 2013, the Obama administration quietly increased its price assumption for the "social price of carbon," used to weigh costs and benefits of proposed federal projects and legislation, from $23.80 to $38 per metric ton by 2015. Originally slipped into a rule on microwave ovens, the planned change elicited squeals of indignation from the business community and congressional Republicans. After the technical document for the executive order was revised in November 2013, the number was reduced to $37 per metric ton, but heavy lobbying to get it reduced further continues — and this was not even an actual carbon tax but merely a price used to evaluate the costs and benefits of projects with federal government involvement.[59]

But one early successful cap-and-trade arrangement designed to address the problem of acid rain, the Acid Deposition Control portion of the 1990 U.S. Clean Air Act, established clear goals to reduce, by the year 2000, annual sulfur dioxide and nitrogen oxide emissions by ten million tons and two million tons respectively from 1980 levels. Sulfur dioxide emissions allowances, issued and allocated by the Environmental Protection Agency (EPA) according to baseline emissions estimates to electric generation facilities operating as of November 15, 1990 (any plants commencing operations thereafter had to obtain them from existing holders), could then be traded at annual open auctions.[60] Importantly, the 1990 amendments to the Clean Air Act made some knowing violations felonies instead of misdemeanors, gave the EPA authority to impose administrative penalties, enabled cash awards for tips leading to convictions, and even provided for citizen lawsuits against corporations, government agencies, or even the EPA for noncompliance: nothing works better than giving the sheriff the tools to do the job. Since then, sulfur dioxide emissions in North America have fallen to levels not seen since the beginning of the twentieth century (while they continue to climb precipitously in China),[61] and at a cost far lower than industry and even the EPA claimed at the time, demonstrating that cap-and-trade schemes can work if designed and executed effectively.[62]

The U.S. EPA has generally been the exemplar of a regulatory agency that successfully protects the public interest since it was created under the Nixon administration in 1970. The EPA is also another example, along with Teddy Roosevelt and George H. W. Bush, of Republican administrations taking dramatic actions to protect the commons. But over the past two decades, Republican legislators have been busy trying to undermine the activities of the EPA and emasculate the agency. In 2014, the Republican-controlled House passed a bill called the Secret Science Reform Act, which would prohibit the EPA from issuing regulations based on nonpublic data such as private industry and personal medical data. As the EPA relies on peer-reviewed scientific research and usually does not have all the under-lying data to share, the bill would severely limit the scope of research to be used by the EPA and impose major costs. Another bill would change the rules for appointing members to the Scientific Advisory Board (SAB), a group that provides scientific advice to the EPA administrator, to allow for more participation by industry experts. The bill would also prevent SAB members from participating in discussions involving their own peer-reviewed research: a bizarre notion that expert researchers are somehow more conflicted than industry insiders. The administration is expected to veto both bills if they progress that far, but combined with the vow from the Senate majority leader Mitch McConnell (from the coal state of Kentucky) to "try to do everything I can to get the EPA reined in,"[63] they give a flavor of the fierce political opposition the agency is up against nowadays.

From control of toxins, such as DDT in pesticides and lead from gasoline, to regulating pollutants, cleaning the nation's freshwater, and protecting the public's right to know about the substances to which they may be ex-posed, the EPA has complied an impressive list of regulation and enforce-ment since its creation, implementing market-based solutions — such as the measures to curb acid rain — when it can to meet the laws enacted by Congress. Moreover, the Office of Management and Budget has estimated that the EPA was the most cost-effective of the major U.S. agencies during a ten-year period to 2012, with the median estimated benefits outweighing costs by eleven to one.[64]

Of course the agency is not without its share of problems and challenges. For example, the Union of Concerned Scientists released a survey in 2008 in which nearly half of the EPA scientists responding to a questionnaire reported experiencing political interference in their work. More recently, the Government Accountability Office suggested in a 2014 report that the EPA should improve the ways in which it conducts regulatory impact analysis.[65] Perhaps the most dubious was the EPA's role in overseeing hydraulic fracturing. In 2004, the agency issued a report, widely criticized as politically motivated, declaring fracking to be safe for the environment and drinking water. The following year, Congress stripped the EPA of its role in regulating fracking in what became known as the "Halliburton loophole," named after then vice president and former Halliburton CEO Dick Cheney, who wanted to include the provision in the 2005 energy bill.[66] Fast forward to 2015, and the EPA released a draft report, requested by Congress, on hydraulic fracking's effects on drinking water. In it, the agency concludes that although there are mechanisms by which fracking can affect drinking water sources, it did not find evidence of widespread, systemic impacts on drinking water supplies in the United States.[67] These travails of the EPA demonstrate that a regulatory agency is only as good as the ability of its political masters to use it effectively.

In August 2015, the Obama administration announced final plans, based on initial proposals made a year earlier, in which the EPA would use its powers under the Clean Air Act to cut the U.S. power industry's carbon emissions by 32 percent below 2005 levels by 2030. Under the Clean Power Plan, the states are assigned goals for emissions reductions and are expected to draft final plans by 2018 to meet their individual goals and work with the EPA to achieve them. Congressional Republicans had been corralling state governors' opposition even before the plan was announced, and a dozen states that rely on coal sued the EPA over it 2014. A federal court dismissed the suit in June 2015, but the legal challenges are sure to continue. Although the Clean Power Plan does little to mitigate human-induced global warming on its own, the fact that the second-largest national emitter is taking concrete steps can only have helped the COP 21 conference held at the end of 2015.

Measures to increase the use of cleaner energy significantly faster than overall energy demand growth must be combined with efforts to enhance broad energy resilience through not only distributed generation, smart grids, and other means, but also the deployment of cheap, reliable, and clean base-load power. We simply cannot keep adding energy sources below the net energy cliff — and that includes wind and solar today when accounting for their fluctuations — with subsidized abandon if we want to maintain the complexity of our current civilization. With the costs of renewable energy declining and potential improvements in energy storage technologies, I hope that renewable energy will account for a large enough portion of our energy mix in time to head off major, irreversible climate change. Unfortunately, hope is not a real risk-management strategy. Similarly, the global slowdown in birth rates brought about by improvements in sanitation and life expectancy in the developing world — so that perhaps the global population peaks at a lower level somewhat earlier than expected even a decade ago — is heartening. But there remain "good news, bad news" aspects to this trend, as we will still likely face a peak global population of nine billion by 2045, many of whom will be looking to improve their lives significantly by using lots of energy. Without dramatic, enforceable commitments by nations to cut greenhouse emissions in time, and in the absence of cheap, reliable, and clean base-load power that can supplant coal economically, the key goal of dramatically reducing human-induced atmospheric greenhouse gas levels over the next several decades will elude us.

The challenges we face in securing the reliable energy we need without messing up our planet further demand that we throw all kinds of solutions at them without undue bias. Abundant energy with a minimal carbon footprint would be a key driver to foster a positive feedback loop of improving quality of life broadly and encourage slower population growth, while alleviating pressures on the Earth's ability to support humanity. Along with renewable energy (paired with effective storage), improvements in efficiency, and possibly measures to absorb greenhouse gases already emitted, nuclear power — increasingly the modern variants that are far more efficient and safer — has an indispensable role to play in this "all of the above" strategy.

5

THE TRIALS AND TRAVAILS OF TAMING THE ATOM

One clear spring morning in 2013, I visited the area immediately north of the Fukushima Daiichi power plant three days after restrictions on entering areas around it were relaxed, taking the route as far south as possible before being stopped at a checkpoint about six kilometers before the plant, beyond which passage was not allowed without passes. I had taken the duck-billed bullet train to Sendai in Miyagi prefecture, where I was picked up at the station by Takahashi-san, a veteran driver who experienced the earthquake while on the job and is familiar with the sites that were devastated by the March 11, 2011, quake and tsunami.

On the expressway from Sendai heading south toward Fukushima slightly inland from the coast, Takahashi-san explains that the highway, elevated on an earthen berm, acted as a breaker for the tsunami as it rolled inland, with everything inside it suffering marginally less inundation. Illustrating the point, there are more earthmovers and dump trucks working on the seaward side of the highway than on the other side. After we get off the expressway and onto Route 6, something like every third vehicle we pass is a dump truck — their plates and markings indicate that they are from as far north as Sapporo, Hokkaido, or far south as Kagoshima, Kyushu — some loaded with soil or gravel, others heading to be loaded. We pass progressively fewer restored rice paddies and fields as we enter Fukushima and head south. Takahashi-san explains that desalination and debris clearing are not the only challenges to recovery: merely the name Fukushima as a point of origin for rice and agricultural products renders them very difficult to sell. Continuing south on Route 6 we pass by two active coal-fired power plants, among the many nonnuclear plants that have taken up the slack since the shutdown of all fifty-four nuclear power plants in Japan,[1] pending policy clarification and potential restarts.

We enter Namie, whose town leaders in 1973 eagerly invited construction of a Tohoku Electric Power plant (not Tokyo Electric Power, the owner of the Daiichi plant), housing up to four nuclear reactors. Although three reactors were eventually built up the coast at Onagawa in Miyagi Prefecture, Tohoku Electric still had plans at the time of the 2011 disaster to build and operate a nuclear power reactor in Namie by 2021.[2] The adjacent town of Minamisoma, under whose jurisdiction the proposed construction area was subsequently placed, finally rescinded the invitation in December 2011 and, citing the "annihilation of the safety myth of our nation's nuclear power industry," called for the closing of all nuclear plants in Fukushima Prefecture.[3] The rows upon rows of abandoned houses we pass remind me of the U.S. communities that were decimated by the 2008 financial crisis — without the vandalism and graffiti. The rice paddies and fields are completely overgrown in this town: no one has even bothered to till the fields so that they may eventually be recultivated without extensive replowing and rehabilitation.

About six kilometers before Fukushima Daiichi, we encounter a roadblock adjacent to an abandoned facility for holding weddings and events, beyond which only vehicles that are registered with the local or central governments or with TEPCO as part of the plant stabilization are allowed to pass. We duly turn back but spot private security guards manning roadblocks at the side roads of Route 6 and ask whether we can proceed. They say yes, but must record the plate number of any vehicle that passes, presumably to deter theft or looting. Slightly up the grassy hill and opposite

Makeshift shrine
to tsunami victims
in Namie, Fuku-
shima, May 2013
(photo by author).

from the roadblock, a herd of feral brown cows, probably abandoned by
their owner after the quake, graze like life-size lawn ornaments. As we proceed down the side road toward the ocean and the fishing port, it becomes
quite apparent that there is nothing to even contemplate looting: smashed
cars tossed about randomly in the overgrown, abandoned fields, fishing
boats mysteriously left inland like the images of stranded vessels in the des-
iccated Aral Sea, and piles of debris and twisted rubble, neatly organized
like funeral mounds. We make our way to the end of the accessible section
of side road, beyond which a sign indicates that only former residents are
allowed but may not stay overnight. Between the sections of rubble, one
can make out the towers of Fukushima Daiichi, only a few kilometers away.
I couldn't agree more with Takahashi-san when he breaks the silence by
remarking, "I wouldn't want to spend a night in this place anyhow."

This is the ground-level view of the havoc, wrought not only by the earthquake and tsunami but by decades of mismanagement and "regulatory
capture"—the handy term for regulatory agencies in thrall to special
political and commercial interests—of the Japanese nuclear power industry. As the Fukushima Nuclear Accident Independent Investigation
Commission of the Japanese National Diet concluded in July 2012, "The
TEPCO Fukushima Nuclear Power Plant accident was the result of collusion between the government, the regulators and TEPCO, and the lack of

governance by said parties. They effectively betrayed the nation's right to be safe from nuclear accidents. Therefore, we conclude that the accident was clearly 'manmade.' We believe that the root causes were the organizational and regulatory systems that supported faulty rationales for decisions and actions, rather than issues relating to the competency of any specific individual."[4]

In light of the utter failure of regulatory governance and safety oversight in its nuclear power industry, Japan is still left with a central dilemma: how does a densely populated island nation with a power-hungry industrial base but no meaningful indigenous sources of fossil fuels, a rapidly aging population, and a debt-to-GDP ratio of 240 percent and rising, ever hope to maintain its standard of living without cheap, safe, and reliable energy?

Son of Godzilla

I was a schoolboy during the early 1970s and fondly remember Godzilla destroying major chunks of metropolitan Tokyo regularly in his starring movie roles. The star of the original film — the movie was first released in November 1954 — was supposed to have been created from thermonuclear tests, inspired by the tragically unlucky encounter of the Japanese fishing vessel *Daigo Fukuryu Maru* (Lucky Dragon 5) with radioactive fallout from a larger-than-designed U.S. H-bomb test at Bikini Atoll a few months earlier. The film was also influenced by the 1953 U.S. movie *The Beast from 20,000 Fathoms*, involving a creature awakened by nuclear testing and wreaking havoc on prime Manhattan real estate. But as a metaphor for the perils of nuclear weapons, Godzilla won claws down with the audience of a nation that had actually experienced nuclear bombardment a decade earlier. As the franchise continued, Godzilla stoically allied himself with humans against other formidable monsters (even battling a "smog monster" in a nod to environmental issues) and, by the twelfth installment in 1972, evolved into a powerful but child-friendly atomic beast. The latter incarnation of Godzilla might as well have been scripted by TEPCO rather than Toho Studios.

Shortly after the dawn of the atomic age, nuclear power generation was touted as a promising means of generating abundant, inexpensive electricity. "Too cheap to meter," a general comment about the future of electricity and not atomic power per se, was uttered by the chairman of the Atomic Energy Commission, Lewis Strauss, in 1954 and went on to become a famous misquote that nevertheless captured the period's zeitgeist. It was during the 1950s that the Eisenhower administration promoted the "Atoms for Peace" program to help spread nuclear power around the globe under what were considered strict IAEA safeguards, though not strict enough to prevent North Korea from simply kicking out inspectors in the 1990s during its nuclear bomb procurement drive, or Syria from trying to build an undeclared nuclear reactor before the site was destroyed by an Israeli airstrike in 2007. The opening of the first commercial U.S. nuclear power plant at Shippingport, Pennsylvania, in 1957 — essentially a navy reactor beached for utility power generation — heralded the construction of a bevy of nuclear power plants in the United States and elsewhere around the world. By 1990, nuclear accounted for about 19 percent of the power generation mix in the United States, and this percentage has remained remarkably stable to the present. But a series of relatively minor accidents and (some allege, suppressed) AEC studies highlighting nuclear plant operating risks focused attention on issues of nuclear plant safety during the 1970s, an era of weakened trust in government, corporations, and institutions in the wake of the Vietnam War and Watergate.

The nuclear power industry was already losing momentum starting from the early 1970s, as costs began to escalate and local opposition to plants grew. Then, in what must be the best-timed follow-up to a theatrical release in cinematic history, the Three Mile Island accident in March 1979 occurred less than two weeks after the premiere of the movie *The China Syndrome*, and nuclear power in the United States has not been the same since. Like many accidents in complex systems, the incident was caused by a series of mechanical problems and human errors. Workers had been trying to dislodge some tiny purifying resin balls in one of the filter tanks called condensate polishers (designed to purify water after being used as steam to operate turbines), with compressed air that had been cross-connected to a compressed-air system used to operate valves remotely from the control room. Someone had forgotten to close an air valve after flushing the tank during a previous shift, and water was steadily forced up an instrument air line until it cut off air going to valves at the top of all eight polisher tanks, shutting them and stopping the flow through the steam and water system. The force of the sudden stop to water flowing through the turbine and secondary cooling loop tore loose a large pipe and pump in the turbine building, and the plant's turbine generator and reactor shut down automatically. With the steam generator connected to the secondary loop no longer removing heat produced by the reactor, pressure increased immediately in the primary, nuclear section of TMI-2.

In a pressurized water reactor, a tank near the top of the reactor vessel adjusts the pressure of the water in the primary loop and, by having a steam bubble atop the water in the vessel, acts as a cushion against sudden jolts to the volume of water in the system. A pressure relief valve on the pressurizer tank, similar in principle to the relief valve on top of a pressure cooker, stuck open and allowed coolant to escape for over two hours. Operators were confused by the valve indicator light suggesting that it had shut (but indicating merely that the signal to close it had been sent), and by a gauge indicating that the water level in the pressurizer was rising and approaching levels beyond which the pipes in the coolant systems would be in danger of bursting. Although the open valve gave the impression that the water level in the pressurizer was persistently high, the operators were actually exposing the reactor core by easing back considerably on the amount of coolant that was being introduced into the loop. The problems of malfunctioning pressure relief valves and in trying to determine water levels in the reactor vessel by looking at levels in the pressurizer had been uncovered previously through incidents in other pressurized water reactors manufactured by Babcock & Wilcox, but the lessons learned were never transmitted by the manufacturer or the Nuclear Regulatory Commission to other operators of B&W reactors.[5] The chain of events culminated in a severe core meltdown, and two days after the initial accident, there were concerns that a large hydrogen bubble — a phenomenon that would play a far greater role in the Fukushima Daiichi accident — had formed in the reactor vessel from the high-temperature reaction of water and zirconium alloy fuel cladding. The operators succeeded in reducing the size of the bubble, although it was determined in any event that the bubble would not explode, owing to a lack of oxygen in the reactor vessel.[6] Unlike the movie title, the melted fuel and cladding collected at the bottom of the reactor vessel and did not melt through the vessel, through the containment building, or hit groundwater to result in a catastrophic steam explosion.

No one was killed in the Three Mile Island accident, nor was there a release of radioactivity sufficient to be called life-threatening, and various presidential, congressional, and state commissions repeatedly investigating the aftermath could not find internal contamination among those living closest to the plant that could be traced to the accident. But even before Three Mile Island, construction periods and costs for nuclear power plants had been increasing steeply, as reactor builders and operators mostly just scaled-up existing technologies without focusing on standardization and modular design to curb costs and for ease of regulatory approval. Merging with the nuclear disarmament movement, growing opposition to nuclear power and the regulatory response slowed or stopped new plant construction: the Tennessee Valley Authority's Watts Bar 1 reactor, which started operation in 1996, remains the newest operational power generation reactor in the United States, pending the scheduled start of commercial operation of Watts Bar 2 during 2016 after decades of delays. Environmentalist Mark Lynas estimates the total capacity of the more than 120 reactors that were canceled in the United States to be about 140 GW, or about half the total generation capacity from coal in the United States today. Had all the nuclear power plants envisaged in the United States during the atomic age been built, the country would have a much lower carbon footprint from power generation.[7]

Nuclear Reactors: The Basics

A nuclear reactor is essentially a device designed to sustain a nuclear chain reaction. When the nucleus of a fissile element such as uranium-235 or plutonium-239 absorbs a neutron, the nucleus splits into lighter nuclei and emits free neutrons, which go on to collide with other fissile nuclei, causing them to split and emit free neutrons as well. To control the chain reaction, solid graphite, water, or heavy water (a form of water that combines oxygen with the hydrogen isotope deuterium) are typically used as neutron moderators (also acting as absorber and coolant in the case of water), which slow down the neutrons and increase the probability that they will hit other fissile nuclei; and neutron absorbers such as boron, cadmium, and hafnium are used to limit the reaction.

Most operating Western civilian reactors use regular or "light" water as a moderator and coolant. Because water density decreases when it is heated, it acts as a less effective moderator at higher temperatures, enabling it to help stabilize the rate of chain reaction and acting as a built-in safety mechanism. Most light water reactors (LWRs) are pressurized water reactors (PWRs), in which coolant water is pumped under high pressure into the reactor core, heated, and pumped into a steam generator to pass on its heat to another system to turn the turbines with steam. The system is used for naval propulsion (with the exception of Russian metal-cooled reactor designs) and in the majority of the world's nuclear power stations. The reactor that experienced the partial meltdown at Three Mile Island was of this type.

Boiling water reactors (BWRs) boil somewhat pressurized coolant water and use it directly to drive a turbine, after which the water is cooled in a condenser and returned for reuse. Although they operate at lower temperatures, at half the pressure, and require fewer components and plumbing than PWRs, BWRs require significantly larger pressure vessels to achieve similar power output. The reactors at Fukushima Daiichi, designed by GE during the 1960s (considered "Generation II"), are BWRs.

Both PWRs and BWRs exhibit "negative void coefficient," a fancy nuclear engineering term for the negative feedback loop described earlier — fewer free neutrons are produced when voids, usually steam bubbles, form in the moderator and coolant, reining in reactivity. LWRs typically exhibit very low rates — under 5 percent — of "burnup," or fuel utilization; in other words, they are not very efficient and leave a lot of radioactive waste behind.

Some civilian nuclear reactors use heavy water (water formed from the hydrogen isotope deuterium instead of common hydrogen, and the famous objective of the frenzied sabotage activity by Allied commandos in Norway during World War II), which captures fewer free neutrons than regular water so can be used in conjunction with unenriched uranium. Although heavy water is expensive to produce — the cost of heavy water alone was about 30 percent of the total capital cost for an Ontario power station[8]—

the ability to use natural uranium, which is overwhelmingly U-238 and contains less than 1 percent U-235, is a major plus, given the complexity and costs traditionally associated with enrichment. Moreover, heavy-water reactors have burnup ratios that are as much as twice that of their LWR cousins, and can be refueled during operation, obviating the need for time-consuming, expensive shutdowns. CANDU (for Canada Deuterium Uranium) reactors have slightly positive void coefficients, as heavy water does not absorb neutrons as easily as regular water. Used extensively by Canada, CANDU-type reactors have been built in India, South Korea, China, Pakistan, Argentina, and Romania.

After the first graphite "piles" at the University of Chicago and elsewhere demonstrated controlled fission, the earliest nuclear reactors at Hanford, Washington, were built in 1944 with the primary objective of producing plutonium for use in atomic weapons. The earliest Hanford reactors were essentially eleven-meter-long graphite cylinders laid on their sides and penetrated by tubes filled with uranium slugs. Water was pumped through the aluminum tubes around the slugs to provide cooling.

Chernobyl

Besides its use in the earliest reactors, graphite was used as the moderator in the Soviet reactor that exploded at Chernobyl in 1986. Called the RBMK reactor — the Russian abbreviation for "high output channel reactor" — the design was essentially a scaled-up, more powerful version of the early graphite reactors used to produce plutonium for the Soviet weapons program. Because it used natural and low-enriched uranium for fuel and regular water as coolant, the RBMK could be run at relatively low cost, but was inherently unstable at low power levels, particularly after the accumulation of fission by-products (such as xenon-135, a powerful neutron absorber or "nuclear poison") through its operation. During the moments leading up to the Chernobyl accident, the operators were conducting an experiment to see if turbines running down after a power grid failure could continue to provide coolant flow until backup diesel generators could be brought up to speed. But in preparing for the experiment, they had initiated a series of actions that made the reactor very unstable, including overriding safety systems and removing nearly all the control rods manually. The RBMK re-actors at Chernobyl had very high positive void coefficients, as the coolant water's capacity to absorb neutrons practically disappears when vaporized, and the reduction in its ability to absorb neutrons is overwhelmed by the graphite moderator. The task of neutron absorption is thus left almost ex-clusively to the boron control rods, which, in the case of the RBMK reactors that were operated at the time, were graphite-tipped. The emergency shut-down procedure produced a massive power spike that deformed the chan-nels in the reactor and prevented the rest of the rods from being inserted completely — the final factor in the cascade of events that resulted in the catastrophe.

The explosions from the overheated core blew the top off the reactor and part of the reactor building roof — there was no proper, reinforced con-tainment structure — and exposure to air ignited the superheated graphite, laced with uranium fuel and cladding. The resulting fire sent a highly ra-dioactive plume into the atmosphere, resulting in fallout over a large area. The amount of radioactive material released by the accident was very large, and many estimate that the release was many times that from the atomic bombings of Japan. Although the approximately 170 tonnes of fuel and fis-sion product in Reactor 4 at the time of the accident was many times more than the 64 kilograms (less than 1 kilogram of which underwent fission) of enriched uranium in the Little Boy bomb dropped on Hiroshima or the 6.2 kilograms of plutonium used in the Nagasaki Fat Man bomb, it is hard to make direct comparisons. Most of the radiation from the bombs' atomic air bursts was released at the time of detonation in conjunction with the blast and heat, while radioactive particles, some of them long-lived, from Cher-nobyl were released over the course of eight days by the fire and dispersed over a wide area.

The Chernobyl disaster was the result of doing just about everything possible wrong: using a reactor design singularly unsuited for civilian pro-duction of electric power, cutting corners by not building proper contain-ment, bypassing safety procedures and systems in its operation, and the pervasive secrecy that not only kept operators in the dark about its han-dling characteristics but also sent first responders to their deaths.

Between 2003 and 2005, a number of UN agencies, including the UN

Scientific Committee on the Effects of Atomic Radiation (UNSCEAR), the World Health Organization (WHO), and the International Atomic Energy Agency (IAEA), investigated the aftereffects of the Chernobyl disaster. They found that, of the 1,000 or so emergency workers and on-site personnel who received the largest exposure to radiation, 134 were diagnosed as suffering from acute radiation syndrome (ARS). Of these, 28 died in 1986 from ARS, another three from other causes, and 19 more died between 1987 and 2004 from various causes, not necessarily directly attributable to radiation exposure. The report suggests that perhaps up to four thousand additional fatal cancers, in addition to the one hundred thousand that could be expected from other causes among the six hundred thousand "liquidators" (those who were called up to Chernobyl to deal with the disaster), evacuees, and residents of the most affected area, might eventually be observed. It goes on to speculate that, among the five million people living in the wider "contaminated" area, the accident could be expected to make a difference of less than 1 percent in cancer mortality.[9] Assuming conservatively that 20 percent of these five million could be expected to die eventually from some form of cancer even without exposure to radiation higher than background levels, a 1 percent increase in cancer mortality translates to ten thousand deaths in addition to the four thousand among the liquidators.

A WHO report released in 2006 estimates that perhaps a total of nine thousand (adding five thousand among the six million people in the greater affected area who were not liquidators, evacuees, and residents to the four thousand figure, though they note that the estimate is very uncertain) additional deaths may occur from the accident.[10] A 2008 UNSCEAR update notes that about six thousand cases of thyroid cancers were observed in the Ukraine, Belarus, and Russia in those who were eighteen or under at the time of the accident, and a substantial part of these are likely to have been due to radiation exposure through iodine: of these, fifteen cases were fatal by 2005. The studies conclude that, though there was some evidence of an increase in leukemia incidence for recovery operation workers from the Russian Federation, the findings were far from conclusive, and that "there appears, at present, to be no hard evidence of any measurable increase of all solid cancers taken together among the population of the Russian Federation and Ukraine."[11]

The reports on Chernobyl's effects published under UN auspices have become a lightning rod for criticism from many quarters, not the least of which concerned the role of the IAEA in compiling the reports and the WHO's contention that economic and psychological problems were far more significant than health or environmental problems in most of the areas affected. It seems that the UN is either a "running dog" of climate-change-religion environmentalists or the stooge of the global nuclear industry, depending on one's viewpoint and the agencies in question.

Much of the criticism is centered not on the deterministic effects of radiation on those who received large doses up to lethal levels in a short time, but on the so-called stochastic effects, which occur randomly and increase in probability as dosages increase. In light of accounts of pervasive secrecy during and immediately after the accident, which led to delays in evacuation and administering iodine tablets to the most vulnerable (potassium iodide tablets help prevent the thyroid glands, particularly those of infants and children, from absorbing radioactive iodine released from nuclear accidents or detonation), it would not come as a surprise if the data collected by the former Soviet government organs during the first years after the event were gathered sloppily and understated the health impact. Conversely, it is quite possible that after the Soviet Union's dissolution, Ukraine, Belarus, and Russia tended to count many illnesses, even those related to higher levels of stress and alcohol abuse, as attributable to radiation from the accident, perhaps inspired as well by the potential for foreign assistance. Either way, estimating dosages for populations affected is fraught with problems, including determining time spent indoors or outdoors immediately following the accident, the amount of contaminated produce or dairy product consumed, and trying to track or identify those who evacuated or moved away.

One study commissioned by a member of the Green Party in the European Parliament in 2006 as a response to the UN reports predicts thirty thousand to sixty thousand excess cancer deaths as a result of the disaster.[12] A 2010 study published by the American Academy of Pediatrics concludes that, though the causation is not definitive because of other factors such as high levels of alcohol abuse, there was a significantly higher rate of birth defects (twenty-seven neural tube defects per ten thousand versus the

European average of below ten) observed in one of the populations most exposed in the Ukraine to chronic low-dose radiation from Chernobyl.[13]

In a 2006 report on Chernobyl's health effects, Greenpeace provides a significantly higher estimate of eventual additional deaths, citing a Russian Academy of Sciences study estimating that about two hundred thousand deaths in Ukraine, Belarus, and Russia between 1996 and 2004 were attributable to the accident.[14] A more controversial study published in the *Annals of the New York Academy of Science* in 2009, coauthored by Alexey V. Yablokov, an editor for the Greenpeace report, estimates that as many as 985,000 deaths (a fivefold increase over the Greenpeace report covering the area most affected) have been caused globally by the Chernobyl accident by 2004 (237,500 in the former Soviet Union, 425,000 in the rest of Europe, and 323,000 elsewhere), though it confounds the imagination that such a dramatic increase in cancer mortality would have gone unnoticed in Western Europe.[15] The authors explicitly reject the utility of attempting to reconstruct received doses from those affected, and its conclusions are based largely on a compendium of numerous Russian-language studies and publications. The study has not been peer-reviewed under Western research standards and has been criticized for its methodology and conclusions.

The sheer range of the estimates provided for deaths eventually attributable to Chernobyl is staggering, spanning from the low end of four thousand, provided by the UN, to several hundred thousand. Many, including the 2006 Torch report commissioned by the European Greens, apply the Linear No-Threshold (LNT) model for estimating eventual cancer deaths, based on a conservative extrapolation for very low radiation doses from data on Japanese atomic bomb survivors. The model assumes that there is no such thing as a safe threshold for ionizing radiation, and that the risk of cancer is proportional to the total dose, regardless of whether it is from a single large dose or cumulatively from very small doses over time.

The WHO's highly uncertain estimate of four thousand to nine thousand lives shortened by Chernobyl is truly tragic if it turns out to be anywhere near that figure, but it is important to keep the number in perspective. There were about 1.24 million road traffic deaths globally in 2010 alone, according to the World Health Organization, but there is no major ideological movement to ban motor vehicles, only to improve traffic safety. Burning dirty fossil fuels over more than two centuries has killed orders of magnitude more people than Chernobyl (and all other nuclear power accidents combined), and the use of nuclear power to generate electricity in lieu of fossil fuels has saved millions of lives, and can save many more in the future.

Radiation: Please Don't Let Me Be Misunderstood

Most of us who do not have an understanding of the subject instinctively recoil when told that radiation levels are elevated, or that a radioactive substance has a half-life of many thousands of years. A brief nontechnical review (given the author's limitations) of radioactive decay, types of ionizing radiation, and relative doses from various sources may, therefore, be useful in gaining perspective. We are often bombarded by the media about the hazards of extremely long-lived nuclear waste, or that uranium has a half-life (the amount of time required before an element decays to half its starting amount) of 4.5 billion years. Despite its scary image, natural uranium-238, along with thorium-232, are thought to be the decay products of elements that were formed by the Big Bang, and produce much of Earth's internal heat through their very slow decay. In their most common natural states, they produce some background radiation (thought to have been four to five times higher a billion years ago) but are not dangerous: even plutonium-239, the bomb core alpha-emitter often touted as the deadliest toxin, can be handled safely with gloves, but can present big problems when inhaled or ingested.

Alpha particles are composed of two protons and two neutrons (essentially the nucleus of a helium atom), and come from the decay of the heaviest elements, such as uranium. Alpha particles use up their considerable energy over short distances as they are heavy, and lack the energy to penetrate even skin. If they get into the body, however, they can cause immense damage to cells and DNA. Readers may recall that the heavy element polonium-210 was used in the assassination of ex-spy and Kremlin critic Alexander Litvinenko in 2006, and was discovered at unusually high levels in Yasser Arafat's exhumed corpse by a Swiss forensics team in 2013.

Beta particles, which are emitted by unstable atoms such as strontium-90, are negatively charged ejected electrons and travel farther than alpha particles but are less damaging to cells and DNA. Though some beta particles can penetrate skin and cause damage, a thin layer of clothing or other materials (such as aluminum) can stop them.

High-energy free neutrons that are emitted during nuclear fission can travel thousands of meters and penetrate several meters of common materials. Though they have no charge themselves, free neutrons are absorbed by other atomic nuclei and cause them to become unstable, making them the only type of radiation that can make other materials radioactive.

Gamma rays are pure energy that are often emitted along with alpha or beta particles during radioactive decay and, without mass, can penetrate several inches of lead, a few feet of concrete or water, or a human body. Though paling in impact when compared to blast and thermal radiation (except for radiation-enhanced weapons), neutrons and gamma rays are the types of ionizing radiation — radiation that carries enough energy to free electrons from atoms — that affect people most immediately in a nuclear weapon detonation because of their ability to penetrate matter. Unlike gamma rays, X-rays are produced outside the nucleus of an atom and are less energetic, making them suitable for the medical imaging role for which they are best known.

For a given element, the amount of radioactivity emitted is inversely related to its half-life: radiation emitted by iodine-131, which has a half-life of eight days, is much more intense than that emitted by iodine-129 with its fifteen-million-year half-life. Some of the most dangerously radioactive elements are in fact quite short-lived. In fallout from reactor accidents the most problematic elements are those that are highly radioactive, have moderately long half-lives, and easily spread throughout the environment or are absorbed into the human body. We have already touched on iodine-131, which is easily absorbed by the thyroid gland, particularly in infants and children, but has only an eight-day half-life. Among the more problematic are strontium-90, with a fairly long twenty-nine-year half-life and biochemical behavior similar to that of calcium, and highly water-soluble cesium-137, which has a thirty-year half-life, so cycles through the environment for quite a while.

Unless we live under tightly controlled laboratory conditions, all of us are subject to some background radiation, from the decay of radon gas, other elements in Earth's crust such as thorium and potassium, and from space. Exposure to cosmic radiation depends largely on atmospheric density: a person living in Mexico City will receive more cosmic radiation than a resident of New York City (although NYC residents may receive radiation from all the granite used for structures and buildings), and a frequent commercial airline passenger or crew will also receive more than those who rarely fly.

A millisievert (mSv) is a measure of radiation equivalent to the background radiation (not including that from radon) to which a person would be expected to be exposed over the course of a year. A sievert differs from another common exposure measure called a gray (Gy), as it adjusts for the type of radiation absorbed (e.g., gamma radiation is dangerous because of penetration power, but alpha is much more damaging once inside the body). The effects of exposure to ionizing radiation can be divided into deterministic and stochastic effects — you are pretty much sure to be affected at high dose levels, but at lower levels, effects from exposure become more a matter of probabilities. Doses over 500 mSv may cause short-term changes in blood-cell production, and it has been demonstrated that doses over 100 mSv increase cancer risk, but death comes pretty quickly whether one receives a dose of 50 or 100 sieverts (50,000 or 100,000 mSv, though at these levels the convention is to simply use gray as the unit of measurement instead).[16] According to the U.S. Environmental Protection Agency, roughly half the annual average dose for Americans of 6.2 mSv comes from background radiation (so a bit higher than the definition originally assumed for the unit), and most of the rest comes from medical diagnosis and treatments.[17] Very high levels of natural background radiation are observed in parts of Kerala, India; Guarapari, Brazil; Yangjiang, China; and other areas, but without noticeable ill effects for their residents attributable to the radiation.

In some areas of Ramsar, a city near the Caspian Sea in northern Iran, residents receive as much as 260 mSv per year, more than ten times the 20 mSv ceiling recommended by the International Commission on Radiological Protection for radiation workers. A 2002 study shows no statistically significant difference in chromosome abnormalities between the Ramsar residents tested and those of control groups, and argues that the risks from high levels of background radiation may be less than those predicted by LNT models. Moreover, the authors suggest that, though different from the beneficial effects posited by the theory of homesis (in which an organism may show a positive response to low doses of toxin), elevated levels of natural background radiation may stimulate an adaptive response that allows cells to withstand higher radiation levels and may play an evolutionary role.[18]

Fukushima Daiichi: Teeing Up the "Man-Made" Disaster

Confusing and changing statements concerning acceptable thresholds for ionizing radiation and known contours of affected areas did nothing to allay the fears of Fukushima residents as the disaster at Daiichi unfolded, particularly among those displaced and told to move repeatedly as the evacuation zones were expanded. About 146,000 residents were evacuated by government order: many of them were not informed initially of the accident's severity or that it had even occurred. Evacuation zones were expanded from a three-kilometer radius to ten kilometers and then to twenty kilometers, all on the same day. By March 15, four days after the initial earthquake and tsunami, residents in the zone between twenty and thirty kilometers from the plant were told to stay put indoors, though they were without adequate supplies; this was revised afterward to voluntary evacuation, with little further information — all while on March 17 the U.S. Embassy, based on a U.S. Nuclear Regulatory Commission recommendation assuming that conditions would worsen, was advising U.S. citizens within fifty miles (eighty kilometers) of the plant to evacuate. Applying the U.S. NRC eighty-kilometer standard to all residents would have meant the evacuation of potentially over two million people. The same guidance, when applied to the Indian Point power station on the Hudson River, would mean evacuating about seventeen million people in the New York metropolitan and surrounding areas in a similar accident. NRC chairman Gregory Zaczko, who issued the U.S. embassy advice for Fukushima and called for the United States to learn from the disaster, resigned in 2012 after he came under withering attack from other NRC commissioners.[19]

Japanese government estimates of the amount of radioactive material released initially by the accident — about one-sixth of the amount released at Chernobyl in terms of cesium-137 and less than one-tenth in terms of iodine-131 — do not seem unreasonable, given that there was far less direct atmospheric release compared with Chernobyl.[20] But the disaster was unique insofar as several reactor complexes and their cooling pools were affected simultaneously, presenting significant challenges in controlling the crisis.

After the Second World War, Japan organized its electric power industry around nine regional vertically integrated electric utilities (ten with the return of Okinawa in 1972) with monopoly over power generation and distribution for households, supplemented by wholesale power generators owned and operated by local governments or joint ventures with major power users. As key enablers for Japan's rapid postwar reindustrialization, each of these regional monopolies was protected from competition, with rates set to produce comfortable profits, and accorded priority in the country's industrial policy: their status is reminiscent of that of the regional daimyo, or feudal lords, during the Tokugawa Shogunate. Tokyo Electric Power is the biggest daimyo of them all and, in a parallel to the Western financial industry, considered far "too big to fail."

A curious legacy of Japan's early industrialization, centered on Tokyo in the East and Osaka in the West, is that there are two separate grids operating at the same voltage but at different frequencies — 50 hertz in the East and 60 hertz in the West. There are only a handful of converter stations between the two grids, with only about 1.2 gigawatts capacity (the Ministry of Economy, Trade and Industry plans to increase capacity to 3 GW, or 3 billion watts, by 2020), which meant that there was not nearly enough power that could be diverted from West to East Japan when the Great Tohoku Earthquake took almost 10 GW of nuclear capacity offline. This major inefficiency made the process of quickly replacing lost nuclear power with fossil-fuel-powered sources, many of them mothballed, more difficult.

Japan passed the Atomic Energy Basic Law in 1955 to pursue the development of nuclear power for peaceful purposes, and its nuclear program was unique at the time in not having a military provenance. The first Japanese nuclear plant, of British design, went online at Tokai in 1966, but subsequent designs were American light water reactors, built in cooperation with companies such as Westinghouse and General Electric. The oil shocks following the Yom Kippur War of 1973 added urgency to reducing Japanese reliance on imported fossil fuels, and construction of new nuclear power plants continued unabated throughout the 1980s and 1990s despite the accidents at TMI and Chernobyl.

The six reactors at Fukushima Daichi were all variants of Generation II boiling water reactors designed by General Electric during the 1960s, and all but the last reactor built were housed in what is called a Mark I containment, with the first reactor commencing operation in 1971. When first approved, the reactors and buildings were supposed to withstand 265 gal (a gal, a unit of acceleration named after Galileo Galilei, is defined as 1 centimeter per second squared), a low number, given the location of the plant near the edge of a major plate subduction boundary. In light of evolving knowledge of plate tectonics, the Atomic Energy Commission of Japan released revised guidelines in 1978 for nuclear reactors and key components to withstand a maximum acceleration of 370 gal.

There was no legal framework to ensure that the guidelines would be applied retroactively to older plants, but the Agency for Natural Resources and Energy demanded in 1992 that nuclear plant operators conduct checks on adherence and report the results. TEPCO's response to the government regarding Fukushima Daiichi was that sufficient safety margins were built in to ensure seismic safety. Several sources cite TEPCO-provided data claiming that the various units at Daiichi were built to withstand maximum acceleration of between 438 and 489 gal horizontal and between 412 and 429 gal vertical, and that the maximum forces observed during the earthquake in only Units 2, 3, and 5 (550, 507, and 548 gal respectively) exceeded their design parameters.[21] Given TEPCO's unfortunate record of fudging facts unless forced to come clean, these numbers must be taken with more than just a grain of salt.

In the wake of several large earthquakes, including the Great Hanshin-Awaji Earthquake in 1995, the Nuclear Safety Commission revised the guidelines further in 2006 for nuclear reactors and key components to withstand acceleration as high as 600 gal. The guidelines also called for the consideration of events associated with major earthquakes, such as landslides and tsunamis. Shortly thereafter, the Nuclear and Industrial Safety Agency (NISA, the main agency responsible for overseeing nuclear reactor safety before its dissolution in 2012) requested that nuclear plant operators conduct

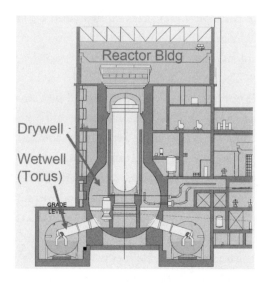

Mark I boiling water reactor
containment (courtesy Sandia
National Laboratories).

back-checks on their facilities, but TEPCO actually performed very few seismic back-checks before the March 2011 accident, and no actual reinforce-
ment work at Fukushima Daiichi except very minor items on Units 4 and 5.

When the earthquake struck, Unit 4 at Fukushima Daiichi did not contain any fuel, and Units 5 and 6 were shut down for scheduled maintenance,
but all the reactor buildings had cooling ponds, containing in total over five
thousand new and spent fuel assemblies. Because spent fuel continues to
decay and generate heat, it must spend several years in cooling pools before
it can be transferred to dry cask storage, and the pools are typically located
next to the reactors in the same building so that the fuel assemblies can be
removed from the reactors and transferred to the pools while immersed.

The three reactors that were operating during the earthquake shut down
automatically (in a procedure with the acronym SCRAM),[22] although they
probably suffered damage including loss of coolant in Unit 1. In some respects, that the reactors and buildings largely withstood the strength of a
temblor that was comparable to the acceleration force and about double
the duration of 2006's 600-gal guidelines, for which they were neither designed nor retrofitted, was pretty lucky. Looking back, TEPCO insisted that
the station blackout would have been avoided if the tsunami had not occurred with the intensity experienced — that is, it was all okay till those

darn waves hit. But this claim was refuted by the Independent Investigation Commission, which found that the times reported for the failure of key backup systems to provide emergency power actually occurred *before* the biggest wave hit the plant, given that the wave measurement buoy was 1.5 kilometers offshore, so the wave arrival time was actually two to two and a half minutes later than when the measurements were taken. In any event, the tsunami that followed forty minutes after the quake overwhelmed the 5.7-meter-high outer seawalls and the ground level at 10 meters above the sea, as later estimates put the height of the waves at between 10 and 13 meters, inundating the plant buildings to a height of over 14 meters.

Throughout Japan's long coast, one can find stone tablets, some hundreds of years old and almost illegible, marking the levels to which previous tsunamis reached, sometimes along with the number of people who perished. They are grim reminders of past catastrophes, as well as warnings to future generations: don't build anything below here. When the application for Unit 1 of Fukushima Daiichi was filed in 1966, the highest wave level assumed was 3.12 meters, based on the Chilean earthquake tsunami that reached the Tohoku coast in 1960.

In 2003, the government Headquarters for Earthquake Research Promotion predicted that, over the subsequent thirty years, there was a 20 percent probability of an earthquake at the level of magnitude 8 along the Japan Trench off northeastern Japan. According to internal documents, TEPCO calculated in 2008 that the tsunami from such a temblor would reach the Daiichi site at a height of as much as 15.7 meters, and the area around Unit 4 would be inundated under 2.6 meters of water. In 2006, the Nuclear and Industrial Safety Agency established a study group to evaluate the potential effects of waves that exceed assumptions, and TEPCO reported to the group that a 10-meter tsunami hitting Daiichi Unit 5 would risk emergency seawater cooling pump failure, and a 14-meter tsunami would risk the loss of all external grid and standby power supplies. Unfortunately, about the only thing TEPCO did in the next several years to address the threat was to raise its maximum tsunami assumption at the plant from 5.7 to 6.1 meters and to raise some seawater pump motor equipment accordingly and make them more water resistant.[23] That the four newer reactors at TEPCO's Fukushima Daini nuclear plant, only twelve kilometers south of Fukushima Daiichi, were able to achieve cold shutdown four days after the tsunami was nothing short of very lucky.[24]

In a striking contrast, since 1988 the Tohoku Electric Power Company (different from TEPCO), the utility servicing its home region, conducted research on tsunami deposits pre-dating available research (which went back only about four hundred years) to construct assumptions for its Onagawa nuclear power station. Located on the coast northeast of Fukushima Daiichi about half the distance from the quake epicenter, the three newer Onagawa boiling water reactors, with the first unit starting operation in 1984, withstood the quakes and tsunami to shut down safely, despite being hit with waves over a meter higher than those that inundated Fukushima Daiichi. Luck surely played a part, as the quake knocked out all but one of the five lines to bring power into the plant and damaged some emergency generators. The plant was also very much a part of the nuclear nexus between the central government, local communities, and the electric utilities, but there was an important difference between it and the TEPCO Fukushima Daiichi facility: a far more rigorous safety culture. In addition to constructing standard seawalls, Tohoku Electric built the Onagawa plant at 14.7 meters above sea level, almost five times more than the initial assumptions about average tsunami heights based on the waves caused by the 1960 Chilean quake, and conducted periodic reviews of its assumptions based on new data. Tohoku also had robust procedures for dealing with accidents, quickly establishing emergency response centers on-site and at headquarters and dispatching supervisors and chief engineers to the reactor control rooms.[25] A 2013 Stanford study that compared Japanese nuclear power plant safety features with those of other countries found that inadequate protection was concentrated among the largest utilities (Tokyo, Kansai, Chubu Electric, and the Japan Atomic Power Company), but that the smaller utilities were indistinguishable from the international average.[26] And, unlike TEPCO, whose far-flung nuclear power plants were tasked with supplying the capital region with electricity, Tohoku Electric is the "home team," supplying power to its own region. Tohoku Electric even invited residents to take refuge at the Onagawa plant following the tsunami, some for months, reflecting the tighter relationship between the utility and the local community it services.

There were many warning signals over several decades suggesting that the way in which the Japanese nuclear industry and its regulators, often called the "nuclear village," conducted themselves was fraught with problems. Among many troubling incidents, highly radioactive water leaked out of a reactor at Japan Atomic Power Corporation's Tsuruga plant in Fukui Prefecture for several hours in 1981, exposing workers to radiation, but the accident was not disclosed to the government and the public for forty days. A more serious "what were they thinking?" incident occurred in 1999, when two workers died from exposure to gamma radiation after causing a criticality accident at a JCO Company (a nuclear fuel processing company) facility by overfilling a tank with aqueous nuclear fuel as they were manually preparing a batch of fuel for the Joyo experimental fast breeder reactor.

These accidents, as well as the Fukushima Daiichi disaster, took place against the backdrop of a traditional phenomenon in many Japanese industries called *amakudari,* or "descent from heaven": retired bureaucrats from regulators and relevant ministries often parachute into senior positions at the companies they previously oversaw, with the most senior bureaucrats finding positions with the largest and most prestigious utilities.[27] It is one side of the "revolving door" often used to help explain the collusive relationships between government and the private sector in other countries, and the direction that is most problematic in Japan. Two months after Fukushima, the *Japan Times* pointed out that, over the past fifty years, sixty-eight former bureaucrats from the Ministry of Economy, Trade, and Industry (which oversaw nuclear reactors through its Nuclear and Industrial Safety Agency) landed in top positions at the nation's twelve electric utilities — and these were only the most senior spots.[28] The practice matters because it allows the ministries to protect and expand their influence over various sectors of the economy and provides the companies with an inside track into, and influence over, laws and ordinance that affect their industry. Despite some attempts to reform the system, the list of *amakudari*-related scandals in Japan is long, ranging from national highways and infrastructure to defense procurement. In the Japanese nuclear industry, the practice allowed the electric utilities and associated companies to water down safety regulations and guidance against the public interest, culminating in the Fukushima Daiichi disaster.

Fukushima: Battling the Hydra

Friday, March 11, 2011, was a pretty typical early spring workday, overcast and chilly in most of Eastern Japan. At 2:46 in the afternoon, a major quake occurred under the seabed seventy kilometers off the coast of Tohoku, lasting about six minutes. Within seconds of detecting the earthquake, the Meteorological Agency issued a strong earthquake warning, which was broadcast automatically on the national TV station NHK and also transmitted to mobile phone carriers to set off early warning alarms on cell phones. Highspeed trains and factory lines around Japan had a precious few minutes to stop, thanks to early warning systems, likely saving many lives. Initial estimates of the magnitude broadcast put it at around 5, but grew within minutes to above 7 on the logarithmic Richter scale. The quake was eventually estimated to have been above magnitude 9 at the epicenter — the strongest ever recorded in Japan — and shifted the seabed about fifty meters, or half a soccer pitch. During the earthquake, Fukushima Daiichi's three operating reactors — Units 1, 2, and 3 — shut down as designed and were cooled by plant controls and cooling systems powered by diesel backup generators. Tsunami warnings were issued along with the initial earthquake report, and initially estimated that waves as high as six meters would reach the coast of Miyagi Prefecture, north of Fukushima, in as little as half an hour. What arrived instead were waves that were about thirteen meters high when they reached the Fukushima Daiichi nuclear power station. With the plant built at ten meters above sea level, its turbine buildings were under several meters of seawater until the levels subsided.

Safety at Fukushima Daiichi was seriously compromised as soon as the waves rolled over the complex. Seven transmission lines heading toward the plant to provide power from outside had been consolidated into three sets of lines, so that failure of two electrical substations and a switchyard would totally deprive Daiichi of all grid power. Most of the emergency generators and power supplies were located in non-watertight turbine buildings, the common cooling pool building, or the control building basement. Even the three diesel generators that were located higher on a hillside went through switching panels that were vulnerable to inundation, and only the panel located in Unit 6 survived. The tsunami inundated almost all the backup diesel generators, emergency battery power supplies, switching panels, and the seawater cooling pumps for transferring the heat from the reactors from the core to the ocean (and for cooling most of the emergency generators). Units 1, 2, and 4 lost all their power supplies, and Units 3 and 5 lost all generated power. The emergency battery power to Unit 3, one of the only on-site power supplies still operating after the tsunami, ran out after about thirty-six hours. On-site workers struggled to restore power to cool the reactors and cooling ponds in the face of almost complete power failure, loss of control room functions, incomplete schematics, and a debris-strewn plant.

With its isolation condenser, a type of heat exchanger atop the reactor in Unit 1, not acting effectively as a heat sink, and a jury-rigged core spray system unable to operate until the reactor pressure was low enough, Unit 1's core of fuel, which requires constant cooling even after shutdown as highly radioactive products of fission decay and continue to produce heat, began to be exposed by the evening of March 11. Commercial nuclear reactors, including those at Fukushima Daiichi, are housed in buildings that are supposed to contain radioactive gases or steam in an emergency. By early the next morning, radioactive gases from the containment vessel, subject to pressures beyond design parameters, began leaking into the containment building from any gaps in the plumbing and electrical systems that could be forced open, and airborne radioactivity began to leak from the building. The falling pressure in the reactor due to the leaks finally allowed the fire extinguisher pumps jury-rigged to the cooling system to begin injecting water, but not quickly enough. Meanwhile, the national government expanded the evacuation zone around the plant from three to ten kilometers. Hydrogen gas, produced by the Zircaloy alloy used as fuel cladding reacting at high temperature with water, began to accumulate in the containment building, raising the possibility of an explosion set off by a spark. The workers at Unit 1 were given permission to vent the dangerous gases at 2:30 p.m. on March 12, but stuck valves had to be opened manually in a quickly deteriorating, increasingly radioactive environment. An hour and a half after the permission to vent was given, the Unit 1 reactor building exploded, showering the vicinity with debris, undoing much of the work being done to route cables to power a standby cooling system for Unit 2 and injuring five workers.

Units 2 and 3 were of slightly more advanced design and in marginally better shape immediately after the tsunami, but shared the same challenges as Unit 1: as core temperatures and reactor vessel pressures continued to rise, it became ever more difficult to inject water to cool them, and pressure had to be relieved through venting before water pumps, jury-rigged to replace the proper cooling units that began to fail, could be effective. The emergency high pressure feedwater pumps (the reactor core isolation cooling system) for Units 2 and 3 appeared to be working immediately after the tsunami, and, in the case of Unit 3, the main high-pressure coolant injection system automatically reactivated on the second day, only to stop again on March 13. Temperatures and pressures in the reactor vessels of Units 2 and 3 continued to rise from the slowing but still considerable pace of residual decay, and the hydrogen building up in Unit 3's containment building exploded at 11 a.m. on March 14 before fire and water trucks could begin attempting to inject seawater. After Unit 2's emergency cooling system stopped working in the early afternoon of March 14, the fire trucks that had been injecting seawater ran out of fuel, the water in the core boiled off, and meltdown ensued. Although Unit 2's reactor containment vessel or, possibly, the torus — a doughnut-shaped ring below the reactor vessel filled with water designed to remove heat from the steam generated by the reactor — probably suffered a breach during the meltdown, the containment building did not explode violently (though a blast was heard), probably owing to gases and steam escaping from blowout panels damaged by debris from Unit 1's explosion. But early in the morning on March 15, Unit 4's containment building exploded unexpectedly, and investigators speculated that backflow of hydrogen from Unit 3 next door leaked into Unit 4's building, providing an explosive atmosphere, which was set off by a fire.

With about three times the number (over fifteen hundred) of fuel assemblies in its cooling pool than were in the pools of Units 2 and 3, as all of its fuel was removed from the reactor for scheduled maintenance at the time, Unit 4 became a major concern after the explosion as white smoke continued to emanate from the pool's vicinity, leading to speculation that the pool was damaged, the remaining water was boiling, and that the fuel assemblies would eventually perhaps even burn. It was on Unit 4 (as well as Unit 3) that Self-Defense Force helicopters, in one of the iconic images of the accident, dumped water several times on March 17 in an effort to replenish water in the spent fuel pools. As it turned out, there was sufficient water in Unit 4's cooling pool to prevent this outcome, but that still left the challenge of eventually restoring water circulation in all the pools to prevent heat build-up. Although Units 5 and 6 were shut down for scheduled maintenance, their cores were still generating decay energy when the tsunami hit. Fortunately, Unit 5 was able to tap into the backup diesel power supply routed through the surviving switching panel in the adjacent Unit 6 and activate a pump on March 13. A follow-up series of jury-rigged pumps and heat sinks allowed the reactor to achieve cold shutdown by March 20.

Reviewing the background and the timeline of Fukushima Daiichi, it is hard to disagree with the Independent Investigation Commission findings: that the accident was "man-made," the result of operating a collusively regulated, inadequately designed plant without enough regard or preparation for safety in emergencies.

Fukushima: The Aftershocks

The most dangerous phase of the Fukushima Daiichi accident was largely over by the end of March, though cold shutdown — when reactor pressure vessel temperatures are below 100 degrees Celsius, radioactive release from the vessel is under control, and the public is not exposed to additional radiation release — was not declared for the whole plant until December 16. The immediate human toll from the nuclear accident was quite small relative to the about twenty thousand people who died from the earthquake and tsunami. Two workers died on March 11 after being trapped in the basement turbine room of Unit 4 when the tsunami hit, and dozens of workers were injured from the subsequent hydrogen gas explosions. About one hundred workers received doses calculated to be over 100 millisieverts (mSv) as of the end of March, and two control room operators received close to 700 mSv (the U.S. EPA guideline for the voluntary maximum dose for emergency workers volunteering for lifesaving work is 750 mSv, the WHO guidelines are a bit stricter at 500 mSv), but no one suffered from acute radiation syndrome as a result of the crisis.[29]

The National Institute of Radiological Sciences (Japan) estimates that of the 14,412 residents of the three most affected towns near the plant during the four months after the accident, fewer than 1 percent received cumulative doses of over 10 mSv, about 42 percent received between 1 and 10 mSv, and 57 percent received less than 1 mSv, numbers that are comparable to typical annual doses in areas with low background radiation.[30] A WHO study conducted in 2012 found that residents most affected by the accident were exposed to between 10 and 50 mSv during the first year after the accident, and that the lifetime risk for some cancers may be somewhat elevated above baselines in certain age and sex groups (such as thyroid cancer in female infants) in the area most affected, based on the most conservative assumptions using the Linear No-Threshold model. But the report concluded that "the increases in the incidence of human disease attributable to the additional radiation exposure from the Fukushima Daiichi NPP accident are likely to remain at below detectable levels."[31]

Much more harmful for the residents of affected areas were the confusion about radiation levels and the inept evacuation from the ever-expanding evacuation zones, particularly of the frailest and most vulnerable. The Nuclear Safety Division of the Ministry of Education, Culture, Sports, Science, and Technology (MEXT) had developed a nationwide network of detectors and an algorithm during the 1990s to measure and provide real-time dose assessments in radiological emergencies. The system, dubbed SPEEDI (System for Prediction of Environmental Emergency Dose Information), proved to be anything but for those affected by the accident. There were uncertainties in the estimates being produced by the system as information from source-measurement instruments to identify and measure the release of radionuclides at the Daiichi plant could not be retrieved for many hours, so the Nuclear and Industrial Safety Agency and MEXT concluded that the system's calculation results could not be used in determining the initial evacuation orders. Although the system would have helped residents to make more informed decisions about evacuation, information generated from it was not released to the general public until March 23, nine days after the data were provided to U.S. military forces stationed in Japan.[32] In a move that did not exactly inspire further confidence in a discredited regime, the government announced on April 19, 2011, without much elaboration, that the amount of radiation to which a child can be exposed is 20 mSv per year, the same level as the International Commission on Radiological Protection's recommended cap for radiation workers (up from the previous limit of 1 mSv, which is one-sixth of the annual dose for a typical American).

As the Fukushima crisis unfolded, it became obvious that, in addition to TEPCO, most government bodies at all levels were woefully unprepared. Japan enacted the Nuclear Emergency Preparedness Act in 1999, shortly after the fatal criticality accident at JCO, which set out roles, responsibilities, and procedures for ministries, agencies, prefectures, municipalities, and nuclear operators in the event of an emergency. But the few simulations that were conducted in the following years were tidy, unrealistic exercises with minimal local resident participation, designed merely to check the boxes.

Evacuating hospitals proved to be particularly difficult, with staff scrounging whatever means of transport they could arrange with local emergency services or the Self Defense Force. In one particularly tragic and avoidable incident, 40 seriously ill patients among 132 evacuated from Futaba Hospital died by the end of March after spending over ten hours and traveling 230 kilometers on a roundabout journey to a high school south of the evacuation zone, where they ended up after the Fukushima Prefecture Headquarters for Disaster Control could not find a hospital to take them in. A study conducted by the Fukushima Medical University reported that mortality rates for elderly evacuees spiked during the three months following the accident, with the mortality rate for residents of care facilities within twenty kilometers of the plant over eight months of 2011 at 2.4 times that for the same period in 2010.[33]

Another key factor exacerbating the crisis was just how low public safety was on the list of regulators' priorities: one damning example revealed by the Independent Investigation Commission was how, in 2006, the Nuclear and Industry Safety Agency (NISA) quashed an effort to upgrade an Emergency Preparedness Guide, originally drafted by the Nuclear Safety Commission of Japan in 1980 in the wake of Three Mile Island. The Nuclear Safety Commission was studying how a Precautionary Action Zone system, one of four alert categories articulated by the International Atomic

Energy Agency (IAEA) and defined as three to five kilometers from a nuclear power plant, could be instituted so that preplanned evacuation or
protective action could be taken shortly after an emergency and preferably
before radiation emissions. NISA requested that the Nuclear Safety Commission halt the review, as NISA's main concern was that the introduction of
a new alert regime would confuse or concern residents near nuclear plants
and perhaps undermine utilities' efforts to introduce a mixed oxide fuel
with plutonium in addition to uranium into their reactors. So international
standards were not incorporated into the revised Emergency Preparedness
Guide released in 2007, and whether they would have become part of another revision, initiated after the IAEA released a new emergency safety
guide in 2010 and incomplete when the accident occurred, is far from certain. In any event, the evacuation zones that were declared after the disaster
turned out to be very similar to those outlined by the IAEA, but with one
vital difference: a woeful lack of preparation.

The aftereffects of the Fukushima Daiichi disaster are still being felt.
For over two years afterward, the complex leaked over three hundred tons
of radioactive water daily into the Pacific, and TEPCO's inability to stanch
the flow of groundwater into the reactor buildings led the Abe administration to decide during the summer of 2013 to shoulder much of the responsibility for dealing with the problem, by providing money (47 billion
yen, or about $480 million) and marshaling technological know-how.[34] In
a major application of a technique pioneered in the United States for containing contaminated sites, TEPCO and the government are constructing an
underground wall of frozen soil to block groundwater seepage, estimated
to be about 400 tons per day. Meanwhile, TEPCO announced in May 2015
that it had finished filtering 620,000 tons of contaminated water stored at
Fukushima Daiichi to lower its radioactivity.[35] In September 2015, TEPCO
started releasing some treated groundwater into the ocean in an effort to
relieve the massive accumulation of water stored at Fukushima Daiichi, but
the battle continues.[36]

In addition to the trauma experienced by those in the Tohoku region
who were displaced or lost loved ones from the earthquake and tsunami,
the residents of the exclusion area experienced the nuclear accident firsthand. Fear of radioactivity and the uncertainty of ever being able to return

to their homes to resume their lives added to their already considerable burden. Like those displaced by Chernobyl, those most affected by the disaster experienced high levels of stress and anxiety, which can become manifest in general health problems. A questionnaire sent to 210,000 evacuees in early 2012 indicated that 15 percent of the 91,000 who replied showed signs of extreme stress, five times higher than the normal rate.[37] During the months after the natural disaster and nuclear accident, the National Police Agency published official figures showing the number of suicides during 2011 in the three prefectures most affected were actually lower than in the previous year. Given anecdotal evidence that the suicide rate in affected areas was quite high, particularly for those displaced, the numbers may have been understated because of a bureaucratic reluctance to report high numbers. Moreover, many suicides among evacuees, particularly among the elderly and the isolated, were not identified as such, as some simply chose not to live useful lives anymore by abusing alcohol or ceased any effort to maintain their well-being—in other words, they decided to die.[38] On June 7, 2013, in an out-of-court settlement with the family of a Fukushima farmer who took his own life twelve days after the meltdown and after authorities banned the shipment of farm products from the area because of fears of contamination, TEPCO conceded for the first time that the 3/11 accident was indeed a factor.[39]

The regulatory capture and lack of oversight in the Japanese nuclear village, which allowed the key players to be so utterly unprepared, can also be observed from differences with other nuclear regulatory regimes at the time of the disaster. France, with its impressive record of nuclear power safety, requires all new and existing reactors to meet regulations regarding the following: (a) failure to shut down the reactor during a reactor event, (b) station blackout, (c) hydrogen build-up, and (d) incorporating filtered containment venting systems to reduce the spread of radioactivity from venting (also called hardened vents). For Japanese nuclear operators at the time of the Fukushima disaster, addressing all these issues was voluntary—in other words, largely ignored.

In the wake of the terrorist attacks of September 11, 2001, the United States initiated a policy to harden nuclear power facilities against terrorists and threats from the air. Whether this would have made much of a difference at Fukushima is somewhat moot, as the U.S. rules, enacted in 2009, applied to new plants only, and Japan took many of its safety cues from the United States. Indeed, the U.S. nuclear regulatory regime comes across as being a bit more "flexible" than its European counterparts in some aspects, as regulations about not being able to shut down reactors and station blackouts, introduced in 1984 and 1988 respectively, applied only to new reactors and not to existing licensed units. As for filter vent systems, which were required in French, German, Swedish, and Swiss nuclear power stations by the late 1980s after Chernobyl,[40] they must now be installed on all Japanese boiling water reactors before they can be restarted (the U.S. NRC came under criticism in 2013 after delaying implementation of a rule that would require them on all thirty-one boiling water reactors operating in the United States).[41]

In September 2012, the Nuclear Reform Monitoring Committee, headed by a former chairman of the U.S. Nuclear Regulatory Commission, was established as an advisory body to the TEPCO board to monitor the firm's progress in improving its technical capabilities and safety standards. With this new regime in place, combined with reforms at the regulatory level with the establishment of the Nuclear Regulatory Authority (NRA), it is hoped that the messy diffusion of responsibility and pervasive regulatory capture that laid the ground for the Fukushima Daiichi disaster will not repeated. But it is far too early to be sanguine: most of the five hundred staff members of the new agency formerly belonged to the old regulator NISA, whose past oversight record is obviously nothing to write home about, and they oversee almost fifty reactors, when the comparable ratio at the U.S. NRC is about four thousand staff — many of them experts in their fields — overseeing about one hundred reactors.[42]

All nuclear reactors in Japan were idled for extensive inspections following Fukushima, and utilities began to file applications in July 2013 with the new Nuclear Regulatory Agency for restarting them. The seventeen applications received by February 2014 were all for units that started operations during the 1980s or later (including those for two advanced BWRs), with a combined capacity of about 16.5 gigawatts of electricity, or less than 40 percent of the total capacity available without Fukushima Daiichi.[43] The Institute for Energy Economics Japan looked for the restart of sixteen

reactors during fiscal year 2014 (ending in March 2015) in its reference sce-
nario for its Economic and Energy Outlook of Japan, for power generation
costs of ¥11.7 per kilowatt-hour, versus ¥8.2/kWh during the year before
Fukushima — a ¥25.4 trillion fossil fuel import bill (40 percent higher
than 2010), and energy-related emissions 4.2 percent higher than in 2010.[44]
But actually restarting reactors has proved far more difficult, with two in
Kyushu going back online during 2015, another two at Kansai Electric's
Takahama plant scheduled for January and February 2016 after a district
court overturned an injunction preventing their restarts, and one reactor on Shikoku Island expected to restart sometime in 2016. Much of the
current discussion in Japan about nuclear power is focused on how many
reactors can reasonably be expected to be restarted, along with measures
to regain public trust in nuclear power. But there is disappointingly very
little discourse about what type of nuclear power — evolutionary improvements of current models or completely different designs, small modular
versus large — may take the place of part of the pre-Fukushima capacity
that is likely to be shut permanently. This lack of debate reflects the continued dominance of traditional conservative incumbents — particularly the
twelve electric utilities, the big business lobby Keidanren, the ruling Liberal
Democratic Party, and the Ministry of Economy, Trade and Industry —
and their interest in getting back to "business as usual" as soon as possible.

Japanese energy policy is a mess at present: the government wants to
restart as many nuclear power plants as possible but faces local opposition
and a new regulator that has (rightly) adopted a more thorough approach
to oversight; the country is more dependent on foreign fossil fuels than
at any time since the 1970s, and renewable energy sources have not been
able to fill the gap fast enough. An energy policy for Japan similar to that
of Germany — closing all current nuclear reactors without replacing them
with modern nuclear, while making up for lost capacity through very expensive LNG and heavy subsidies to renewable energy — would be potentially catastrophic for a nation with unsustainable government borrowing
and a rapidly aging population. Japan, unlike continental Germany and its
imports of electricity from nuclear-powered France, does not even have the
near-term option of importing cheap electricity from its neighbors.

On the morning of August 26, 2011, the Japanese legislature passed a bill calling for the establishment of feed-in tariffs for renewable energy, to take effect in July 2012. Feed-in tariff regimes aim to encourage the buildup of renewable energy capacity by establishing long-term, cost-plus contracts for power produced from renewable sources at prices higher than the spot rate for electricity, as well as ensuring access to the grid, with the cost passed on by the utilities to electricity users. Over fifty countries have introduced feed-in tariff policies, and several European countries, such as Denmark, Germany, and Spain, are often cited as the most successful in building renewable energy capacity, although in exchange for some of the highest electricity costs in the world. The bill had met fierce opposition from the Ministry of Economy, Trade, and Industry (METI, the ministry then responsible for promoting nuclear power and overseeing its safety, and now responsible, ironically, for overseeing the renewable energy build-out), electric utilities, and the Keidanren big-business lobby. Later that afternoon, Naoto Kan resigned as prime minister, making it the last piece of legislation passed during his watch. News of the new feed-in tariff scheme was welcomed by much of the general public (including the author) as a vital first step to wean Japan from its two-pronged dependence on imported fossil fuels and discredited nuclear power. But the devil is in the details, as they say, and the details may not be as comforting.

The initial Japanese feed-in tariffs, designed to maximize renewable energy build-out during the first three years, were generous: for example, solar power players producing over 10 kW would be paid ¥42/kWh for twenty years, while those below 10 kW would receive the same but for ten years; wind power producers over 20 kW would receive ¥23.10/kWh for twenty years, and those under 20 kW would be paid ¥57.75/kWh for the same period.[45] The tariff paid to larger Japanese solar producers was almost three times as much as those offered by Germany and France (about 50 percent more than Spain), over twice that charged for wind power produced by large farms in France and Germany, and the highest rate in the world for wind power produced by installations under 20 kW (all using 2012 foreign exchange rates). Since then, the feed-in tariffs have been revised downward — to ¥36/kWh in 2013 and ¥32/kWh in 2014 for large solar PV power producers, for example — as one would expect for policies designed to adjust to improved scale and technologies, and the weaker yen has made international comparisons less extreme.[46]

Feed-in tariffs are typically designed to attract investors, big and small, to install capacity by providing predictable rates of return, usually in the range of 5–10 percent. But it is no accident that, in an age of near-zero interest rates, many very large companies and financial players, including telecom conglomerate Softbank and leasing giant Orix, have become major players in the Japanese solar PV build-out. One cannot help but look at examples like Spain and worry that Japan is following a similar path in attempting to add renewable capacity quickly, even if it significantly erodes the energy return on (energy) investment for society. Overall, Japan's initial feed-in tariff policy failed to learn from Germany's renewable energy mistakes (more on this later) and was set too high, while not doing enough to en-courage investment in grid infrastructure and more-balanced deployment of other forms of renewable energy, such as wind and geothermal.[47] With the utilities that are obliged to buy renewable power reportedly unable to keep up with the backlog of applicants, METI has recently decided to freeze new solar PV approvals pending a national policy review on renewable energy — a positive move, particularly if accompanied by specific policies that would lower the bureaucratic and NIMBY hurdles to other forms of renewable energy that have been left behind.[48]

So what are the main lessons to be learned from the Fukushima Daiichi disaster? Many antinuclear ideologues feel that the big take-away, like that of TMI or Chernobyl, is that using nuclear fission to produce electricity is inherently too dangerous and should be scrapped altogether. The Interna-tional Atomic Energy Agency classifies it as a "major accident" at the same rating as Chernobyl (the ultimate nuclear power fiasco), making it sound as bad to the general public. The disaster at Fukushima, involving three melt-downs and radioactive release, was a serious accident. But to call it another Chernobyl is simply wrong for several reasons. No workers were killed by radiation or explosions at Fukushima, while the Chernobyl catastrophe killed fifty people directly or following the event. As for radiation dispersed into the atmosphere at Fukushima, the IAEA estimates it to be 10–20 per-cent of that released at Chernobyl, much of it dispersed over the ocean.[49] Some of the release from Fukushima has been the result of water leaks that flowed into the ocean, which is still very problematic, but less so than an intensely burning reactor spewing radioactive fallout over a land area spanning several countries. The real lesson from Fukushima Daiichi is that, to tap the energy of atoms safely, you simply cannot have the degree of regulatory capture seen in the Japanese nuclear power industry going into the disaster. No human-made system is perfect, but the absence of a proper safety culture, eroded by decades of collusion, results in a nuclear power industry that amplifies imperfections and severely undermines the public interest. I can only hope that meaningful regulation, combined with new and safer "human-proof" technologies (which I will cover later), will enable nuclear power to finally fulfill its promise of providing, in conjunction with renewable energy, the means of powering our future.

In the wake of Fukushima, the global "nuclear renaissance" anticipated since the turn of the millennium came to a screeching halt as many countries reviewed their nuclear power industries. The biggest impact outside Japan was felt in Germany, where Angela Merkel's coalition government ordered in May 2011 that eight old reactors be shut down and the remaining eleven be phased out by 2022. But there are signs that the much-touted German goal, articulated in 2000 and known as *Energiewende*, to produce 80 percent of electricity and 60 percent of overall energy use from sun, wind, and biomass by 2050 while lowering greenhouse emissions by over 80 percent compared to 1990, is running into serious trouble. Subsidies to renewable energy, projected at €24 billion in 2014 alone, make electricity in Germany among the most expensive in Europe (three times that of the United States, four times that of China and India), while electricity-intensive industries have been exempt from paying subsidies so as to remain competitive, a situation that has become increasingly unpopular. Meanwhile, Germany's emissions rose in 2012 and 2013, and some point out that most of the drop in emissions in 2014 can be attributed to a warmer winter, making it ever-more challenging for the nation to meet the emissions reduction goals (20 percent less than 1990 by 2020, 40 percent less by 2030) articulated the 2015 Paris climate summit.[50]

The scheduled shutdown of nuclear plants has increased the use of cheap brown coal (Germany is the among the world's biggest producers) for power generation to the highest levels since 1990, instead of more expensive but cleaner natural gas, which would be dependent anyway on Russian supplies (about 36 percent of the total in 2012), even if its use could be increased. The German minister for energy and economy Sigmar Gabriel has indicated that he would like to cut feed-in tariffs to renewable power generators to an average of €0.12/kWh from €0.17/kWh, but costs are unlikely to come down quickly as the high, fixed prices for the renewable power capacity already in place, which accounted for 23 percent of electricity production in 2013, are guaranteed for twenty years under the 2000 renewable energy law.[51]

During the same month in 2011 as Germany's decision, Switzerland decided to cancel plans for new reactors and to not replace its five existing units when they are retired. In Italy, which had revived plans to build new plants to overturn a 1987 referendum closing down all nuclear power plants, 94 percent voted in June 2011 against building any new capacity. In France, a 2012 campaign pledge by François Hollande, as part of an effort to cement an alliance with the Green Party, called for cutting reliance on nuclear power to 50 percent from the current 75 percent. The policy may not undermine the country's resilience to interruptions in fossil fuel supplies so long as the 25 percent reduction (about twenty reactors) could be replaced with renewable energy and cost-effective storage over time. But the French industry minister commented in November 2013 that the government has no plans to close any reactors beyond two reactors scheduled to be shut down by the end of 2016.[52]

Like Japan, South Korea is very dependent on fossil fuel imports and had plans to increase nuclear power's share of power generation from 26 percent to 41 percent by 2030. But the ambitions have been scaled back to about 29 percent (43 GW) recently, because of growing opposition following Fukushima and charges of large-scale corruption among the domestic industry—the so-called "nuclear mafia." But the reassessment and scandals have not deterred South Korea's push to export its nuclear technology to Asia and the Middle East.[53]

On March 16, 2011, China halted the approval of all new nuclear plants and ordered that safety checks be conducted on all nuclear projects, delaying the construction of twenty-six reactors being built. In May 2012, China resumed granting approval for new nuclear plants, with preferential treatment to projects utilizing up-to-date Generation III technology. The

National Energy Administration stated at the end of 2011 that China intends to make nuclear power a foundation of its energy policy by adding as much as 300 GW of nuclear capacity over the following ten to twenty years. Although the country's pre-Fukushima target of 70–80 GW of installed capacity by 2020 (about 6 percent of total electricity output, up from 2 percent today) was scaled back to about 60 GW in 2012, the target for nuclear capacity, increasingly relying on fuel-breeding fast reactors, remains moderately high at 150 GWe (providing 10 percent of electricity) by 2030 and 240 GWe by 2050.[54]

Following the Fukushima Daiichi accident, much of the developed world slammed the brakes on nuclear power, and the developing world slowed its adoption. Although an understandable reaction to the accident, the loss of momentum came at a time when, driven by global warming, the imperative for replacing fossil fuels for generating electricity was intensifying. Deployment of new nuclear power plants has resumed since, with 66 reactors (70 GW of electrical generation capacity) under construction globally and another 158 (179 GW) ordered or planned.[55] Although the numbers look impressive, the world had about 5,550 GW of total installed electrical capacity in 2012, with 3,600 GW provided by fossil fuels.[56] So the pace at which nuclear power is being deployed today isn't anywhere near enough to make a meaningful dent in replacing fossil fuels, perhaps until the day that renewable sources and storage can provide almost all the energy we need to power society cost-effectively. Meanwhile, construction of new large light water reactors, at least in the West, has continued to be plagued by cost overruns and delays, even in countries with good track records of reactor deployment and safety, such as France. So what is to be done if modern nuclear power is to fulfill its promise? In the next chapter, we will examine the current and imminent generation of nuclear reactors, as well as the regulatory environment required to scale up and operate them safely.

Just pick the biggest idiot in the plant
and put the plutonium in his bag.
—**Charles Montgomery Burns (b. 1890)**

We must learn to set our emotions
aside and embrace what science tells
us. GMOs and nuclear power are two of
the most effective and most important
green technologies we have. If—after
looking at the data—you aren't in favor
of using them responsibly, you aren't
an environmentalist.
—**Ramez Naam (technologist and author)**

6

INVITING BACK THE TOILET-TRAINED GENIE

Fans of the animated series *The Simpsons* will remember Mr. Burns, the
evil owner of the Springfield Nuclear Power Plant, where Homer Simpson
works. A strange fusion of extreme old age and embodiment of modern
corporate values, Mr. Burns just cannot memorize his employee's names,
including Homer's. He would regularly blackmail and bribe officials to get
his way, including the town's mayor and nuclear regulators. A gross, funny
caricature of the nuclear industry and a reflection of just how low it stands
in the eyes of the public, the portrayal is nevertheless uncannily accurate
in an unexpected way: Mr. Burns's affinity for dated technology and old
ways of doing things reminds us of much of the real nuclear industry today.

Although humanity has used nuclear energy for over six decades, the
nuclear power industry often appears to be caught in a dimension where
time stands still. Power companies and regulators have managed to extend
the service lives of second-generation reactors to sixty years in some cases,
and to gain approval and begin construction of new plants at a pace that can

only be described as glacial. The nuclear power industry in the developed world is leading itself to slow extinction — not a problem if energy sources with low or no carbon footprints take their place quickly. But unfortunately this is not the case.

The nuclear industry is very conservative: it likes to focus on proven technology and takes considerable time in developing improvements or new technologies. True, for most of its existence the industry has been under intense scrutiny born of doubt and fear, but its self-proclaimed safety culture often focuses too narrowly, and not enough on some of the most important risks. (Filtered vents? It'll never get that bad. Tsunami? Who knew?) The nuclear industry is one of the few in which building more units means higher costs and slower deployment, a state of affairs that stems from the tradition of building every plant from scratch and needing to go through approval and licensing periods that can stagger on for decades. Nuclear power is currently the best clean way to replace base-load power provided from fossil fuels in large scale. But if nuclear power is to have a future, its hopes lie in introducing significantly cheaper, safer, and efficient third- and fourth-generation technologies as soon as possible. So let's move on from the wood-paneled station wagons of nuclear technology (the bulk of reactors operating in developed countries today), to what the Priuses and Teslas of the nuclear world look like.

Modern Nuclear Power: Not Your Grandparents' Pot Boilers

Third-generation (Gen III) reactors are essentially safer, evolutionary developments of second-generation reactors. They are designed to burn fuel more efficiently and produce less waste than Gen II designs, and are generally standardized to streamline licensing and construction. Although many modern nuclear power plants can adjust their power output in accordance with electricity demand (the European Utilities Requirement calls for nuclear power plants to be capable of changes in output from 50 percent to 100 percent at a rate of 3 to 5 percent per minute), making them suitable for producing variable power in addition to base load, Gen III reactors can adjust their power output more quickly.[1] More importantly, Gen III reactors are simpler and more rugged, and are designed to substantially reduce the odds of core accidents by incorporating safety systems that do not involve electrical or mechanical processes initiated by operators, but only physical phenomena such as convection and gravity. Most are designed so that the reactor requires no active intervention for seventy-two hours or more after shutdown. Core damage frequency (CDF) is a term used to indicate the likelihood of an accident that causes damage to a reactor core, based on an application of probabilistic risk-assessment models. Gen III reactors are claimed to have expected CDF rates that are more than ten times better than those required by the U.S. NRC for commercial reactors and for current U.S. plants.[2] In a parallel to the unfortunate reliance on models as a factor in the subprime mortgage crisis, people should of course know better than to rely excessively on estimates that do not incorporate nonlinear feedback loops adequately or may be limited by failures of imagination. At Fukushima Daiichi, for example, the bigger-than-envisaged tsunami shut off all external power, flooded almost all the generators and electrical switches, damaged seawater pumps and their water inlets, and wiped out fuel tanks for backup generators, so that the overwhelming event initiating the chain of failures washed away just about all the assumptions going into the plant's risk assessment.

An example of a reactor design safer than those of the second generation is the advanced boiling water reactor (ABWR), evolved from the BWRs that caused so many problems at Fukushima Daiichi. Among many improvements, the design incorporates ten reactor internal pumps mounted at the bottom of the reactor pressure vessel to minimize complex piping and their perforations of the vessel, and the emergency core cooling system comprises three separate sets (two in the earlier models like the ones at Fukushima Daiichi), each capable of providing water to cover the core in the event of off-site power loss. Two high-pressure core flooding loops, with fully separated mechanical and electrical systems, use power generated from backup generators. In addition, the steam-driven reactor core isolation cooling pump produces high pressure and has extensive battery backup for its control systems to allow it to operate in the event of full station blackout and failure of all three backup diesel generators. All the piping and equipment for the emergency cooling systems outside the containment structure housing the reactor and recirculation system are protected by watertight, reinforced concrete pump rooms.[3]

The most advanced Gen III designs, often called Gen III+, allow about seventy-two or more hours of cooling without operator action following shutdown by incorporating redundant, passive safety features that rely on heat resistance, gravity, or convection. One example is the Economic Simplified Boiling Water Reactor (ESBWR), a boiling water reactor design by GE Hitachi that improves upon the ABWR by incorporating passive safety systems — such as a gravity-driven cooling system in the event of an accident as well as a passive, closed-loop cooling system that transfers decay heat into the atmosphere in the event battery power is lost — to safely cool itself for more than a week without human interference or grid or generator power. It is also designed for an operational life of sixty years, and received final U.S. NRC certification in 2014.[4] Another is the AP1000, a Westinghouse pressurized water reactor design certified by the NRC in 2005. China has made the AP1000 the centerpiece of its nuclear build-out, with twenty-four units under construction, and four units are being built in the United States.

The Evolutionary Power Reactor (EPR), developed by Areva NP, Électricité de France (EDF), and Siemens, incorporates four independent cooling systems as well as significantly hardened containment structures. EPRs being built in France and Finland have faced significant delays and cost overruns, with the French Nuclear Safety Regulator warning of cooling system and reactor vessel faults in the units under construction at Flamanville, France.[5] The two units under construction in Guangdong, China, since 2009 have faced shorter delays of about two years thus far, with the first completed and scheduled to come on line in the first half of 2017.[6] Two units are currently scheduled for construction by EDF, with Chinese minority investors, in the UK. But the scheduled UK plant at Hinkley Point has stirred controversy, both for the high price being set by the government to buy the power produced and for the £2 billion in government guarantees offered to the Chinese investors.[7]

Marketed but not yet built, the Canadian Advanced CANDU reactor differs from pervious CANDU designs in its use of light water instead of heavy water, which allows for negative void reactivity (temperature up, nuclear reaction down), deemed a desirable safety feature in Gen III machines. The use of light water, however, means that it must use enriched uranium for fuel. The Russian VVER-1200 is an evolutionary development of a series of pressurized water reactors deployed in Russia and Eastern Europe since the 1970s, and advanced versions of the VVER series have been built or are planned in Turkey, Iran, Finland, India, and China, in addition to the former Soviet bloc countries. To enhance safety, the VVER-1200 has a passive cooling system with water tanks above the containment dome, designed to provide seventy-two hours of core cooling without human intervention.

According to a tally kept by the World Nuclear Association, 66 reactors are currently under construction and another 158 on order or planned around the world. China leads the pack with 64 reactors under construction and planned, 44 of which are Gen III. With 33 reactors under construction or planned, most of them Gen III, Russia has ambitious plans to increase the share of electricity production from nuclear power from 16 percent currently to about 25–30 percent by 2030 and 45–50 percent by 2050. India is building or planning construction of 30 reactors, mostly indigenous versions of the CANDU heavy water reactors developed by Canada, but about a third of them of various Gen III designs described earlier. Although work on all of them has been deferred, and getting them licensed is going to be a lot tougher than before Fukushima, Japan still has 11 commercial reactors being built or on the drawing boards, all of them Gen III.

Most of the Gen III reactors being built around the world today are big, designed to produce over 1,000 megawatts of electricity: some, like the European Pressurized Reactor, are designed to produce 1,700 MW or more per unit. And many of the Gen III reactors being built in China today, and the new heavy water reactors in India, have been built with a view to connecting them to the grid within five to seven years of the start of construction, and most of the projects have met their schedules. But the trend of nuclear power reactor projects becoming ever-larger continues largely unabated, and, at least in the G-7 countries, delays and costs continue to rise despite industry claims that standardization will bring them down over time. And even in the rest of the world, where the idea of replacing fossil fuels with nuclear power does not engender the degree of phobia seen in the West, nuclear is not making enough progress to meet the growth in electricity demand. While the World Nuclear Association's tally for nuclear reactors being built and planned totals 249 gigawatts (579 GW including those proposed) the IEA expects global electrical capacity to grow by 2,496 GW between 2012 and 2025. So for Gen III reactors, the current state of affairs doesn't exactly sound like the recipe for overwhelming success in replacing fossil fuels.

Gen IV and Beyond

In 2002, the Gen IV International Forum, composed of representatives from ten governments plus Euratom (the European Atomic Energy Community), narrowed down the many concepts for the next generation of nuclear reactors into six types that were thought the most promising for further development:

- Sodium-cooled fast reactor
- Lead-cooled fast reactor
- Supercritical water-cooled reactor
- Very high temperature reactor
- Gas-cooled fast reactor
- Molten salt reactor

Many are designed as modular units to be built on assembly lines instead of on-site, for quicker licensing, cheaper construction, and safer operation. All of them use fuel much more efficiently than light water reactors, which extract less than 1 percent of the energy contained in mined uranium, and most are potential breeders — in other words, they can produce more fissile material than they consume. They also burn the long-lived radioactive dregs of fission — minor players in the group of elements including uranium and thorium, called actinides — more effectively.[8]

As we reviewed earlier, traditional reactors use a moderator (water) to slow down neutrons after they are emitted, from above 9 million meters per second to around 2,200 meters per second (in the so-called thermal energy spectrum), increasing the chances that they will collide with a uranium-235 or other fissile atom to sustain a fission chain reaction. Fissile materials are capable of sustaining nuclear fission chain reactions and include (in addition to U-235) plutonium-239, which comes from U-238 capturing an additional neutron, and U-233, produced from thorium-232 through neutron capture. As the nonfissile U-238 (which accounts for about 92 to 97 percent of the fuel in light water reactors) absorbs a neutron and becomes Pu-239, it also contributes to a reactor's energy output.

If slowing down neutrons is so important for the nuclear chain reaction of U-235, why develop reactors that use fast neutrons? While Pu-239 gives off an average of almost three neutrons when it fissions, it also tends to absorb neutrons traveling at slower thermal energies without causing fission. But when the neutrons are very fast, Pu-239 tends not to absorb them and gives off more than the two required to split another Pu-239 atom and also turn a U-238 atom into Pu-239. So fast neutrons reduce the amount of Pu-239 that undergoes fission (thus initially requiring more fissile material in the fuel) while increasing its creation. It is in this way that fast reactors can be used to produce, or breed, more fuel than they consume.[9]

Given the need to maintain neutron speeds, fast reactors typically use a coolant other than water, such as liquid (metallic) sodium or lead-bismuth, requiring extra care in reactor design and coolant use. On the other hand, these coolants are better than water at transferring heat and also make possible the use of metallic fuel with better thermal conductivity than oxide fuels, so that reactors can be designed to shut down naturally without operator intervention.

Fast reactors are often described as having "closed" fuel cycles, as opposed to "open fuel cycles" for most traditional reactors. In a closed fuel cycle for traditional reactors, spent fuel is reprocessed to extract the remaining fissile material to be reused in reactors. Fast reactors can recycle nuclear materials, even those that have been through traditional reactors, and leave little residual waste for disposal — much closer to an intuitive understanding of a closed fuel cycle, and what it means in this book. Calling the process of fueling traditional reactors a cycle at all seems misleading, as uranium is typically mined, enriched, used in reactors, stored, reprocessed in some countries to recover some fissile fuel, and finally disposed of, if proper sites can be developed. Several countries, including the United States, practice a "once through" nuclear fuel chain, in which fuel is used once and then sent to permanent disposal without reprocessing; of course the challenge is to find suitable sites for the depositories, which must be secured for a very long time. And while many countries, such as Japan, have been developing fast reactors so that nuclear fuel can be genuinely recycled, for many of them their nuclear fuel chains have actually been stuck somewhere between storage after use and reprocessing.

Sodium-Cooled Fast Reactor (SFR)

The sodium-cooled fast reactor uses liquid sodium as a coolant and typically operates at near atmospheric pressure and at around 500–550°C. Its ability to burn minor actinides and its closed fuel cycle minimize waste. The idea of using sodium as a coolant is not new: the U.S. Navy considered using it for their reactor program during the development of nuclear propulsion in the 1950s but decided on water, as sodium has an annoying habit of exploding when exposed to water and burning when exposed to air. The latter is precisely what happened when Japan's experimental 714 MWt ("t" for thermal output) Monju breeder reactor sprung a piping leak in its secondary (so not radioactive) cooling system in 1995, caused a fire, and an all-too-familiar type of scandal over a cover-up of the extent of the accident, which delayed the reactor's restart until 2010. After yet another technical glitch, the Japanese government decided to shut down Monju in February 2014 after spending over $10 billion, pending a decision on assigning a new operator.

There are several experimental SFR reactors around the world today, in Russia, China, and India. In the United States, the Fermi 1 prototype fast breeder reactor began operation in 1963 but suffered a partial meltdown in 1966 after a blockage reduced the amount of sodium coolant entering the reactor; the reactor was shut down in 1972.[10] The Clinch River Breeder Reactor Project, a joint effort of the Atomic Energy Commission and the private sector to construct a 1,000 MWt prototype breeder reactor, took a decade to eat through $8 billion and failed to produce a working prototype before it was canceled in 1983. France's large 1,200 MWe ("e" for electricity generated, which will be less than the thermal energy because of conversion losses) Superphenix SFR operated for a decade before being closed down by the Jospin government in 1996, ostensibly because of high costs but also influenced by the government's political alliance with the Green Party. In one of the most misguided decisions in the history of U.S. nuclear power (more on this later), the Argonne National Laboratory operated the passively safe 62.5 MWt Experimental Breeder Reactor (EBR) II for thirty years before the program was canceled in 1994.

On a much smaller scale, Japan's Central Research Institute for Electric Power Industry (CRIEPI) and Toshiba have developed a 30 MWt sealed fast neutron sodium reactor called 4S — for super safe, small, and simple. The 4S is a small, modular reactor that would be contained in a thirty-meter-deep underground cylindrical vault beneath a small turbine generator building and retired after thirty years of operation. The reactor uses metallic instead of oxide fuel, sodium for coolant, and, instead of complicated control rods, employs a neutron reflector around the core that slides very gradually over its life to maintain efficient fuel burn. The 4S removes heat passively, regulates itself through negative temperature reactivity feedback (temperature up, reaction down), and uses few moving parts to minimize maintenance.

Sadao Hattori, now a senior adviser at CRIEPI and the driving force behind the 4S concept, is a longtime insider of the Japanese nuclear government-industrial complex: his biographer Eiji Ohshima writes that Hattori always harbored reservations about the unnecessary size and complexity of commercial nuclear reactors and hoped that safe modular reactors would provide power and water to developing nations.[11] Although there has been interest from remote "off-grid" communities and projects such as Galena, Alaska, Toshiba has yet to submit a time-consuming and extremely costly full license application with the NRC. An unfortunate reality in the nuclear power business today is that major incumbents appear focused on selling big-ticket, large-scale power plants around the world and do not pay nearly as much attention to very small reactors that, once produced, can be churned out like commercial airliners. So perhaps this is a field best advanced by start-up companies and others who are not wedded to the "big is beautiful" business model, but these firms will need a supportive (or nonobstructive) regulatory framework.

Lead-Cooled Fast Reactor (LFR)

The lead-cooled fast reactor uses molten lead (or lead-bismuth mix), the inert stuff to which uranium and thorium ultimately decay, as its coolant at low pressure and between 480 and 570 degrees Celsius. A major advantage is that, because lead has a very high boiling point, complete core melt is very unlikely; conversely, the reactor has to be kept a lot hotter than lead's melting point of 327°C (lead-bismuth is better at 123°C) to prevent the reactor from solidifying into the ultimate paperweight. During the Cold War, the Soviet Union used lead-cooled reactors to power its very fast, titanium-hulled Alfa-class attack submarines, and a Russian company is trying to build a larger 300 MWe commercial prototype called the OD-300 based on the naval design.

Europe is in on the act with its 600 MWe European lead-cooled fast reactor (ELFR) project, and the Lawrence Livermore Laboratory is developing a 20–100 MWe version called SSTAR (for small, sealed, transportable, autonomous reactor), basically like a big (fifteen by three meters for the 100 MW version) returnable battery with an operating life of thirty years. SSTAR operates with passively safe natural convection cooling and is meant to be a tamper-proof design that would prevent developing nations that lease the units from using them for weapons proliferation.[12] A U.S. company called Gen4 Energy has also developed a 25 MWe uranium-fueled, lead-bismuth cooled fast reactor, which would be marketed as a modular reactor to provide power to off-grid regions and energy-intensive projects. The company was awarded an R&D grant from the Department of Energy (DOE) in 2013 (along with GE, Westinghouse, and General Atomics) to develop its concept further, though it does not expect a prototype to be rolled out until 2030, and the major hurdle of NRC licensing would remain.[13]

Supercritical Water-Cooled Reactor (SCWR)

The supercritical water-cooled reactor is basically an LWR with much thicker walls and plumbing that can withstand very high pressures. Supercritical does not refer to difficult in-laws, but to any substance at a temperature and pressure above its critical point, where it displays characteristics of both liquids and gases. Because the supercritical coolant water (either regular or heavy) is used to drive its turbine directly, its thermal efficiency — the proportion of heat converted for useful work — can be close to 45 percent, as opposed to about 35 percent for most current LWRs. The technology has been used extensively in fossil-fueled and even concentrated-solar power plants to make them more efficient, but the challenge is to make it work in the extremely harsh conditions of nuclear reactors. According to the Gen IV Forum, studies have indicated that the operating costs for a SCWR could be about 30 percent less than current PWRs. One significant hurdle for the SCWR is that, in its supercritical state, small changes in temperature or pressure can change the coolant density and cause changes quickly in the reactor, potentially making it hard to control. So a major challenge for this system is to develop robust, passive safety systems that can withstand and offset the massive instantaneous loss of coolant that can occur if there is a leak.

Very High Temperature Reactor (VHTR)

As its name denotes, the very high temperature reactor is designed to operate at temperatures as high as 1,000°C, making it suitable for producing hydrogen in addition to electricity, although initial Gen IV designs may concentrate on producing electricity at 700–950°C. It uses helium as coolant and graphite as its moderator, either in graphite pebbles embedded with TRISO particles (fissile material coated with layers of flexible coating) or as a prismatic matrix surrounding TRISO particle fuels molded into rods. The use of tennis ball–size fuel in the pebble-bed design allows coolant to circulate and obviates the need for pumps and complex plumbing, simplifying design. Moreover, as the fissile fuel temperature rises, a wider range of neutron speeds results in more absorption and reduces the neutrons available for fission and slows the reactor. Although this phenomenon, called negative reactivity feedback, is observed in other reactor designs, the effect is particularly pronounced in the pebble-bed design and acts as a good passive safety mechanism. The benefits of the pebble-bed VHTR approach are offset by the use of graphite, which is combustible if exposed to oxygen at high temperature (as we all learned from Chernobyl) and by the potential volume of waste that must be managed and stored.

The helium-cooled, graphite-moderated VHTR is not new. The UK and the United States operated experimental reactors from the mid-1960s to the mid-1970s, and the 330 MWe Fort St. Vrain power station in Colorado was connected to the grid from 1976 to 1989. Although it demonstrated the viability of a scaled-up graphite matrix approach, the Fort St. Vrain reactor was a commercial failure, with water infiltration, corrosion, and electrical issues causing it to be unavailable much of the time.[14] Japan's atomic energy agency has operated an experimental helium-cooled graphite reactor called HTTR (High Temperature Test Reactor) since 1998, but it has not been restarted after shutdown and inspections following the Great Tohoku Earthquake. A 15 MWe demonstration pebble-bed reactor was operated by a consortium called AVR in West Germany from 1967 to 1988 with a very high availability rate. But later analysis of the AVR found that temperatures in parts of the pebble bed were probably as much as 400°C higher than the designed outlet temperature of 950°C (and higher than the fuel pellets' design tolerance of 1,250°C), causing the reactor vessel to be heavily contaminated with cesium-137 and strontium-90.[15] A follow-up commercial reactor fueled by uranium and thorium called THTR-300 started operating in 1985. In May 1986, a fuel pebble became lodged in a feed pipe to the core, and some radioactive dust was released into the atmosphere during attempts to dislodge it.

The THTR-300 accident was minor and highlighted the need for technological refinements, but was exacerbated by a clumsy cover-up attempt by the operator, which occurred against the backdrop of the Chernobyl disaster and an atmosphere of zero tolerance for nuclear mishaps.[16] After a long shutdown in 1988, when damage to one of the hot gas ducts was found during routine inspection, the operator and the government decided to deactivate the reactor in 1989.[17] A South African effort to refine the pebble-bed technology, supported by the state utility Eskom, was shelved in 2011, mainly for financial reasons. Among its many nuclear projects, China is actively pursuing a pebble-bed technology as well, starting construction of a 200 MWe demonstration plant in 2013.[18]

The United States has taken a different route, with the DOE inviting design submissions for the Next Generation Nuclear Power (NGNP) project in 2007. The Idaho National Laboratory (formerly Argonne National Laboratory), tasked with picking the winner among several concepts, chose a design based on Areva's Antares prismatic block high temperature graphite reactor (a helium-cooled reactor that burns coated particle fuel embedded cylindrically in blocks of graphite moderator), to be coupled with a neighboring hydrogen production or other plant. It is designed to take advantage of the "reactivity feedback" mentioned earlier and to keep the core temperature within limits by transferring heat to the surrounding ground in which the containment is buried, even if all active and passive cooling mechanisms are unavailable.

Although the spent fuel from the NGNP can be cooled by natural air circulation (unlike current spent fuels), this once-through process does not really address the problem of spent fuel piling up at nuclear plants around the world.[19] The design is modular, with each module providing 200 to 625 MWt, so it can be tailored to specific output and a mix of applications such as power generation, oil shale and oil sand processing, cogeneration of electricity and steam, desalination, and hydrogen production. U.S. companies (and Areva) have formed the NGNP Industry Alliance to enter into a cost-sharing arrangement with the U.S. government to roll out a prototype by 2021.[20] Whether they have picked the winning long-term technology remains to be seen, but the government's track record of prematurely aborting potential winners and sticking with losers should arouse concern (the DOE's enthusiasm for funding the project has reportedly waned since the Alliance was formed in 2009).

Gas-Cooled Fast Reactor (GFR)

Like the very high temperature reactor, the gas-cooled fast reactor operates at high temperatures and uses helium as its coolant and to drive the turbine. Its high thermal efficiency and generated heat make it suitable for hydrogen production. Like the sodium-cooled fast reactor, the GFR is a fast-spectrum reactor with a closed fuel cycle — in other words it would breed fuel while burning the dregs. It also has the advantage of being able to burn a variety of fuels, including thorium. No commercial examples have been built to date, and according to the Gen IV Forum, its development would take advantage of structural, material, and power-conversion technologies developed for the VHTR.

General Atomics, a diversified U.S. company best known for its Preda-tor drones, is developing a factory-fabricated version of the gas-cooled fast reactor called the Energy Multiplier Module. The 265 MWe reactor would use a ceramic fuel cladding that can tolerate much higher temperatures (2,000°C) than the Zircaloy (which begins to oxidize at around 1,230°C) used in light water reactors, and also incorporates passive safety with no need for water. At the end of its thirty-year fuel cycle, the fissile material left over from the core would be used to start another generation of reactors, and the remainder would go into storage for a few hundred instead of about three hundred thousand years required for conventional unreprocessed nu-clear waste storage. Aiming to beat the levelized cost of energy produced by coal and gas, the company is looking for funding to build a commercial model in a little over a decade.[21]

Start-up companies have presented numerous ideas on Gen IV reactors: some of them, like variations on the pebble-bed concept, overlap consid-erably with those chosen by the Gen IV Forum, while others are quite dif-ferent. Many of the concepts share a common trait: smaller size. They can be used in a stand-alone capacity for distributing power generation across more locations and closer to where the power would be used, to enhance energy resilience; or modular units can be bundled efficiently for more centralized applications, such as providing lots of power to urban areas. The Gen4 Energy 25 MWe uranium-fueled, lead-bismuth cooled fast reac-tor mentioned earlier is one example of a design by a new company trying to make inroads into making small nuclear reactors. Another is NuScale Power's 50 MWe units, which are basically passively safe, modular pressur-ized water reactors that each produce about 50 MWe. Like the Toshiba 4S, some of the designs have come from larger incumbents: the Babcock & Wilcox mPower reactor is designed as a modular light water reactor, each unit producing 180 MWe. As part of its support program for small modular reactors (SMRs), the DOE selected Babcock & Wilcox to receive a cost-share grant to develop the reactor in 2013, but the company has since indicated its desire to decrease its investment in SMRs. In its next round of funding in 2014, the DOE chose NuScale to receive up to $226 million to develop its small modular light water reactors, once again demonstrating its institutional preference for simply scaling down traditional reactor technologies, which do not address the current fundamental shortcomings of nuclear power.[22]

Standardized smaller reactors are designed to be built quickly from factory-prefabricated parts and, in the smaller versions, meant to be factory-built in the kinds of volume seen in the commercial airliner industry — for example, Airbus Industries delivered a total of 635 aircraft across four models in 2015, or about forty per month for its most popular A320 model. Let's assume for a moment that advanced modular reactors, with 300 MW of electrical generation capacity each, can be stamped out at a pace of one hundred units per month by several manufacturers. The twelve hundred units that come online every year would provide 360 gigawatts of clean power — significantly more than the annual growth in total electrical capacity of about 200 GW envisaged by the IEA from 2012 to 2025, and enough to replace about two thousand of the 2,245 GW of coal-generated capacity forecast by 2025.

One company, TerraPower, is particularly notable because it combines innovative technologies with the credible financial backing that other nuclear start-ups often lack — Bill Gates. Edward Teller, the father of the H-bomb, proposed in the 1990s to make fuel-breeding burn waves travel through a gas-cooled, thorium-fueled fast reactor core. TerraPower calls its modern adaptation of this "burn and breed" concept the Traveling Wave Reactor (TWR). Capable of burning a range of fuels (unenriched uranium, spent uranium fuel, thorium) and cooled by liquid sodium, it is designed to produce up to fifty times more electricity from the same amount of fuel and produce less than one-seventh of the waste compared to conventional LWRs during a life cycle of over forty years. When TerraPower began work on the TWR in 2006, it envisaged a complex array of coolant and control systems that would enable the burn region to travel through the core. But two years later, the designers were able to successfully simulate a variant in which shuffling fuel in the core periodically would achieve the same effect as a traveling wave, but as a "standing wave," greatly simplifying the design.[23] The company plans to start up a 600 MWe prototype by the mid-2020s.[24]

Molten Salt Reactor (MSR)

The molten salt reactor is fundamentally different from the other Gen IV Forum reactor designs. Its genesis can be traced to the U.S. effort during the 1950s to develop a nuclear-powered bomber aircraft — not quite as loony as it sounds, given the perceived need to keep strategic bombers aloft for long periods to maintain an around-the-clock nuclear weapons delivery capability, but also laced with "me too"-ism, in light of the naval nuclear propulsion program. The "salt" in MSR refers to the fluoride to which the various components of the chemical cocktail attach themselves. Headed by Alvin Weinberg, a protégé of Nobel laureate Eugene Wigner and the principal driver of the MSR concept, Oak Ridge National Laboratory produced a 2.5 MWt reactor called the ARE (for aircraft reactor experimental), fueled by a molten salt mixture of sodium and zirconium fluorides into which enriched uranium was dissolved, moderated by beryllium oxide, and cooled by helium. The reactor, which operated at an outlet temperature of about 850°C, was shut down after nine days of operation in 1954, as it had achieved its objective of running for 100 megawatt-hours and because of concerns about heat-induced weakness in its fill line — a good decision, as the fill line opened completely several days later and released radioactive gas into the reactor compartment.

Overall, the air force considered the test a success and commissioned Pratt & Whitney to develop an indirect cycle engine powered by a compact version of the ARE. But the project was killed shortly after John F. Kennedy took office in 1961, as defense planners by then were focused more on developing land- and submarine-based missiles than an atomic-powered bomber.

The ARE demonstrated the feasibility of using molten salt fuel, and Oak Ridge got funding for studying molten salt reactors further. The lab developed two design concepts, both using thorium and uranium; the thorium would be the "fertile" fuel that would capture neutrons from uranium fission to become fissile uranium-233. One concept mixed the uranium fuel with the thorium in the same fluid, while the other blanketed a uranium molten salt core with the fertile thorium molten fluid, separated by parts of the graphite moderator. The "two fluid" design was judged to be better for breeding fissile material, but to keep the experiment simple, the molten salt reactor experiment used one fluid without thorium. The fuel salt was a mixture of the fluorides of lithium, beryllium, zirconium, and uranium, and the heat from the core was transferred through a heat exchanger through which another coolant salt circulated. The salts were stored below the reactor in heated vessels, to be forced into the plumbing by gas pressure as needed, and pumps atop the reactor vessel could be used to extract noble gases such as xenon-135, add fuel, or take samples.

After winning against two competing concepts for further development, the molten salt reactor project proceeded with constructing an experimental reactor in 1962. Although the project encountered a few teething problems at first, the MSR went critical using U-235 in June 1965, went critical on U-233 in 1968, and was operated until December 1969. In one extended run, the reactor operated near full power with 80 percent availability for fifteen months — a very impressive feat for a pioneering technology.[25] The project encountered a few problems during its operation, all solvable: tritium, a radioactive hydrogen isotope, diffused through the heat exchanger tubes and would have to be captured in later reactors; the interior surfaces of Hastelloy-N alloy (developed for molten salt reactors and later used widely in many reactor types) used in the reactor became brittle from radiation; and the fission product tellurium caused fine cracks on the surfaces of Hastelloy-N piping.[26]

When the MSR was shut down at the end of 1969, most of those who worked on it expected that they would build follow-on reactors using thorium and that the technology would become central to the future of nuclear power.[27] Under the Nixon administration, however, the Atomic Energy Commission was focused on developing a sodium-cooled fast breeder reactor (LMFBR). The AEC fired Weinberg, who was an advocate of enhancing reactor safety and of the MSR, as director of Oak Ridge in 1973. Budgetary constraints, combined with a bureaucratic preference for the sodium-cooled fast breeder reactor, consigned the MSR to purgatory for several years before cancellation in 1976.[28] After years of development and a final cost of $8 billion (versus an original estimate of $400 million), the LMFBR prototype at Clinch River, Tennessee, the centerpiece for the U.S. nuclear energy policy based on fuel reprocessing, was canceled before completion in 1983.

Interestingly, the pioneering light water reactor at the Shippingport power plant was fueled with U-233 and thorium in 1977, ran for five years, and ended up producing about 1.4 percent more fissile material than it used, proving the thorium breeder concept, though not nearly as efficiently as it could be done in a molten salt breeder. But if anyone had hoped that the breakup of the AEC into the Department of Energy and the Nuclear Regulatory Commission in 1975 would lead to a fresh review of reactor technologies for further research, it was in vain, and the MSR was never again given serious enough consideration for a revival under the aegis of the U.S. government, though various companies (and the Chinese government) are now trying to carry on the work.

Although the Clinch River Breeder Reactor, which won out over the molten salt reactor, was canceled during the Reagan presidency, it was already in trouble during the Carter administration: the president himself (a nuclear engineer by training) felt that producing plutonium in breeder reactors was bad for the cause of nonproliferation and that the focus should be on improving the safety of widely used nuclear technology, presumably like that at Three Mile Island.[29] In 1984, the year following the Clinch River cancellation, the Argonne National Laboratory initiated the integral fast reactor (IFR) program, based on an experimental sodium-cooled reactor — Experimental Breeder Reactor II (EBR-II) — that the laboratory had successfully operated since 1965. Like the EBR-II prototype, the IFR was designed to use metal alloy fuel instead of the Zircaloy-clad uranium oxide pellets usually used in light water reactors, sodium at near-atmospheric pressure for cooling, and to convert nonfissile uranium-238 into plutonium-239 for further burning. Like other fast breeders, the IFR could also be fueled by waste products from once-through reactors, and extract almost all the energy contained in its fuels. During EBR-II's operation, Argonne scientists found that the uranium fuel alloy used would swell under irradiation and burst its cladding if left in the reactor for more than a few months, requiring them to melt the fuel down again. But the melting process purified the fuel, introducing the thought that on-site fuel processing could be simple and desirable. The fuel swelling for a range of fuel types was a technical issue to be tackled under the IFR program to allow extended, scaled-up operation. But, as the name implies, the hallmark of the integral fast reactor was its ability to process used fuel on-site for further use, extending fuel resources by more than a hundredfold over the traditional once-through fuel cycle. The reactor's fuel processing cycle also extracted much of the long-lived radioactive substances from the waste, to be reintroduced into the reactor to be destroyed, easing the need for long-term waste storage considerably.[30]

The standard method for reprocessing nuclear fuel today is the PUREX (plutonium and uranium recovery by extraction) method, an aqueous technique developed during the Manhattan Project to extract fissile material for nuclear weapons. Spent nuclear fuel needs to be carted around, sometimes over great distances, to a handful of commercial reprocessing plants around the world (in England, France, India, Japan, and Russia). There, the spent fuel is subjected to a series of chemical processes to extract some of the plutonium and uranium, to increase the energy extracted from the original uranium by about 25–30 percent. The World Nuclear Association puts the total capacity for reprocessing at about 5,370 tonnes annually and estimates that about 90,000 out of 290,000 tonnes of used fuel discharged from commercial power reactors has been reprocessed to date. The major challenge is that an additional 400,000 tonnes of spent fuel will be generated between 2010 and 2030.[31]

Pyroprocessing, the type of on-site reprocessing used in the integral fast reactor program and envisaged for the molten salt reactor, uses molten salts or metals at high temperature to separate out fuel and long-lived radiotoxic actinides, which are returned to the reactor to be destroyed through fission. Actinides, the fifteen elements starting with actinium on the periodic table, are radioactive to varying degrees and release energy during decay, including thorium and uranium. The exotic ones that add to the long-term radiation in spent nuclear fuel have great names like americium (which is used in household smoke detectors), neptunium, and curium, and many have medical and other applications. The final dregs from pyroprocessing take several hundred years instead of hundreds of thousands of years to return to background radiation levels — a manageable disposal problem.

Pyroprocessing is much less suited than PUREX for producing weapons-grade material and is said to cost less than one-tenth as much. Why, then, has the process not been embraced and widely adopted by the nuclear-government complex around the world? Perhaps it goes too far to picture Mr. Burns chanting "PUREX, PUREX!" but fuel processing and reprocessing are very big business for industry incumbents. The biography of nuclear insider Sadao Hattori describes how he was asked by Japanese bureaucrats to explore cheaper and safer alternatives to PUREX during the early 1990s and visited Argonne repeatedly with other Japanese engineers. Though he advocated pyroprocessing for the Japanese nuclear industry, the decision was made for Japan Nuclear Fuel Limited to build a large PUREX plant at Rokkasho in Northern Japan, with technical assistance from France's Areva.[32] The project has cost over $20 billion to date, spreading its largesse to hundreds of companies, about three times the original cost estimate, and is not yet operational pending final approval (about fifteen years later than the December 1997 planned completion date in the original government filing).[33]

Fuel reprocessing in Japan brings up another smoldering issue: nuclear proliferation. Since the late 1960s, Japan has abided by a parliamentary resolution called the "Three Nuclear Principles," which states that Japan will neither possess nor manufacture nuclear weapons, nor shall it permit their introduction onto Japanese territory. Popular support for the principles remains very high, with one Asahi poll conducted in April 2014 indicating over 80 percent in favor, as one might expect in the only country to have ever experienced atomic bombardment.[34] Originally intended for Japan's fast breeder reactor program, about forty tons of plutonium was separated from spent Japanese reactor fuel by France and the UK during the 1990s. When the fast breeder program ran into trouble, the plutonium was used to produce uranium-plutonium mixed oxide (MOX) fuel for Japan's light water reactors, though operators were leery of paying for the significantly costlier fuel. The program was plagued with MOX fuel quality problems and was a public relations nightmare as well, with ships carrying nuclear fuel to and from Japan (back to the UK for return to the producer) regularly tracked by Greenpeace and making the evening news. Intended to be used to produce MOX fuel eventually (starting in 2016), the Rokkasho reprocessing plant has already produced 3.6 tons of separated plutonium from a test run in 2006–2008. Combined with other stocks scattered over ten locations throughout the country, Japan has over nine tons of plutonium suitable for use in weapons — the "Fat Man" dropped over Nagasaki used 6.4 kilograms, so enough for over one thousand similar nuclear devices.[35]

During the 1960s, against the backdrop of the Cold War and the development of the Chinese bomb, the Japanese government weighed the option of developing a nuclear weapons capability but decided to rely on the U.S. nuclear umbrella instead. More recently, conservative thinkers and politicians have become increasingly open in their view that Japan should keep the nuclear option open. Former defense minister and ex-secretary-general of the Liberal Democratic Party Shigeru Ishiba expressed his view that though Japan chooses not to develop such weapons, its civilian nuclear plants demonstrate its latent nuclear weapons capability.[36] Combined with its stockpile of separated plutonium, this kind of talk makes Japan's Asian neighbors take note and has even raised alarm in the United States, not so much because Japan is about to fast-track bomb development, but for the message that is conveyed when endeavoring to stem proliferation in Iran and trying to convince South Korea that uranium enrichment and fuel reprocessing is a bad idea.[37]

But let's get back to the integral fast reactor. One of the truly outstanding characteristics of the IFR design was its passive safety. In two tests conducted in 1986, the EBR-II shut itself down safely from full power, once after power to the primary pump was cut off, and then after the primary system was isolated from any heat sink.[38] The reactor was able to shut itself off both times because the metal fuel and sodium coolant expanded as they grew hotter, and more neutrons were able to escape from the core — that good old negative reactivity again, but much more pronounced than in traditional light water reactors like the ones at Fukushima Daiichi.

But in yet another fine example of the suboptimal U.S. government management of civilian nuclear power research, Senator John Kerry and Hazel O'Leary, secretary of energy in the Clinton administration, led an opposition campaign against the IFR, and the government cut off funding to the IFR program in 1994, three years before scheduled completion. The stated reason for the cancellation was that it would threaten efforts to curb proliferation of nuclear weapons. But all nuclear power plants produce plutonium, and would keep on producing plutonium even without breeder reactors. And because fuel processed by IFRs is a highly radioactive cocktail of elements and requires remote handling, it is significantly less suited for weapons fabrication than, say, plutonium-239 produced through the PUREX process.

GE Hitachi has carried on the work at Idaho National Laboratory to commercialize the IFR. Its modular design, called Power Reactor Innovative Small Module (PRISM), would have rated thermal power of 840 MW and 311 MW of electrical output, and two reactors per unit would power a turbine generator to produce 622 MW of electricity. The design has been considered by the UK government to burn its stockpiles of plutonium (a vital application for Gen IV nuclear reactors), and GE Hitachi has filed a letter of intent to submit a license request to the U.S. Nuclear Regulatory Commission. PRISM is one of the best examples of a safe and cost-effective design that could be operational in several years if the licensing process does not delay the process unduly. While it is encouraging to see private enterprise trying to develop very promising concepts, one cannot help but wonder how strongly motivated traditional nuclear industry incumbents will be to aggressively push ideas that may cannibalize their current business models.

Several private companies have also re-embarked on continuing the development of molten salt reactors, using thorium as fertile fuel. One firm, called Flibe Energy, is working on developing and deploying a modular liquid fluoride thorium reactor (LFTR), a modernized descendant of the Oak Ridge MSR. The company takes its name from FLiBe, a mixture of lithium fluoride and beryllium fluoride, the molten salt that would be used as coolant and moderator in the reactor. Like the design originally envisaged at Oak Ridge, the reactor would use two molten salts in the core: one with U-233 as the starter,[39] the other with thorium as the fertile fuel. As the thorium produces more U-233, it would be separated out from the blanket salt and be fed back into the fissile core. For generating power, a secondary salt loop would transfer heat into a closed gas-turbine loop, which would then drive a generator.

The design is very scalable, so units as small as 10 MWt could be used to

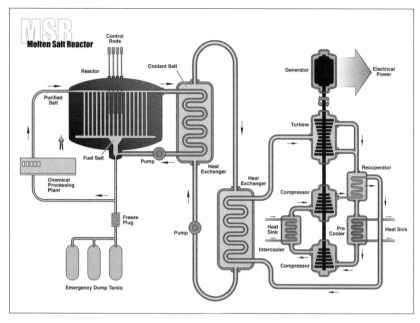

Molten salt reactor schematic from the Gen IV International Forum
(https:/www.gen-4.org/).

power remote locations, and units of 250 MWt, for example, could be bundled for utilities. The LFTR would operate at about 650°C, some 300–400 degrees higher than pressurized water reactors, for greater thermal-to-electric conversion efficiency, but at a much safer, near-atmospheric pressure. The residual heat from the turbine could also be used to desalinate water, a particularly attractive option for regions of high water stress. The LFTR can also be refueled, and nuclear poisons removed, without shutdown, which would improve availability significantly over current and most Gen IV reactors. An elegant safety feature of the LFTR is an idea that has survived from the concept's genesis at Oak Ridge — a plug of frozen salts, cooled by an electric fan, in a drain below the reactor vessel, which will melt quickly if all power goes out, allowing the salts to drain into a tank where it will be impossible for the chemical cocktail to regain criticality.

The light water reactor uranium fuel cycle used around the world today typically uses less than 5 percent of the total fuel mass by the time the buildup of fission products stops its reaction, and its leftovers, mainly U-238 with some U-235, Pu-239, and assorted fission products, must be stored, re-processed, or buried for a very long time (ten thousand years if reprocessed, three hundred thousand if not). In comparison, the LFTR would convert almost all the thorium into energy and would produce only a small fraction of the waste that is the focus of long-term disposal headaches today. Kirk Sorensen, founder of Flibe Energy, makes the comparison as follows: to make 1,000 MW of electricity for a year would require 250 tonnes of natural uranium to be enriched to 35 tonnes of enriched uranium (while leaving 215 tonnes of depleted uranium), which would produce 35 tonnes of spent fuel for very long-term storage, while 1 tonne of natural thorium would produce the same amount of electricity but leave only 1 tonne of fission product, 83 percent of which would become stable after ten years and 17 percent would go to geologic isolation for three hundred years.[40] Robert Hargraves, an advocate of molten salt reactors, at the Osher Lifelong Learning Institute at Dartmouth College, argues that by being so efficient, the LFTR can re-place fossil fuels for power generation by providing electricity at a total cost (capital cost, fuel, operations) of less than half that from gas- or coal-fired plants, even without carbon taxes.[41]

Under the very successful "Megatons for Megawatts" program, which started in 1995, enriched uranium from over fifteen thousand Russian nu-clear warheads was reprocessed into nuclear fuel for U.S. power plants. But the LFTR can go much further in the efficient use and recycling of fission-able material, as it can be used to burn plutonium or other transuranics in its fissile core, just by adding them as fluorides to the molten salt cock-tail. The advantages of the LFTR (and other molten salt reactors) can be seen in comparison to other reactor types in the matrix of Gen IV reactors below—its ability to breed in the thermal neutron spectrum, low-pressure operation, and a fuel cycle that minimizes waste.

A Japanese start-up called Thorium Tech Solutions, also inspired by the Oak Ridge research, is also looking to develop a thorium-fueled reactor, but with a one-fluoride core for plumbing simplicity and using alternatives to beryllium (a controlled toxin) in the molten salt. Although thorium is spe-cifically mentioned, along with uranium, in the Atomic Energy Basic Law of 1955, Japan has never fielded a thorium-fueled reactor, and its nuclear power industry has been wedded to uranium-cycle LWRs and fast-breeder

Main characteristics of Gen IV reactors

Gen IV reactors (typical)	Neutron speed	Primary fuel(s)	Fuel form	Coolant	Pressure	Outlet temp. (°C)	Fuel cycle	Breeder?
SFR (sodium-cooled fast reactor)	Fast	U-235, Pu-239, U-238, Th-232	Metal or oxide	Sodium	Low	500–550	Closed	Yes
LFR (lead-cooled fast reactor)	Fast	U-235, Pu-239, U-238, Th-232	Metal or nitride	Lead-bismuth	Low	480–570, possibly over 800	Closed	Yes
SCWR (supercritical water-cooled reactor)	Thermal	U-235, Pu-239, possibly U-238 or Th-232	Oxides clad in non-zirconium alloys	Water (light or heavy)	High	510–625	Open or closed	Possible
VHTR (very high temperature reactor)	Thermal	U-235, Pu-239, possibly U-238 or Th-232	Coated particles in pebble beds or prismatic blocks	Helium	High	900–1,000	Once-through	No
GFR (gas-cooled fast reactor)	Fast	U-235, Pu-239, U-238, Th-232	Ceramic-clad carbide fuel pins	Helium	High	850	Closed	Yes
MSR (molten salt reactor)	Thermal	Th-232, U-235, Pu-239, U-238	Molten fluoride salts	Fluoride salts	Low	650–1,000	Closed	Yes

SOURCE: Adapted from the Generation IV International Forum website, https://www.gen-4.org/gif/.

reprocessing despite a fair amount of basic research being done at companies and universities on alternatives. How a start-up attracts a big backer and fares in this environment remains to be seen.

Taking a totally different approach, a Norwegian company called Thor Energy is also developing thorium nuclear power, but as a mixed-oxide fuel containing thorium and plutonium. The goal would be to develop pellets for use in the fuel assemblies of current LWRs that would both burn up the plutonium and extend the fuel cycle through production of U-233. The Norwegian government has also gotten in on the act, announcing recently that it would establish a center for thorium research.[42]

LFTRs and other molten salt reactors also promise to be much more proliferation-resistant than current LWRs. Because the fuel salts are a highly radioactive mix of many isotopes, separating out enough weapons-grade plutonium or uranium-233 or 235 from molten salt reactors is very challenging compared to PUREX or centrifuge enrichment. Plutonium is a by-product of producing nuclear power from uranium and has been piling up for decades. The United States has ceased civilian processing of spent fuel from commercial reactors through the PUREX process since 1974 (though the government continues to run several reprocessing plants), citing proliferation concerns. Fair enough, but it is equally bad to let spent nuclear fuel pile up in cooling ponds and dry casks around the country without a final disposal plan. It is imperative that we use this resource to produce plentiful energy instead of weapons, along with the spent fuel that would otherwise have to go into long-term storage.

To stop producing nuclear power does little to prevent determined state and other actors from acquiring nuclear or radiological weapons. When the Treaty on the Non-Proliferation of Nuclear Weapons came into force in 1970, five countries — the United States, the Soviet Union, the UK, France, and China — were recognized as "nuclear weapons states" that would pursue the ultimate elimination of nuclear arsenals, and other signatories would not acquire them. Since then, India, Pakistan, and North Korea, three nonsignatories, have acquired nuclear weapons, and Israel, a signatory that has not ratified the treaty, is commonly thought to have possessed nuclear weapons since the late 1960s. The weapons programs that have successfully produced nuclear weapons in those countries have produced and processed bomb-grade material from dedicated or experimental reactors and processing facilities, and not through clandestine diversion from commercial power-producing reactors under international safeguards. Moreover, like North Korea did in 2003, any national player can choose to remove itself from (or only participate partially in) the IAEA regime if it really had its heart set on going nuclear. If anything, civilian nuclear power has furthered the cause of nonproliferation by burning through the tons of weapons-grade uranium, equivalent to over fifteen thousand warheads, left over by the decommissioning of former Soviet weapons.

The dangers of proliferation lurk much more menacingly in substate actors getting their hands on enriched fissile materials or, in the case of "dirty bombs," highly radioactive isotopes. Although some embedded fuel particle concepts for very high temperature reactors are perhaps just as unsuitable for nuclear weapons production, the LFTR, unlike light water reactors, leaves very little plutonium (the nuclear weapons material of choice), and the U-233 produced and suspended in the molten salts is laced with U-232, which decays into heavy gamma-emitters that would make it very dangerous to handle for use in weapons, and much easier to spot with gamma ray detectors. This, of course, may not be a sufficient deterrent against substate actors trying to use it, but it does make it much more difficult. Critics can point to the production and burning of U-233 as a potential proliferation risk in LFTRs, but the most ideologically driven choose to miss the point that, among the various technologies out there for nuclear power, LFTRs are among the most proliferation-resistant of the Gen IV technologies and much better than current light water reactors.

One other emerging fission reactor technology merits mention: the accelerator-driven subcritical reactor (ADSR). The basic concept is a proton accelerator coupled with a thorium core. The proton beam would hit a heavy metal target in the core, chipping away neutrons from its nuclei. The neutrons would convert the thorium into U-233, which would provide the fission energy and would leave very little waste. Moreover, this technology could potentially be used to transmute radioactive waste from existing nuclear reactors, addressing the problem of disposal. The approach relies on the development and refinement of small, reliable particle accelerators, which would derive their power from tapping a small part of the reactor output.[43] The inherent safety of the concept is obvious (kill the beam to turn the reactor off) and, coupled with the use of thorium fuel that does not require enrichment, is a very promising avenue of research, though many issues for its development, such as accelerator power and beam availability, remain.

A number of countries — the EU, the United States, Japan, and Russia — are working on the ADSR, while a Norwegian company called Aker Solutions is developing a 600 MW version of the concept, which would not require massive containment.[44] Perhaps this is an example of development that is better left to start-ups and quasi-governmental efforts than to established players who have so much staked on the current infrastructure and the established fuel cycle.

Finally, nuclear fusion — the fusing of hydrogen atoms into helium under the super-intense pressures and temperatures found in the sun — has been a dream of scientists for decades, since the development of thermonuclear weapons. Controlled, sustained fusion could theoretically provide tremendous energy from plentiful hydrogen but with little waste. Soviet dissident and Nobel laureate Andrei Sakharov and colleagues developed the concept during the 1950s of using powerful electromagnets around a hollow ring (torus) to produce a current inside and confine plasma that would otherwise burn through just about anything. The device would produce the high temperatures and conditions necessary for fusion to take place, its magnets cooled to below −250°C lest they be obliterated. Called the Tokamak (a Russian acronym), the design has been adopted for use in the International Thermonuclear Experimental Reactor (ITER), a multinational facility — with Russian, U.S., EU, Japanese, South Korean, and Chinese participation — being constructed in Provence, France, to demonstrate the principle of producing significantly more fusion energy than the energy required to initiate it. The project has been plagued by numerous delays, cost overruns ($20 billion projected, up from $6 billion originally), and governance issues given its multinational structure, and it remains uncertain whether the completion and first experiment targets will be safely met by 2019 and 2020 respectively.[45]

Another approach to achieve fusion, adopted by the innocuous-sounding National Ignition Facility at Livermore, California, is to fire powerful lasers on fuel pellets of frozen heavy hydrogen (deuterium and tritium) shrouded in heavy metal cylinders. After spending about $5.3 billion to date, the facility recently announced that it had finally succeeded in producing flashes of energy like mini H-bombs — but the long-term goal of achieving sustained ignition and controlled fusion still seems some way off.[46] The difficulties and delays encountered thus far in creating sustained fusion in a safe manner would suggest that the technology will not be able to make a significant dent in meeting the need for clean power within the next two decades or more, so its immediate potential pales in comparison to the safer nuclear fission technologies that are available now for deployment.

The Nuclear in Our Portfolio

As in all energy sources, examining the energy return on investment (EROI) of nuclear power is important in determining the proper role in the power production mix. As we reviewed earlier, societies like ours need EROI that are reasonably above the "net energy cliff" of about 8 — say, somewhere in the teens — to sustain their complexity. The EROI for fossil fuels are high but falling (a mean estimate of 46:1 for coal, 20:1 for oil and gas), while EROI for solar PV and wind are likely lower than often claimed, owing to issues such as installation lives and power variability. Unfortunately, EROI estimates for nuclear power, mostly Gen II LWRs, have varied widely, from above 90 to less than 1, based more on ideology and selective boundaries than on clear analysis. In his paper reviewing the EROI of various power sources, EROI doyen Charles Hall and colleagues point out that meta-analysis of EROI for nuclear power suggests a mean of about 14, though he also notes that the extended service lives of U.S. reactors, more efficient centrifuge enrichment, and, in the United States, the just-ended program of Soviet weapons uranium denatured for fuel fabrication should impact the results favorably.[47]

The recent study by Weißbach and colleagues examining the EROI for various power sources mentioned earlier analyzed nuclear EROI incorporating uranium extraction, refinement primarily through centrifuges, eight thousand annual full-load hours based on U.S. mean utilization rates of 90 percent, and sixty-year lifetime (including the energy used for plant decommissioning), and comes up with 75:1 (no difference for buffered), a number that is sure to raise controversy, particularly among those who find nuclear power highly problematic.[48] The study derives its nuclear EROI based on the assumption that 83 percent of the fuel is enriched through centrifuges and 17 percent from gas diffusion, but the much more efficient centrifuge technique will likely become universal over the next few years. Although some U.S. units have been granted twenty-year extensions to their forty-year service lives, it may be more conservative to use forty years, as other units have been retired earlier: using the Weißbach et al. spreadsheet on Google Docs, the corresponding EROI results are lower, but only to 69. An even more conservative set of assumptions, combining forty-year service lives with six thousand annual full-load hours (so a bit under 70 percent) still gets to 52 EROI.[49]

A controversial subsidy for the nuclear power industry is the U.S. Price-Anderson Act of 1957 (similar laws exist in other countries), which caps the liability for commercial nuclear power at the level of an industry-funded fund ($12 billion), over which claims would be covered by the government. Critics of nuclear power point to its use as incontrovertible proof that nuclear energy is, by, definition, unsafe, or that its inherent value added to society, shorn of subsidies, is very low. One interesting study concludes that the estimated $33 million per reactor per year (so about $4 billion per year) subsidy to the U.S. nuclear industry would be much better applied to loan guarantees for solar PV,[50] but the idea is not very convincing given the very low (2.4) EROI, driven by massive subsidies, derived by Hall and Pieto in their 2013 study of solar PV in Spain. The more important point is that, unless the opposition to nuclear is largely ideological, the right trees to bark up to garner more backing for renewable energy would be the massive government subsidies — the U.S. post-tax subsidies to oil, gas, and coal that amounted to over 8.5 percent of U.S. government revenues in 2011[51]— to dirty fossil fuels.

Nevertheless, a nuclear industry that relies on newer, safer technology should eventually stand on its own feet and persuade the insurance industry to cover it, and Price-Anderson should be reduced or phased out over a set schedule when it comes up for renewal in 2025. While the act was instrumental in encouraging the early development of the U.S. nuclear power industry, it has been around for almost forty years, during which the U.S. nuclear industry has not met its full potential. And although some of the most established players with the biggest investment in legacy technologies would squeal — just as U.S. utilities did when faced with the Clean Air Act — a phase-out would encourage the adoption of significantly more efficient and safe nuclear technologies instead of trying to squeeze out extended operations from aging units.

Other portions of the Energy Policy Act of 2005, which authorized the extension of Price-Anderson, include cost overrun support and standby support for delays in new nuclear reactors that are beyond the industry's control, measures that would tend to reinforce the "business as usual" proclivity for cost overruns associated with typical U.S. nuclear power projects. Although loathsome to anyone ideologically opposed to nuclear power, $18.5 billion in loan guarantees offered for the construction of advanced nuclear power plants by the end of 2008 do not seem totally misplaced in the context of $78.5 billion offered for renewable energy projects ($8 billion for "clean coal"), and a production tax credit for new nuclear plants during the first eight years of production that is less generous than one offered to wind energy. The U.S. nuclear industry duly tried to take full advantage of these provisions, with about twenty applications for new reactor licenses: these shrank to only a handful after the Fukushima Daiichi accident, but have recovered somewhat since,[52] and there are currently six nuclear reactors under construction in the United States.

Critics of nuclear power often point to the problem of high-level nuclear waste, some long-lived, that is piling up around the world with no permanent means of storage or disposal. Although only about 3 percent of the total waste is considered high level (most of it spent fuel), it emits 95 percent of the radioactivity. Spent reactor fuel generally spends several years in cooling ponds, after which it is either reprocessed or moved to dry cask storage. Russia, China, India, Pakistan, Japan, France, and the UK have active reprocessing programs. The problem is that current PUREX reprocessing can separate out pure plutonium, the material of choice for nuclear weapons, and the United States has not reprocessed fuel for years now, based on a policy of discouraging global nuclear weapons proliferation. According to the World Nuclear Organization, nuclear power reactors worldwide produce about 10,000 tonnes of high-level waste each year, and about 240,000 tonnes are in storage around the world, mostly at reactor sites. The Obama administration's decision to cut off funding to complete the Yucca Mountain nuclear waste depository in 2009 (despite a federal law in effect designating it as the nation's nuclear waste repository, as well as $32 billion received from utilities to fund it) has left the United States without a permanent home for its high-level waste.

Nuclear fuel reprocessing today extracts uranium and plutonium from spent fuel and still creates high-level waste that must be disposed of properly. Technologies such as the traveling wave reactor, the molten salt reactor, and pyroprocessing promise to transform the nuclear fuel cycle altogether by using fuel of all types — uranium (unenriched, enriched, or recycled), plutonium, thorium — very efficiently. They will also cut high-level wastes — which will remain harmful for three hundred years, rather than from about ten thousand years for wastes that have been reprocessed through PUREX to three hundred thousand years for unreprocessed spent fuel — to a small fraction (less than 1 percent, given the same generation capacity) of what is produced today. Uranium mining would need to continue during a transition period to new nuclear technologies, and long-term disposal sites would still have to be built, but the problem of disposal will become much more manageable.

Another question often raised about nuclear power revolves around getting uranium out of the ground cost-effectively, as well as potential long-term depletion issues. Despite one-off factors for uranium supplies such as the "Megatons to Megawatts" program, opening a new uranium mine in developed countries takes a decade or more, so mined supply is inelastic in the short term. After spending the previous twenty-plus years under $20 per pound, spot uranium prices spiked to above $130 (nominal) from 2005 to 2007, possibly due to short-term supply uncertainties combined with expectations of greater demand from China and India. The froth has largely subsided since then, and the price stood at $35.5 per pound ($78/kg) as of October 2014. The World Nuclear Organization estimates that the world's current recoverable sources of uranium, 5.9 million tonnes, will last about ninety years if divided by current usage, in conventional reactors, of 66,000 tonnes a year. There may be another 7.3–8.4 million tonnes if all conventional resources are considered, providing about two hundred years at current consumption.[53]

Like estimates of any resource, however, there are many moving parts to uranium supplies: price, technologies for exploration/extraction, total reactor capacity, and technologies for its use. And the argument used by Cornucopians like Julian Simon — that innovation allows for ever more efficient extraction and use of a resource — also applies to uranium. In 2012, DOE's Oak Ridge National Laboratory (the same lab that developed the molten salt reactor) announced that it had improved upon a Japanese technique to extract uranium from seawater using braided plastic fibers coated with a uranium binder, and cut production costs to extract a kilogram of uranium from $1,232 to $660.[54] The world's oceans are estimated to hold about 4.5 billion tonnes of uranium, or close to seven thousand years' worth at the current rate of use. And though it would be uneconomical to extract currently unless uranium prices increase eightfold, there are several points to consider: extraction technologies continue to improve, and modern breeder reactors burn enriched fuel up to fifty times more efficiently and can burn a range of fuels, from unenriched uranium to plutonium or thorium. So the nuclear fuel depletion argument is largely a red herring, especially when presented by fans of alternative energy who argue that technological developments will continue to race ahead for renewables but stand still for nuclear power. As for thorium, it is about as abundant as lead in the Earth's crust and is estimated to have more potential energy than the combined world supply of coal, gas, and uranium.[55]

Although no detailed EROI studies of Gen III or IV reactors are available, all are designed to burn fuel more efficiently and, in breeder types, produce more than they consume. They also promise to be significantly safer than those operating today. Some of the Gen IV designs, including the TWR and the LFTR, save a great deal of cost in fuel enrichment, and, in the case of the LFTR, in both fabrication and disposal. Most are designed as modular units that would cut capital costs considerably by taking advantage of production and licensing efficiencies. Moreover, modular concepts make more distributed power generation possible, which, when combined with localized and smart grids, enhances resilience considerably. Whichever technologies are used, modern breeder reactors or thorium fuel cycles promise multiples better efficiencies and only a small fraction of the long-lived waste compared with the current once-through uranium fuel cycle.

All the recent developments in nuclear power promise improvements in nuclear EROI from current technologies. Based on the EROI estimates for conventional reactors by Weißbach et al., the EROI of reactors that can use unprocessed fuel such as TWRS or LFTRS and use very little energy for expended fuel disposal may well surpass 100. There is no doubt great scope for discussion about the detailed assumptions for advanced nuclear, but the point here is that their EROI are better than those of reactors most widely used today. And, as seen in the illustration of the net energy cliff, the whole point of developing and deploying a new generation of safer nuclear power is not to beat hydro or coal EROI handily per se, but to replace dirty coal for base-load power at an EROI that is comfortably above the net energy cliff—a zone they will be able to exceed.

Nuclear power, in its appropriate and modern forms, can provide among the most efficient, clean base-load power of all the current energy alternatives. As we discussed earlier, the means of generating the electricity to sustain modern civilization from now on must meet three requirements:

- Be reliable.
- Have sufficiently high EROI.
- Be clean.

Energy portfolios composed of renewables, combined with modern nuclear power to provide base-load capacity and to compensate for renewables' intermittencies, can wean countries from dependence on dirty coal for power generation while maintaining sufficient energy return on investment.

Perhaps eventual advances in power storage, smart grids, and materials will reduce or even eliminate the need for nuclear, though betting on timing for mass commercialization is quite risky, given the planetary thresholds, particularly for greenhouse gases, we are blowing through. Maybe someday there will no longer be sufficient reason to develop modern nuclear power solely for producing electricity, but the need to get rid of the high-level waste that is accumulating today will remain just as compelling. As mentioned earlier, the UK is currently considering using Gen IV reactors such as the GE Hitachi PRISM to burn its plutonium stocks instead of converting them to mixed-oxide fuel to burn in its new generation of light water reactors; perhaps this is a (welcome) harbinger of things to come in the nuclear industry.[56] With the means to both reduce (much shorter-lived) nuclear waste to manageable levels while providing plentiful power on a mass scale so tantalizingly close, to neglect modern nuclear technology would be a terrible waste. Moreover, the need for mass desalination to address chronic water stress, or an eventual move to a hydrogen economy for transport, may well require advanced nuclear power even in a longer-term post-carbon world. But condemning all nuclear power by pointing to Chernobyl is like banning all cars over the safety record of the Chevy Corvair, and ideological opponents of nuclear power often refuse to recognize that new generation reactors, whether uranium or thorium fueled, are orders of magnitude safer than the light water reactors commonly built in the West during the 1960s and 1970s. Moreover, most Gen IV nuclear reactors are designed for modularity to cut construction and licensing costs, are more efficient, produce far less waste, and, in many concepts, obviate the need for expensive fuel enrichment or fabrication. Phasing out subsidies like Price-Anderson will encourage innovation, efficiency, and greater safety for nuclear power, and, combined with government oversight and regulation that is not as biased against nontraditional technologies, would finally allow nuclear power to fulfill its initial promise. Nothing humans build is foolproof. But we all engage in a risk-acceptance exercise when planning for a new technology or even going about our daily lives — what level of risk would we bear for the mobility provided by motor transport, for example — and decide to bear the risk when weighed against benefits. So it is with modern nuclear power when thinking about our energy future.

Nuclear in the Global Mix

Nevertheless, power generation through uranium fission in Gen II reactors is chained to a legacy of military provenance, perceived proliferation dangers, examples of gross mismanagement, and fear-inducing accidents. A poll taken across many countries about a month after the Fukushima disaster showed that, of the respondents who opposed nuclear energy in each country, a significant proportion (52 percent in Japan and China, 50 percent in

India) decided to oppose nuclear power because of the accident.[57] The true costs of nuclear power, including those of waste management, have been underestimated historically by the industry and have proved burdensome, just as the environmental movement has tended to overstate the dangers and costs. The conservatism that pervades much of the industry, particularly among the established players in the developed nations, concentrates efforts on extending the service lives of reactors that rely on 1960s technology instead of focusing on replacing them quickly with new, significantly safer technologies. In his book about power from thorium, energy author Richard Martin calls this nuclear power establishment of physicists, engineers, utility executives, and regulators the "nuclearati," and they have thrived under the sponsorship of successive political leaders and their taxpayer subsidies.[58] Thousands of words have been devoted to explain that people live in areas of background radiation substantially higher than the maximum permissible for workers in the nuclear industry, with no statistically significant ill effects, or to point out that several digits of more deaths are attributable, either through emissions or from accidents, to the operation of conventional power plants than of nuclear power plants — but in popular culture there is no horrifying Godzilla-equivalent born of exposure to coal ash.

Trying to increase grid nuclear power generation significantly in many developed nations with democratic decision making — even France has discussed reducing its dependence on nuclear plants, though the UK is actually planning on building new ones — is a tough slog: electorates are wary of buying it. Despite the significantly increased safety of Gen III nuclear reactors, many developed, democratic nations may find it hard to accept a meaningful resurgence of nuclear power, even when viewed from the framework of reduced carbon emission benefits versus risk acceptance, until Gen IV or other materially different technologies are commercially viable.

For Japan, the chairman of the Institute of Energy Economics has advocated an energy mix composed of 25 percent nuclear, 25 percent renewables, 35 percent fossil, and 15 percent cogeneration, given the often conflicting imperatives of minimizing both cost and environmental impacts.[59] METI and the Abe cabinet have since articulated their take on the best mix in 2030: 23–25 percent renewables, 30 percent coal, 25 percent LNG, 5 percent oil, and 21–22 percent nuclear.[60] The broad energy mix suggested by both makes sense only if coal use can be curbed further among fossil fuels, and it is just too cheap for many nations to leave off the table today, especially when its real environmental and societal costs are not accurately reflected.

But getting Japan back to the pre-Fukushima level (or higher) of reliance on nuclear energy very quickly will require, if not enough buy-in, sufficient apathy by the electorate to allow the government to restart most of the reactors currently idled. There are obviously problems with such an outcome: it's no way to run a (democratic) railroad, and simply restarting much of the current capacity without replacing those reactors that are old, or in suboptimal locations, with more modern capacity (ideally modular) is also not a good answer. Indeed, an analysis by Reuters — incorporating plant age, required safety enhancements, proximity to faults, evacuation plans, and local opposition — suggests that, of forty-eight operable reactors, fourteen will likely eventually become operational again, the fate of seventeen are uncertain, and seventeen will probably never be restarted.[61]

Perhaps the most sensible way for Japan to make best use of its nuclear capacity would be to restart only the reactors of most recent vintage and technology (Gen IIIs, with a smattering of the most recent Gen IIs) that pass safety standards incorporating the Fukushima experience and are not built on the most seismically vulnerable areas, while limiting plant lives to forty years and encouraging the deployment of more Gen III and IV plants to replace aging Gen II plants. In any event, the Abe government's policy of encouraging existing reactor restarts runs contrary to public opinion, as expressed by, among others, another Asahi poll indicating that 59 percent of respondents oppose bringing them back online versus 28 percent in favor, so the nuclear industry and the government have quite a task ahead of them to drum up broad public support.[62]

But many citizens of developing nations, though well aware of nuclear power's controversial history, experience firsthand the need for cheap, reliable energy in fostering economic development and bettering their lives. A poll conducted by WIN-Gallup immediately after the Fukushima Daiichi disaster saw the percentage of respondents supporting nuclear energy fall from 83 percent to 70 percent in China and from 58 percent to 49 percent in India: big drops, but with many still supportive of nuclear power, unlike in Germany (from 34 percent to 26 percent) or Japan (from 62 percent to 39 percent).[63] Interestingly, support for nuclear power in the United States in the poll didn't drop by as much as one might have expected: by 6 percentage points to 47 percent, versus 44 percent against (up by 7 percentage points). And when resource and waste constraints are increasingly planetary issues, many governments will also no longer be able to largely ignore environmental issues, as the developed world did during its phase of rapid development. Indeed, despite the pause seen immediately following Fukushima, fifty-four (excluding two in Taiwan) of the seventy-two nuclear reactors under construction worldwide in April 2014 were located in non-OECD countries.

Unless newer, modular technologies can be rolled out quickly on a large scale, the dramatic growth of greenhouse gas emissions from the increasingly urban developing world would argue for an accelerated rollout of Gen III nuclear power in developing nations. Pundits can opine all they want that their definition of better lives should not include living like Americans, which would require an extra four or so Earths, but the reality remains that most of the world's denizens hanker to live better, however defined. So, with accelerating urbanization and rapidly growing energy demand, the energy consumers most likely to drive the large-scale adoption of modern generations of nuclear power can be found in the developing world.

The appropriate power mix of the future will be different for every country and region: Indonesia, like Iceland, has its thermal resources, many island nations have the potential to deploy seaborne generation, and even Saudi Arabia recently expressed its intention to become a leader in producing power from the sun (great place to do it, if it can be executed well), but many densely populated, rapidly urbanizing emerging nations will need nuclear if they are to reduce or forgo emissions meaningfully. Asia and Africa, where the bulk of the population growth and urbanization is expected to take place over the next three decades, will be pivotal in establishing the power mix of the future. As we discussed earlier, Africa has the potential to leapfrog development in many sectors — including energy — because many African nations are starting from a very low base and have a "late-mover advantage" with so many technologies.

Sub-Saharan Africa is one of the most underserviced regions of the world when it comes to cheap, reliable electricity — about half its 1.3 billion residents have no access to grid electricity. Many businesses are forced to buy generators that are many times more expensive to run than tapping grid power, and the poorest of the continent have to pay much more for power — one estimate puts it at $10/kWh, or about one hundred times more — and a much higher proportion of their income for energy than in the developed world.[64]

In a recent report, McKinsey & Company expects electricity consumption in sub-Saharan Africa (where the proportion of urban households will increase from 38 percent to 50 percent) to more than triple by 2040, to a level about equal to the 2010 consumption in Latin America and India combined. Their analysis projects that sub-Saharan Africa needs to build about 292 gigawatts of new capacity (for total installed capacity of 345 GW) over the next twenty-five years to meet demand. These investments will require big money: an estimated $490 billion for generation and $345 billion for distribution and transmission. Gas and coal use are forecast to grow from 28 to 710 terawatt hours (TWh) and 225 to 371 TWh respectively, so will remain the biggest power technologies in 2040 (44 percent and 23 percent respectively) if each country builds capacity to meet domestic demand. McKinsey estimates that renewable sources will account for about 26 percent of energy supplied in 2040, compared to 21 percent in 2010. But the continent is blessed with tremendous untapped potential for renewable energy: not only an estimated 11 terawatts of solar, according to McKinsey, but about 350 GW of hydroelectric potential that can be used for base-load power to support urbanization.[65]

Even if the huge growth in fossil fuel use expected in Africa comes largely from gas rather than coal, emissions from fossil fuels would still increase outright about 400 million tonnes (727 million tonnes if all from coal) from 2010 to 2040, based on McKinsey's projections: a very large increase, even if it looks small compared to the UN Environment Programme's estimated 15 billion tonne total annual emissions "gap" that needs to be closed by 2030 to prevent warming by over 2°C.[66] If the most efficient renewable sources can be tapped more aggressively, to between one-third and half of total capacity by 2040, with the balance composed of gas and, increasingly, advanced nuclear, Africa's power mix — reliable, clean(er), with sufficient aggregate EROI — would become the envy of the world.

As an example, a simplified, highly resilient power mix of 25 percent each of hydro (35 buffered EROI according to Weißbach et al.), solar PV (4 EROI), combined-cycle gas turbines (28 EROI), and modern nuclear (75 EROI) would give a blended EROI of 35, well above the net energy cliff. By eliminating the use of coal, this mix should also reduce fossil fuel emissions (by about 60 million tonnes) as of 2040, despite the projected tripling in total power consumption. The argument that nuclear would be far too capital-intensive for widespread adoption on the continent, or that training so many personnel is an insurmountable challenge, would be much less relevant for "drop-in" modular Gen IV designs if they can be deployed quickly enough. Security and proliferation concerns would also be minimized through the deployment of designs that would be built overseas, dropped into place, and repatriated at the end of their service lives.

At a more aggregate level, let's examine a hypothetical global power mix that, if built over the next two decades or so, could deliver resilient, reliable power at a decent EROI, and cleanly enough to help prevent runaway warming. The exercise is far from a detailed plan: its purpose is to demonstrate what can be achieved in shifting to a power mix that meets the required criteria. As coal consumption is responsible for about 40 percent of total global GHG emissions today, one of the biggest steps that would help keep warming to within 2°C would be to dramatically reduce coal-fired power in China, the United States, and the EU, and to prevent others, mostly notably India, from expanding their coal-fired capacity. Effectively eliminating coal from the power mix would also obviate the need to expend tremendous effort to capture and sequester the carbon emitted.

In its report published ahead of COP 21, the IEA constructs a "bridge scenario," one that is slightly more optimistic than if all the emissions reduction commitments made by various countries were honored (Intended Nationally Determined Contributions, or INDC, scenario), but much less ambitious than its by-now familiar "450 Scenario" (in reference to the parts per million of GHGs consistent with an even shot at staying within 2°C). Under the scenario, total global electricity generation would rise from

23,234 terawatt-hours (TWh) in 2013 to 26,734 TWh in 2020 and 30,620 TWh in 2030.[67] About half would still be generated from fossil fuels, with renewable sources accounting for over one-third and the balance from nuclear power. Replacing 7,478 TWh generated from coal and 487 TWh from oil by 2030 in the IEA's bridge scenario with modern nuclear power would provide a mix of 24 percent gas, 39 percent nuclear, and 37 percent renewables for power generation. Such a mix would offer EROI well above the net energy cliff while shaving about 7.4 gigatonnes in GHG emissions.

Many readers will notice that 7.4 Gt is only half the 14–17 Gt total excess GHG emissions that need to be cut annually from the United Nations Environment Programme's "business as usual" scenario in 2030. The rest would need to come from continued technological progress and diffusion across not just power generation but total energy use, such as efficiency improvements for industry, buildings, and vehicles. But replacing most fossil-fueled vehicles with electric vehicles, for example, and providing their power from far cleaner sources than coal and oil (instead of pretending that they are clean even when powered by coal-generated electricity) would make a genuine contribution to curbing emissions from transport. And relying on a renewables/nuclear/gas power mix, combined with efficiency improvements from technological progress, is surely a more realistic way of eliminating the emissions excess by 2030 than hoping, as in the Greenpeace Energy Revolution scenario discussed earlier, for total energy demand to fall back gradually to 2009 levels after 2020, with 58 percent our electricity (39 percent of energy demand) to be supplied by renewable sources by 2030, and over 17 Gt in emissions to be saved by then through these and other means.

The Juggernauts

China and India are among the biggest users of coal today, and, at about 29 percent and 7 percent respectively in 2013, the two countries together produce over one-third of global CO_2 emissions. The good news is that the annual growth rates of China's emissions have begun to slow to about 3–4 percent since 2012, compared to the around 10 percent rate (omitting the 6 percent rates during the Great Recession) observed over the preceding decade. Much of the slowdown reflects reduced coal generation growth, consistent with State Council plans to cut the share of coal to 65 percent of energy consumption by 2017 (from 68 percent in 2012), leading some observers to even talk of "peak coal" use in China by sometime between 2020 and 2030.[68] The bad news is that, in order to help meet a carbon budget consistent with keeping global surface temperature increases within 2°C, total global emissions have to begin to decline — instead of merely peaking — during the period. As it is the single largest emitter of GHGs, China's latest stated aim ahead of the Paris COP to cut GHGs by 60–65 percent from 2005 levels by 2030 is encouraging, but it is hard to imagine that such a goal can be met without a far more significant decline in the share of electricity produced from coal in 2030 than the 65 percent projected in the State Council's 2013 plans. And it is far from clear that the shortfall from significantly curtailed coal use can be made up through renewable sources. Meanwhile India, the forth-largest emitter, where coal-related emissions continue to grow annually at over 10 percent, may be on the path to overtake China's current growth rate of about 7 percent soon. So it is these two countries, along with the rest of developing Asia, that will be central to developing and deploying new generations of nuclear power.

The father of India's nuclear program, Homi Bhabha, formulated a three-stage nuclear power road map during the 1960s, starting off with natural uranium for fuel, moving on to converting thorium into U-233 or depleted uranium into plutonium in breeders, and achieving the final objective of perpetuating a thorium and U-233 fuel cycle. The reason for the focus on thorium is simple: India has one of the largest known thorium reserves in the world, while its uranium reserves are relatively limited. The Soviet Union, the United States, Canada, and France all vied to provide technology to the Indian nuclear program during the 1960s and early 1970s, until India conducted its "Smiling Buddha" nuclear bomb test in 1974, with plutonium diverted from its Canadian and U.S.-supplied heavy water power reactor program. Western nations responded to the test with the formation of the Nuclear Suppliers Group (NSG), a multinational body focused on controlling the export of technologies that may be used for nuclear weapons development, and India thereafter largely developed its nuclear power technology alone.

In 2006, the George W. Bush administration provided a "get out of jail free" card, in the form of the U.S.-India Civil Nuclear Agreement, under which India agreed to separate out and place all civil nuclear reactors under IAEA safeguards in exchange for full civil nuclear cooperation with the United States. In 2008, the NSG granted a waiver to India to access civil nuclear technology, making it the only known nuclear-armed country to be allowed to carry out nuclear trade with the rest of the world in spite of being a nonsignatory to the Non-Proliferation Treaty. The agreement with the United States and the NSG waiver did not lead to a massive influx of foreign reactor technology, as a 2010 Indian law would make nuclear plant suppliers liable for damages beyond those outlined by an international convention on compensation in the event of an accident — not a shocker, given India's searing experience at Bhopal. During his visit to India in January 2015, President Barack Obama announced that the issues holding up civilian nuclear cooperation between the two countries — the Indian liability law and how to track nuclear materials provided by the United States — had been resolved; whether the details can be worked out to the satisfaction of American companies involved in nuclear power remains to be seen.[69]

The Fukushima Daiichi disaster has also stoked a vocal grassroots opposition movement in India against nuclear power — government assurances about nuclear power safety, without undertaking a comprehensive review as other countries have done, do not inspire confidence — resulting in violent clashes with police at the sites of plants under construction. Since then, India has expressed its objective to add about 60,000 MW nuclear power generation capacity by 2032 to the twenty reactors (eighteen of them pressurized heavy water reactors) currently producing about 5,000 MW. India's three-stage nuclear power program is still stuck in between the first and second stages, however, with power generation to be reliant on uranium fuels until the 2030s, when fast breeder reactors may begin to take over.[70]

For now, India shows no signs of modifying its nuclear road map so as to leapfrog the fast breeder reactor phase to just get on with a mainly thorium-based fuel cycle. This is somewhat puzzling but perhaps understandable, given that the nation's long-term nuclear needs are to be met by a heavy water moderated, light water cooled reactor design — called the Advanced Heavy Water Reactor (AHWR) — using a combination of thorium/U-233 and thorium/Pu-239 mixed oxide solid fuels.[71] While few would doubt the technological prowess of India's scientists and engineers, one cannot help but wonder about whether the bureaucracy, graft, and corruption so endemic in the system — as illustrated by the scandals surrounding the 2010 Commonwealth Games — will undermine nuclear power safety.

China's approach to developing nuclear power has been more flexible and encompasses a wider range of technologies. After conducting a review of existing and future nuclear plants following the Fukushima Daiichi disaster, China reiterated its commitment to increasing the nuclear component of its power mix, but with an emphasis on employing Gen III (and beyond) technologies. In a method reminiscent of Deng Xiaoping's famous dictum "It doesn't matter whether it's a white cat or a black cat, a cat that catches mice is a good cat," China has imported and deployed advanced PWRs based on French and American designs, as well as Canadian heavy water CANDU-6 and Russian VVER PWRs. While the process of "indigenizing" this wide range of models will allow China to pick and choose the best, it raises major challenges for regulating such a diverse array of reactor types and plants safely.

China eventually seeks to become self-reliant in nuclear power technology, become a leading nuclear power technology exporter, and to commercialize fast breeder technology as well. In the interim, one of China's major projects for the next generation of nuclear power is the small high-temperature gas-cooled reactor, a modular concept using pebble-bed fuel, that may be used for a variety of applications, including hydrogen production, much like the U.S. NGNP. Another major project is to perfect the thorium-fueled molten salt reactor pioneered by Alvin Weinberg and his team at Oak Ridge.

Spearheaded by Jiang Mianheng, son of former president Jiang Zemin and a member of the Chinese Academy of Sciences, the team working to develop thorium MSRs is armed with a budget of US$350 million and has partnered with Oak Ridge National Laboratory in their efforts after striking an agreement with the DOE to share developments arising from the research.[72] Originally scheduled to deploy its first thorium MSRs in twenty-five years, the project has reportedly greatly accelerated the deadline to ten years.[73] The focus on thorium makes eminent sense for China, as its uranium reserves are limited but thorium is plentiful, as illustrated by its preeminent position in the mining of rare metals. With its commitment to developing various nuclear technologies and to deploying a portfolio of low-carbon power sources, China, the economic powerhouse led by cadres of engineers, promises to be at the forefront of the next generation of nuclear power: it should not come as a big surprise if, a decade from now, other countries (including the United States) are looking to deploy thorium MSRs under license from China.

As with any nation ramping up the construction of nuclear power plants, getting China's regulatory regime right will be vital for the endeavor to succeed without serious mishap. China's record on safety is mixed: though clearly suboptimal in many industries such as food, drugs, construction, mining, and — in a highly publicized 2011 accident — high-speed rail, the safety record for civil aviation in China has improved considerably since the 1990s despite its continued rapid growth. As with its goal to institute the highest standards in aviation safety, China has worked closely with the U.S. NRC and other national regulators as well as the IAEA in adopting best practices for plant safety and conducting regular external safety reviews.

In January 2011, a couple of months before Fukushima Daiichi, the State Council Research Office (SCRO, an agency empowered to provide strategic policy analysis for the Chinese leadership) even recommended that provincial and corporate overenthusiasm for building nuclear power capacity should be limited to a target of 70 GWe by 2020, to prevent quality-control problems in the supply chain. The SCRO also noted that to meet the need for regulatory staff per reactor, the National Nuclear Safety Administration staff of one thousand would not only need to more than quadruple by 2020, but also have to be imbued with the proper safety culture. In 2012, following the post-Fukushima safety review of all nuclear power projects, the State Council called for improving nuclear regulation and spending on safety at all nuclear reactors operating and under construction so as to ensure that no International Nuclear Event Scale Level 3 event ("serious incident," or one level above the worst Chinese incident on record) or greater occurs.[74] One thing that can be said about stated domestic policy objectives in China: when they are sufficiently important, the State Council and the organs of the state generally have a knack for meeting them.

Elliot Ness, Where Art Thou?

Nuclear power, in its current form and dominated by the traditional players, evokes fear and animosity among much of the public in developed nations. And the nuclear industry, often including its regulators, has been its
own worst enemy in many countries. Let's look at the U.S. example. After
calls for more effective oversight of civilian nuclear power, the Atomic Energy Commission was broken up in 1975 into the Nuclear Regulatory Commission and the Energy Research and Development Administration — the
precursor to the Department of Energy. The latter was tasked with developing and producing nuclear weapons as well as exploring various sources of
energy, and it was hoped that leaving the NRC to be the primary regulator
of civilian nuclear power would lead to better focus and fewer conflicts of
interest. So what went wrong?

In the wake of Three Mile Island, there was much public hand-wringing
about whether the regulatory oversight of the U.S. nuclear power industry
was being conducted appropriately. But eight years after the accident, in
1987, Congress issued a report titled "NRC Coziness with Industry," the output of a six-month investigation. Its conclusions: "First, the Nuclear Regulatory Commission has not maintained an arms-length regulatory posture
with the commercial nuclear power industry. Second, the NRC has, in some
critical areas, abdicated its role as regulator altogether. Third, the NRC has
tried to stifle its Office of Investigations (OI) from performing independent
investigations of wrongdoing by licensees." Ouch!

The report made five recommendations, the most significant of which
called for the establishment of an independent Office of Investigations, and
to make it easier for NRC staff to justify requirements for improving safety
at plants through equipment back-fits. But what was most illuminating was
the dissenting view of the report by two committee members who felt that
the solutions proposed were mere Band-Aids instead of the major recon-
structive surgery needed. They proposed instead to completely reorganize
the NRC by replacing management by five commissioners with a single
administrator answerable to the president and the people.[75] NRC commissioners are appointed by the president and confirmed by the Senate for five-
year terms, so the dissenters' point was that government by committee is

ineffective, and we need only to look at the positive example of the EPA to see that agencies headed by an administrator can work quite effectively.

In March 2002, workers discovered a large indentation in at the head of the shut down reactor at the Davis-Besse nuclear plant in Ohio. Acidic borated coolant water had leaked through cracked control rod mechanisms above the reactor and eaten through the reactor head until there was less than 10 millimeters of steel holding in the high-pressure reactor coolant — an invitation for a catastrophic loss-of-coolant accident. This was the same Babcock & Wilcox reactor that experienced a stuck pilot-operated relief valve two years before a reactor of similar design experienced the same phenomenon at Three Mile Island, with more serious consequences. With mounting evidence of cracks and leaks around the plumbing that penetrates reactor heads, NRC inspectors asked twelve nuclear power plants in August 2001 to conduct inspections, giving then until the end of the year to comply. FirstEnergy, the owner of Davis-Besse, insisted that it would inspect the reactor in March 2002, when it was due to be shut down for refueling, and the NRC backed down. The plant was subsequently closed for emergency repairs for two years, a couple of engineers were convicted of lying, and the company paid $33.5 million in civil and criminal fines. The plant's forty-year operating license expires in 2017, and FirstEnergy has applied to the NRC for a twenty-year extension.[76] Filed in 2010, the application is still pending, but the NRC has never turned down outright a renewal application since the first was issued in 2000.

To be fair, the NRC has stood firm on some notable issues, such as inspectors at the Oconee plant in South Carolina insisting in 2008 that the operator inspect the remaining two reactors after workers found that a broken gasket blocked a key line in one of the reactors' cooling systems. The NRC has pointed out that safety system failures and the number of emergency shutdowns (SCRAMs) at U.S. power plants had been trending lower. But many would contend that the NRC could still do a much better job of regulating the nuclear industry and ensuring public safety.

David Lochbaum, the director of the Nuclear Safety Project for the Union of Concerned Scientists and a nuclear engineer by training, noted in testimony before a congressional subcommittee in 2004 that the technologies supervised by the NRC, in a parallel to NASA, are dominated by high-consequence, low-probability events, and that the vast majority of the NRC managers rose through the ranks and are of the same mold. Lochbaum articulated the need for fresh perspectives from outside managers, better timeliness for regulatory action, and improved clarity of communications.[77]

In a *New York Times* article about the NRC two months after the Tohoku earthquake of 2011, a former investigator with the NRC's inspector general's office characterized the agency as a "prep school" for many who hope to land lucrative jobs at the companies they regulate, and argued that this prospect almost certainly helped soften the positions of some employees.[78] This characterization is hauntingly similar to the criticism heaped on the Japanese nuclear regulator after the Fukushima Daiichi accident.

A year later in a *Science* magazine article, Stanford physicist Sidney Drell and coauthors called for steps to be taken to strengthen safety and security in the nuclear power industry and weapons programs, particularly in nations that are new to nuclear undertakings. The authors emphasize the need for organizations involved in nuclear matters to "embrace" an overarching safety culture, and call for incorporating independent peer reviews for nuclear projects globally (citing the U.S. Institute of Power Operations, which evaluates commercial nuclear power plants), as well as strengthening the International Atomic Energy Agency. In addition, the authors stress the need to protect against "regulatory capture" by industry to ensure safety and security.[79]

Improving regulatory effectiveness may well be one the most important issues to tackle if the nuclear power industry is to play a major role in securing a clean energy surplus for society writ large. Over the past decade, we have seen numerous examples of regulatory capture facilitating major disasters, from the global Great Financial Crisis to the Deepwater Horizon spill. But scholars of regulatory capture point out that the criteria for defining the phenomenon have historically lacked clarity, tended to be characterized in binary terms (good or bad regulation, absence or ubiquity of capture) instead of degrees, and often been used to argue for the elimination or reduction of regulation.

Of course, instituting "light touch" regulation of the type Wall Street (and Mr. Burns) loves is just not an option for the nuclear power industry. But regulating fleets of standardized, passively safe reactors effectively would be far less daunting than overseeing hundreds of reactors, each very complex, powerful, and slightly different from the others. One way in which regulators are "captured" by industry incumbents is by perpetuating procedures and policies that act as hurdles to entry for new players: the current regime of nuclear reactor licensing and approval, geared to big, customized projects that take many years to design and construct, effectively acts as a barrier to entry for smaller players, particularly those with revolutionary technologies.

Students of regulatory capture today distinguish between its strong and weak forms: the former violates the public interest so extensively that regulation should be eliminated or policies and agencies to administer them completely replaced, while the latter still serves the public interest even if effectiveness is diminished by the influence of special interests. We touched upon the effectiveness of the U.S. Environmental Protection Agency in protecting the public interest. Perhaps the EPA's very broad remit since it was created in 1970 — to "permit coordinated and effective government action on behalf of the environment"— has, along with appropriate staffing policies, helped prevent strong regulatory capture.

In the case of Japan, the Fukushima Nuclear Accident Independent Investigation Commission's extensive revelations of "strong capture" led the government to replace NISA with the NRA. Although the NRA has been more thorough to date than its predecessor in the process of granting permissions for plant restarts, the jury is still out on how it will perform over the long term in protecting the public interest. Japan often looked to the U.S. NRC (and European regulators) for "best practices" in regulating the nuclear industry but did little to go beyond or, in some cases, even meet, the standards. Given the long history of collusion and capture, the Japanese government decided that a brand-new agency must regulate the Japanese nuclear industry. Perhaps the United States — where the regulatory functions of the AEC were assumed by the NRC after the AEC was split up in 1975, but without game-changing improvement — in a role reversal, has something to relearn from the example.

Modern Nuclear: Making It Adoptable

If we conclude that Gen III–Gen IV nuclear power, using advanced, safer technology, is an indispensable part of a cleaner portfolio of power sources for society, what steps can we take — policy prescriptions or otherwise — to encourage its faster, widespread adoption? Historically, the up-front construction and debt servicing costs have been very high for nuclear power plants, with common estimates of 70–80 percent of the cost of the electricity produced. Moreover, delays and cost overruns have often plagued new projects, especially under developed countries' regulatory regimes. But many new nuclear power designs are modular for lower costs and easier licensing, promising to lower capital costs significantly.

High capital costs are a characteristic shared by renewables, making fixed feed-in tariff regimes and other subsidies important in raising their share of power production, but we choose to subsidize them because of their perceived contribution to sustainability by reducing aggregate pollution and greenhouse gas emissions, and to encourage scale increases to bring down unit costs. Subsidies to develop nuclear power, whether through indemnification or through government-sponsored research, can be viewed similarly when stripped of the ideological aversion to anything nuclear. But we have seen that subsidies of all kinds (pretax, post-tax, producer, consumer) can be associated with suboptimal EROI outcomes, such as corn ethanol, as well as help perpetuate the use of dirty fossil fuels, so must be applied very carefully.

High fossil fuel prices are good. Fans of unencumbered economic growth would recoil at that statement — and, as we have discussed, high energy costs over the long run undermine society's capacity for maintaining complexity. But making fossil fuels reflect their true, unsubsidized prices, including their social and environmental costs, is the single best way to encourage the development and deployment of cleaner alternatives through the market. A world in which we pile subsidies on fossil fuels and then institute tax breaks and feed-in tariffs to steer society away from them and toward renewable energy is hardly efficient, and borders on crazy. Crude oil prices began to plunge from over $100 per barrel in mid-2014 to around $30 at the beginning of 2016, as Saudi Arabia refused to cut production (presumably to squeeze out marginal U.S. shale oil and gas producers) and exacerbated by the prospects of Iranian supply hitting the market. Periods of very low prices provide an ideal opportunity for many countries to withdraw wasteful fossil fuel subsidies and to introduce measures to incorporate their social and environmental costs.

Some nuclear proponents argue that, in its modern forms, nuclear power would be both safe and cheap enough to supplant coal and other dirty fuels without any help from policy makers. Although it is important to let modern nuclear power stand on its own feet, it is quite optimistic to assume that it can replace fossil fuels without properly pricing in the negative impacts of the latter. The most elegant solution would of course be to institute schemes in which all major polluting nations set mutually agreed targets for substantial carbon emissions reductions, institute either emissions trading or carbon tax regimes, initially price them correctly, and let the emitters and the markets figure out the best ways for them to get there; however, this approach would need to be applied globally (and include the top ten emitters who account for almost 70 percent of the total) to be most effective, and the failure of regional initiatives like the European Emissions Trading System and successive global efforts to address greenhouse gases do not provide grounds for optimism.

According to the IMF, total global post-tax fossil fuel subsidies (the difference between a benchmark price, adjusted to reflect efficient taxation and correct for negative externalities, and those paid by energy consumers) cost a whopping $2 trillion in 2011, or about 2.9 percent of global GDP.[80] The IMF estimates for pretax subsidies — the difference between world prices for fossil fuels and the price paid by consumers — amounted to $493 billion during the same year, close to the IEA 2011 global fossil fuel subsidy estimate of $524 billion.[81] Since then, an IMF working paper has raised its estimate of aggregate annual post-tax subsidies dramatically to $4.9 trillion in 2013 and projects that the 2105 number will reach $5.3 trillion (6.5 percent of global GDP).[82] These kinds of numbers make the total global budget suggested recently by a group of British scientists for developing technologies to mitigate climate change through an Apollo-type program — $150 billion over ten years — look like an incredible bargain.

Post-tax subsidies are especially pervasive and large in developing countries — close to 20 percent of GDP in some cases — and represent a considerable drag on national budgets. Unwinding inefficient subsidies to fossil fuels that depress long-term growth, encourage overconsumption and depletion, and, in developing economies, tend to benefit the rich more than the poor (in monetary terms, but somewhat different when one is poor and the subsidy is *the* key enabler for cooking or heating one's home), must be an important objective for societies looking to build more sustainable energy infrastructure. This, of course, is far easier said than done: witness the political clout of the U.S. fossil fuel industry, or the misfortunes that befall political elites in developing nations that attempt to wean their people from energy and food subsidies (like Egypt, Yemen, and Sudan).

One policy prescription for developing countries would be to target subsidies, such as capped prices for essential goods or cash transfers, specifically to those who need it most, although this approach can open up its own avenues for potential abuse. The money saved could then be better used to provide education, improve medical care, and develop sustainable energy infrastructure. Though the jury is still out on its effectiveness, Malaysia has given this approach a try in cutting fuel and sugar subsidies. It is also mildly encouraging that a diverse group of countries have recently begun to address the subsidies problem: Indonesia and Egypt have begun to cut fuel subsidies, India has embarked on a program to end diesel subsidies, and Morocco ended diesel subsidies at the end of 2014. Whether other countries that heavily subsidize fuel consumption — Iran and Saudi Arabia both cover about three-quarters of the total cost for fuel, for example — can follow suit remains to be seen.

Ditching fossil fuel subsidies and pricing carbon appropriately represent the Holy Grail in getting to a much cleaner and sustainable energy mix. Those who depend exclusively on cheap coal or gas to produce base-load power today will find it necessary to look for alternatives only if their costs rise to incorporate emissions that are priced appropriately. And utilities are far more likely to adopt (and accommodate) a more sustainable mix between cleaner gas, nuclear, and renewable energy, and between centralized and distributed power generation, in response to increased price liberalization, proper carbon pricing, and emerging smart grid and other technologies. But are there additional measures that need to be taken to ensure that national or regional entities that are responsible for regulating emissions meet their commitments?

William Nordhaus, the doyen of climate change economics at Yale University, argues in a recent paper that forming a club of nations to undertake harmonized emissions reductions, while penalizing nonparticipants through import tariffs, would minimize the "free-riding" endemic to climate accords and induce significant reductions.[83] Such a club, utilizing optimized carbon pricing and tariffs (the study suggests a carbon target price of up to $50 per ton, combined with tariffs on imports from nonparticipants of 5 percent or more), together with the elimination of fossil fuel subsidies, promises to be very effective in reducing GHG emissions to the levels necessary to keep global temperature increases within the limits articulated by much of the scientific community.

But perhaps the Holy Grail lies more in the realm of hope than pragmatism. Some proponents of renewable energy or modern nuclear also call for a present-day "Apollo Project" (that is, "where there's a will there's a way") to develop and deploy clean power technologies. But the general degree of concern regarding the adverse human influence on the Earth is probably not yet at the levels required for such an effort: perhaps such alarm will come only fairly late in the game, when we would need to spend a lot more to undo, if possible, the damage already done.

So it makes sense to outline specific, more realistic steps to encourage the rapid development and adoption of advanced nuclear power, the only reliable and cheap enough source of clean base-load power for the next couple of decades. For example, the U.S. government can learn from China's diverse approach to research and development and not be so determined to pick winners that so often end up as losers — the Clinch River Breeder Reactor Project during the 1970s, and potentially the next generation nuclear plant today. One of the most promising avenues for advanced nuclear development and deployment is exemplified by Bill Gates's involvement in Terrapower: perhaps tech entrepreneurs with deep pockets and intellectual honesty will back promising technologies and, one hopes, bring them to market far more quickly than the traditional incumbents, wedded to large-scale legacy systems and the once-through uranium fuel cycle.

An important part of making it easier for safer, more efficient nuclear power technologies to be introduced more quickly is to make the licensing process efficient while preserving public safety. In 1989, the NRC streamlined its procedures for the construction and operating licenses for a nuclear power plant by combining them (Combined Construction and Operating License, or COL) into a process that would allow licensing and construction to take place within ten to fifteen years. By the time the Energy Policy Act of 2005 was passed, very few applications were received under the new procedure, inspiring inclusion of a "standby support" program, designed to reduce uncertainty about the process and provide coverage for delays caused by the NRC's failure to follow its own rules![84] Whether things have improved since then, particularly the approval process for new nuclear reactors, remains a question, as illustrated by several start-ups looking to get their initial contracts from the Department of Defense first before having to undergo the tortuous process for licensing at the NRC.[85]

There are lessons, mostly positive, to be drawn from the experience of France with nuclear power. Like Japan, France has little to no oil, gas, or coal, and in the wake of the 1973 oil crisis, the French government embarked on a huge nuclear power program with the objective of producing all the country's electricity from nuclear power. France put fifty-six reactors online during the following fifteen years, and now produces 75 percent of its electricity — among the cheapest in Europe, and exported to other countries such as Germany — from its fifty-nine nuclear power plants. Despite several accidents that made it onto the International Nuclear Event Scale (INES) incident rating system, including two rated 4 or "accident with local consequences" (Three Mile Island was 5, Chernobyl and Fukushima Daiichi were rated the highest at 7), France has had an admirable nuclear safety record, particularly when adjusted for the high number of reactor operating hours.

So what accounts for France's ability to run a large nuclear power industry effectively and safely? Observers like to point out that the best and the brightest in France study science and engineering and go on to staff the ministries that direct and regulate the country, or that the country has a tradition of top-down, centralized management — of course not always a plus, as seen at its extreme in the Soviet Union. The French Nuclear Authority (ASN), the regulator, was transformed in 2006 from a multi-ministerial agency into an independent authority, with its chairman and commissioners appointed by the president. France has one main-grid electricity generation and distribution company, Électricité de France (EDF), and one nuclear construction and services company, Areva: both are majority government-owned. After Areva racked up record losses of €5 billion in 2014, due mainly to delays in building a plant in Finland and from investments made in anticipation of customer commitments, the French government agreed to allow EDF to take over Areva's reactor business: the details are still being worked out.[86] But the factors that made French nuclear power successful are simply not very applicable, for example, to the United States, with its fragmented regulatory institutions, privately owned nuclear power industry, antitrust traditions, strong judiciary, and distrust of state-directed industrial policy. Several factors, however, offer lessons for running nuclear power industries in the United States and other countries.

The first lesson is standardization. Although the first French nuclear power reactors were gas-cooled, graphite-moderated reactors of local design, almost all subsequent nonexperimental reactors were highly standardized, Westinghouse-type pressurized water reactors: thirty-four 900 MWe, twenty 1,300 MWe, and four 1,450 MWe reactors of the same basic designs. Although French nuclear reactors have been criticized for frequently being delayed and over budget, greater standardization has allowed for shorter average construction periods and lower construction and running costs than in the United States. A 2001 study comparing the U.S. and French nuclear power industries points out that, during the ten-year period between 1974 and 1984, the average delay for plant construction in the United States was 33.9 months longer than the average delay for French plants of 5.5 months. Such delays are associated with higher costs, including interest charges per kilowatt of electricity produced, which have been estimated to be 42 percent lower in France than in the United States in 1987.[87] One can only hope that the recent experience of significant delays and cost overruns for the generation of French reactors now being deployed are not the harbinger of sustained deterioration.

The second lesson, effective regulation, stems largely from the first and is also a major factor affecting costs. Standardization allows for uniformity in operator training, safety protocols, and inspections, as well as quickly applying, across the industry, lessons learned from specific reactors. So although the structure of the French system, which is not applicable to all nations, may make for more effective regulation, standardization surely is a huge plus as well, regardless of systems.

Modern nuclear power can help provide a more secure energy future through the deployment of modular designs, preferably that produce only a small fraction of the long-term waste produced by those in use today, and that can be mass-produced and bundled as needed after much quicker licensing. But large players in the nuclear power industry are dependent on the whole range of businesses involved in the once-through uranium fuel cycle: Areva, one of the only major stand-alone "pure play" nuclear equipment makers in the West, derived 62 percent of its 2013 revenue from uranium mining, the "front end" (enriching and fabricating fuel), and the "back end" (treating used fuel and cleaning up sites), compared to 36 percent from the design, construction, and maintenance of reactors.[88] So it comes as no surprise that Toshiba-Westinghouse, GE Hitachi, and Babcock & Wilcox, the other incumbents in the Western uranium-fueled nuclear industry, have also stuck to uranium-fueled designs for their advanced modular reactor designs that will probably be brought before the NRC for licensing.

You might have noticed by now a pattern in the nuclear industry: promising technologies are developed, from MSRs to pyroprocessing, often under the aegis of the government, but are then waylaid before sometimes being taken up by the private sector again years later. This must stop. One does not have to be Mr. Burns to feel apprehensive about giving up a proven business model, to replace it with one that may be far better for society but likely less profitable in the short-term. But it is very difficult to effect major change when the most influential players in the nuclear power business — from uranium miners and fuel fabricators to plant manufacturers and fuel reprocessors — and their regulators are all facing the same, often inefficient, way. We have repeatedly seen that efforts to develop safer and more efficient technologies, whether sponsored by the government or the private sector, have languished because of bureaucratic neglect or a regulatory regime that strongly favors incumbents. Governments need to ensure that fundamentally different technologies that may offer major leaps in efficiency or safety are not unduly handicapped against incremental improvements to current technologies that are much easier to gain regulatory approval.

One way to encourage more progress is to reduce regulatory capture, while cultivating a more consistent governmental and regulatory environment. National and international nuclear regulators must be weaned from a long tradition of capture and even replaced completely when the condition is so severe as to undermine public interest. Effective, possibly newborn regulators should provide incentives — more challenging license renewals for older plants, significantly streamlined licensing for new modular designs, perhaps specific tax abatements, etc. — to retire Gen II reactors and replace them with newer, safer technologies.

Public acceptance will remain a major factor for nuclear power. Technologies that are truly different from those in use widely today, such as the thorium-powered molten salt reactor or the accelerator-driven subcritical reactor, will likely have a far better shot of gaining public acceptance, especially in the developed world, given the degree of public distrust for the traditional once-through uranium fuel cycle.

Finally, as we have discussed, nuclear power has the greatest potential to provide cheap, reliable, and clean base-load power in the rapidly urbanizing emerging world. But the emerging world has traditionally preferred "big is beautiful" infrastructure and energy projects, often procured through foreign aid tied to buying goods and services from donor countries. One does not have to be a conspiracy theorist to recognize that, historically, there has been a confluence of interests between donor countries, companies based in the donor countries, and the political/business elites in the recipient countries. But the outcomes of tied aid were often inefficient and inimical to the broad pubic interests of the recipient nations, with the European Network on Debt and Development (Eurodad) estimating that tying aid increases the cost of projects by 15 to 30 percent, and as much as 40 percent when it comes to food aid.[89]

In 2001, the Development Assistance Committee (DAC) of the OECD recommended that aid from its member states to the least developed countries should be untied so as to reduce costs and improve ownership in the recipient countries. From 1999 to 2007, the percentage of fully untied bilateral aid from OECD donors rose from 46 percent to 76 percent — a positive trend overall.[90] But a 2011 Eurodad report found that two-thirds of formally untied aid contracts still go to firms from developed donor countries.[91] Among donor nations, the United States still ties much of its food aid to buying from U.S. farmers and transporting it on U.S.-flag vessels: one of the most inefficient forms of aid. And, as a rapidly emerging donor, China is notorious for tying much of its aid — often targeted to secure natural resources or build key infrastructure — to the use of Chinese (especially state-owned) companies, as well as shipping battalions of Chinese workers to work on overseas aid projects in lieu of hiring local labor.

If the future of nuclear power is in smaller, modular reactors that do not operate according to the traditional wasteful once-through fuel cycle, emerging nations must be able to access and procure the technology in a timely and cost-effective manner to make a difference. Much has been written about how small-scale and community-based renewable energy projects in emerging countries have high success rates in bringing reliable electricity to the rural poor. Perhaps we can even hope that the EROI required to support the complexity of these communities can be attained through renewable sources alone. But much of the emerging world is rapidly urbanizing and therefore requires plenty of clean base-load power. So while "small is beautiful" applies also to modern nuclear technology, bundling reactors to meet the energy needs of rapidly growing emerging cities can make them even more beautiful. And although much of the manufacturing for modern modular reactors will likely remain in developed countries, and decommissioned units should be recovered to be disassembled, aid for energy infrastructure that is not tied to government-backed megaprojects will be essential to ensure that recipient countries make informed, rational choices about meeting their power needs, from the rural to the urban.

For I dipped into the future, as far as human
eye could see, saw the vision of the world,
and all the wonder that would be.
—Alfred, Lord Tennyson (1809–1892)

The future ain't what it used to be.
—Yogi Berra (1925–2015)

7

INNOVATION | STEVE AUSTIN OR GRAY GOO?

In England during the First Industrial Revolution, textile artisans, seeing
themselves steadily replaced by machinery operated by low-wage workers,
smashed power looms and other machines in protest. Called the Luddites,
perhaps after a lad named Ned Ludd who allegedly smashed stocking
frames in a fit of rage in 1779, the movement gave a name to those who
oppose or are slow to embrace new technologies. While new technologies
were displacing skilled workers during the Industrial Revolution, the aggregate demand for labor continued to rise across many evolving and growing industries, driving employment and consumption. Economists came to
call the view that technological advances lead to structural unemployment
the "Luddite fallacy." But the sheer pervasiveness, generalized applications, and accelerating development of technology today, particularly in
computing and automation, behoove a rethinking of the relationship between technology and structural unemployment. It is one thing to refer
disparagingly to the Luddite fallacy when the pie is growing reliably and
sufficient employment supports consumption; quite another when even

the more skilled jobs in the service sector — accountants and lawyers, for example — are at risk from increasingly sophisticated automation.

Innovation is generally seen as the "magic sauce" that allows for endless socioeconomic growth. One only has to scan the book reviews and Amazon nowadays to encounter a bewildering universe of books on innovation, its importance, and how we can deliver more of it. In spite of all this focus on "innovation," prognostications of a bright, technologically driven future are often juxtaposed with the reality of a sluggish "new normal" for the vast majority of people in developed countries, exemplified by the growing number of underemployed young people still living at home while enjoying the fruits of digital technology (a 2012 study found that social media is harder to resist than alcohol, cigarettes, and even sex, inspiring one academic to call it the new opiate of the masses).[1]

In the developed world, high levels of structural unemployment, particularly among the young, are often attributed to sluggish growth and the effects of "off-shoring" of jobs to lower-wage countries. But what if the persistent structural unemployment and underemployment observed today is just a prelude to artificial intelligence and robotics eventually replacing human jobs permanently across a growing number of industries, including those of the service sector and even among the most highly skilled today?

Moreover, many people in the developed world perceive an increasing stasis in truly life-changing technologies, and a growing number of economists argue that the economic impact of today's innovations compare unfavorably to past major innovations. What if the big innovation that has allowed for continued exponential growth over the past two centuries was the widespread tapping of fossil fuels — a onetime inheritance? A long-term innovation slowdown, if it exists and encompasses key sectors such as food production, energy, and some areas of medicine (e.g., antibiotics), would have serious implications regarding our ability to continue unabated development as a species. On the other hand, accelerating developments in nanotechnologies, artificial intelligence, robotics, and genetics may eventually enable innovations that help meet basic human needs much more effectively and efficiently than we can today. Such a process, however, is in a race against how quickly we make the Earth a far less hospitable place on which to live.

Innovation: Eyeballing the Numbers

To examine the concern that the pace of technological innovation is slowing to the detriment of civilization it is worth glancing at actual numbers. According to the World Intellectual Property Organization (WIPO), there has been a steady increase in the number of patents granted annually around the world, from 379,580 granted in 1980 to 1,134,500 in 2012. In the United States, the number grew from 61,827 in 1980 to 253,155 in 2012. While all the technologies categorized saw growth globally, the magnitudes were most pronounced in areas such as semiconductors (2,614 to 48,103), computer technology (5,974 to 87,450), digital communications (1,093 to 45,178), and biotechnology (2,452 to 19,771), while more mature sectors such as "textile and paper machines" (10,828 to 21,043) experienced rather milder growth. One category, "micro-structural and nanotechnology," went from 3 grants in 1980 to 1,960 in 2012. The numbers jibe with what we would intuitively expect — that the areas where the most dramatic innovations appear to be taking place are where growth in number of patents granted is strongest.

Let's do a reality check on the growth numbers by seeing how they look within the context of other metrics. Resident patent applications (applications filed with patent offices by residents in the countries in which those offices have jurisdiction) globally per million people — grants would have been preferable but unavailable — show fairly steady growth globally, from 135 in 1980 to 271 in 2012. The same metric for the United States displayed more dramatic growth, from 273 in 1980 to 856 in 2012, and applications in China (excluding Hong Kong and Macao) grew from 4 per million in 1985 to 396 in 2012. Although resident applications per US$100 billion GDP (2005 purchasing power parity) grew globally from 1,772 in 1995 to 2,032 in 2011 (14.6 percent), the same metric for the United States grew faster, from 1,374 to 1,873 (36.3 percent) during the same period. Patent applications globally per US$1 billion in research expenditure (2005 PPP) were fairly steady at 1,767 in 1997 and 1,709 in 2011, with a range between 1,520 and 1,797 and a mean of 1,691. U.S. applications per US$1 billion in research expenditure grew faster, from 693 in 1997 to 948 in 2010, and Chinese applications grew at a similar pace during the same period, from 2,104 to 2,846.[2] The WIPO data series, though admittedly short, seems to indicate that all is hunky-dory in the world of innovation, perhaps vindicating Julian Simon's theories that more population means more innovation and not just mouths to feed. So what are some researchers and economists so concerned about when it comes to innovation?

Have the Easy Pickin's Been Picked?

Jonathan Huebner, a scientist working for the Pentagon, published a paper in 2005 arguing that the rate of human innovation peaked in the 1870s and had been on a decline since. Huebner bases his assertion on measuring the number of important technological developments per year divided by the world's population and observes that the rate of innovation has followed a bell curve. The list of important scientific and technological developments since the so-called Dark Ages is subjective by definition, taken from a list compiled by B. Bunch and A. Hellemans in *The History of Science and Technology*. Additional evidence presented includes patents issued by the U.S. Patent Office each year to U.S. residents since 1790 per population unit, which shows that the rate of invention peaked around 1915 and has been declining since, though there has been a noticeable upswing since the 1980s. Huebner concludes that the pace of innovation follows a bell curve rather than exponential growth, and that we may be approaching an economic or intelligence limit.[3]

In a 2010 research paper, D. Strumsky, J. Lobo, and J. Tainter contend that scientific fields follow a common evolutionary pattern, with early work establishing basic theories that are broadly applicable, and subsequent questions becoming increasingly narrow and expensive to solve. As such, research grows increasingly complex, and yields from investments in research decline, as illustrated by the trajectories of patents per inventor in a variety of fields, from energy to computing, even in fields where the pace of innovation appears high. Using U.S. Patent Office classifications and data, Strumsky and colleagues point out that patents per inventor in gas power technologies fell from about 0.75 in 1973 to below 0.60 in 2004, while the same metric for wind power during the same period fell more dramatically, from about the same starting level to below 0.45. Even sectors such as biotechnology and nanotechnology, areas usually considered the cutting edge of innovation, display similar declines over a shorter period. The study's authors also note that the increase in patents per unit of GDP observed in the United States since the 1980s is associated with changes to the patent regime — a system of patent appeals to pursue infringement cases more efficiently, and transformation of the U.S. Patent Office into a fee-for-service operation — that encourage patent activity.[4]

Economist Tyler Cowen posits that most modern innovations are private rather than public goods that offer only slight additional benefits to the vast majority of people. As he pithily puts it, "Contemporary innovation often takes the form of expanding positions of economic and political privilege, extracting resources from the government by lobbying, seeking the sometimes extreme protections of intellectual property laws, and producing goods that are exclusive or status related rather than universal, private rather than public; think twenty-five seasons of new, fall season Gucci handbags."[5]

Many would respond that the Internet, originally funded by the U.S. Department of Defense to develop resilient computer communication, is a fairly universal and public innovation that continues to diffuse downward and outward throughout social strata globally. But Cowen points out that although the Internet has been very influential, its economic impact on revenue and employment has been modest when compared with the impacts of previous universal innovations.

Another American economist who has focused extensively on productivity and growth, Robert J. Gordon, points out that there was "one big wave" in multi-factor productivity growth in the United States since 1870, accelerating and peaking between 1928 and 1950 and decelerating since 1972. Gordon explains the phenomenon as the product of four great groups of inventions: electricity (light and motors); the internal combustion engine; petroleum-based products; and innovations in entertainment, communications, and information developed before World War II. These inventions had far greater impact, in his view, than computers and the current information revolution.[6] The common thread running through most of these innovations is that they were enabled by tapping fossil fuels — a onetime inheritance.

Pharmaceutical research and development is notable for its contribution to (mostly fictional) tales of malfeasance and conspiracy: it is also an area in which innovation is slowing visibly. For example, only two new antibiotics were developed between 2008 and 2012 (versus sixteen between 1983 and 1987), while their overuse by humans and livestock have enabled the emergence of "superbugs" that are resistant to a wide array of agents. Without significant new breakthroughs and more effective ways to slow resistance, we may be entering an age in which previously treatable minor infections could mean death.

A team of pharmaceutical analysts at Sanford C. Bernstein & Company pointed out in a 2012 article that the number of new drugs approved by the U.S. Food and Drug Administration per inflation-adjusted billion dollars of R&D spending has halved every nine years since 1950. They dubbed the phenomenon "Eroom's Law"—Moore's Law spelled backward—to denote the opposite of semiconductor pioneer Gordon Moore's 1965 observation that the number of components in an integrated circuit doubled about every year (he later revised this to every two years), which has proved remarkably prescient to date about the pace of technological developments in computing. The analysts attributed the trend to the industry's unique problem of an ever-expanding catalog of generic drugs that used to be blockbusters (called the "better than the Beatles" effect), combined with regulatory caution and the tendency to use brute force (the rapid screening of millions of compounds to target particular molecules instead of looking at a disease as a complex whole) and money in developing new drugs.[7] In the case of antibiotics, pharmaceutical companies appear much more willing to develop drugs that treat chronic disease such as high cholesterol or diabetes, which produce revenue for extended periods. The Infectious Diseases Society of America is concerned that the goal of its "10 × '20" initiative to gain FDA approval for ten new antibiotics to combat multidrug-resistant bacteria by 2020 will not be met.

Some economists point to other possible reasons for innovation stasis. In his work *The Gridlock Economy*, which spread his concept "tragedy of the anti-commons," Michael Heller argues that too much ownership stifles innovation in a variety of fields. A commons has traditionally been considered a classic setting for overuse, and private property is often associated with optimal use, with gradations in between (such as access for a limited number of commoners). But Heller makes a strong case that the concept of the anti-commons, in which very fragmented ownership leads to underuse, occurs more frequently than is usually appreciated, with research indicating that the loss of efficiency from underuse may be greater than economic theory predicts.[8] He provides illuminating examples of tragic underuse in drug development, in which "too many overlapping patents can push drug-makers away from the most medically promising lines of research to those that are least legally challenging" and points out "the threat of gridlock erodes the incentive to produce drugs particularly for diseases that afflict the poorest people with the least ability to fend for themselves."[9]

Heller also cites the more positive example of "Golden Rice," designed to reduce blindness and childhood mortality in developing countries through the production of beta-carotene to provide vitamin A. Developed by a non-profit organization called the International Rice Research Institute, which makes the special rice available to researchers without cost, the project has been able to overcome a number of patent holders and technology owners. Heller points out, however, that "Golden Rice" might be an exception rather than the rule, as "plant geneticists worry that agricultural biotech patenting is closing off a thousand-year-old tradition of hybridizing crops to improve health and nutrition."[10] Indeed, agricultural biotech companies have come under scrutiny for patenting crops, such as Monsanto's seed products that are genetically modified for resistance to the company's brand of herbicides. But it is far more difficult to portray Golden Rice, as well as other efforts by nonprofits such as the Gates Foundation to develop crops tailored to addressing the nutritional needs of the developing world, as a conspiracy by huge corporations to control agriculture through patented crops.

Almost fifteen years after its media debut, however, Golden Rice still meets resistance (protesters destroyed field test plots in the Philippines in 2013) and is not approved for general use anywhere in the world. Opponents of initiatives such as Golden Rice see them as a thin end of the wedge to garner support for genetically modified organisms (GMOs), to the eventual benefit of huge agricultural businesses while hurting small farmers and the public.[11] Meanwhile, a 2013 study by a pair of researchers at Technical University Munich and UC Berkeley estimated that a ten-year delay in introducing Golden Rice in India has cost the loss of at least 1.4 million life years, not including the indirect health costs of vitamin A deficiency.[12]

Innovation gridlock presents a problem as a contributory cause for the possible slowdown in major innovations arising from increasing complexity. Governments and the private sector need to devise ways — including patent reform, patent pooling conventions, and even possibly a form of eminent domain — to minimize the phenomenon. While it is encouraging that the Obama administration has recently stepped up its efforts to curb the excesses of "patent trolls," who sit on portfolios of patents without using them in the hope that someone will infringe them so that they can collect fees, much more can be done.[13] Although patents, as a form of temporary intellectual monopolies, can lead not only to innovation but also to underuse, particularly when abused or standards for granting them are not set appropriately, we have seen that semipermanent economic monopolies and oligopolies can also impede human progress and innovation, particularly when they are regulated collusively or inappropriately. One need only look at the consequences of the Tohoku earthquake to appreciate that decades of oligopoly, political favoritism, lax oversight, and regulatory capture in its power industry have left Japan with antiquated nuclear technology and tremendous problems in securing energy at reasonable cost.

Gee Whiz

Cornucopians — the futurists who believe that we have all the resources and innovation at our disposal to give us pretty much unlimited potential for growth — in general do not agree with the somber observations of "technological stasists" and believe technological progress is accelerating in ways that will profoundly change our lives. MIT economists Erik Brynjolfsson and Andrew McAfee argue that innovations are not fruit to be picked but are additive and lead to combinations that accelerate the process. They contend that we are at an inflection point for digital technologies that will lead to a dramatic acceleration in innovation — what they term "the second machine age." They add, however, that the characteristics of digital innovations tend to cause dislocations and even inherent "winner-take-all" income inequalities that will require policy actions to address.[14] Let's take a quick tour of some of the technologies that Cornucopians believe will allow us to prevent decline and perhaps even undo some of the damage already done. Many of the technologies, although often categorized separately, reinforce and at times blend into each other. And although some of them, like developments in genetic mapping and medicine, do not at first appear to be directly related to the issue of energy, these developments are integral to the suite of technologies that Cornucopians contend will enhance the quality of life for all and help allow continuous growth.

"It's Alive!"

Nanotechnology commonly refers to the ability to create and use matter at the molecular or atomic level and represents a broad technological advance that promises to affect a diverse range of applications dramatically, from semiconductors to molecular biology. For example, carbon nanotubes are microscopic cylinders that can be used in myriad applications, from superstrong, lightweight structures to solar PV and transistors. In the latter application, scientists at Stanford University successfully built a one-bit carbon nanotube computer in 2013, which may mark the beginning of moving beyond current silicon-based computer technology. That existing technology, because of power wastage through heat, will eventually bump into physical limits to stuffing more transistors onto a chip and threaten Moore's Law. Because carbon nanotubes consume very little energy to turn on or off, they open up a whole new frontier for transistor densities.[15]

The walls of carbon nanotubes are one-atom-thick sheets of carbon called graphene, made famous by the method of lifting layers from graphite using adhesive tape for their initial laboratory production (the Scotch tape method). Graphene is the best conductor of heat at room temperature, the best conductor of electricity, the strongest compound known, and the lightest material for a given area. It may open up a bewildering variety of promising applications including solar PV, power storage, electronics, optics, advanced materials, and water treatment. For example, ultra-capacitors that increase storage capacity by using the large surface area of graphene may one day provide performance similar to that of lithium ion batteries while being recharged in minutes instead of hours. Or graphene filters may be used to desalinate water at lower cost than the reverse osmosis techniques commonly used today. In computing, graphene nanoribbons could potentially be used to increase the density of transistors on a computer chip by ten thousand times, even more efficiently than nanotubes.[16]

Solar PV cells using nanotechnology, such as nanoscale antenna arrays, may potentially be used to convert about 70 percent of the energy hitting a cell into electricity. The level of efficiency would blow way past the current commercial solar PV limitations of about 20 percent and even more experimental techniques to capture 40 percent, paving the way for genuine grid parity and beyond with the cheapest fossil fuels, particularly when paired with transformational energy storage techniques incorporating nanotechnology.[17] Solar power satellites, which would beam power from the sun down to Earth, could also become feasible as superefficient PV and superstrong lightweight materials make it more economically viable to launch the apparatus. Graphene filters may reduce the energy costs of reverse osmosis desalination to a very small fraction of the pressure required today. The ubiquitous Bill and Melinda Gates Foundation is even funding research into developing a condom using graphene composite materials, taking advantage of its strength and high thermal conductivity. And nanoscale medicine will allow for the maintenance and treatment of our biological systems at a molecular level, through techniques such as delivering drugs, proteins, and imaging agents for the treatment of cancer and other disease.

A potential but controversial nanotechnology application is "molecular assemblers," devices that would guide chemical reactions by manipulating molecules with precision. Similar to the way in which RNA can direct the synthesis of specific proteins, human-made assemblers could be used for extremely precise manufacturing at a molecular level. Researchers have produced early stage molecular machines and are working on developing nanorobots that can be manipulated remotely. Medicine and semiconductors are the most obvious applications for nanoscale factories or robots, but many other applications have probably not even been conceived yet. Molecular assemblers may be designed to make copies at a molecular level and to move, consume energy, and self-replicate like organisms. First coined during the 1980s, the term "gray goo"— a superb image of technology run amuck — was used to describe low-probability, high-consequence scenarios in which nanoscale replicators would slip out of control and consume everything on Earth or even beyond, but has since taken on the contours of a modern version of Dr. Frankenstein's famous exclamation: "It's alive!"

We Can Rebuild Him/Her

In the 1970s TV series *The Six Million Dollar Man*, astronaut Steve Austin was brought back from the brink of death and rebuilt to higher specs with bionic parts after a test-flight crash. Although blind people have regained some eyesight from incorporating electronic technology that sends signals to the brain, for example, bionics have not developed yet to the degree envisioned in the series forty years ago. But developments in other aspects of medical technology appear to be accelerating, and it is quite possible that life expectancy at birth may reach one hundred years by the end of this century, perhaps even more if there are breakthroughs in genetics or anti-aging medicines. The life expectancy for women in the United States at birth was 48.3 in 1900, but this had increased to 71.1 by 1950 and now stands at 81 (2010), according the U.S. Centers for Disease Control and Prevention.[18] Vastly improved sanitation and housing did wonders for extending life spans during the nineteenth century, and in the early twentieth century much of the improvement in life expectancy was due to the development of vaccines and antibiotics, which helped decrease early and midlife mortality. By the second half of the century, old folks living longer took over as the principal driver of improving life expectancy. Although often very rewarding individually for those living longer lives and their families, this trend threatens to strain our general socioeconomic resilience. Often used as an example of the pessimistic aphorism "demographics is destiny," Japan is already a laboratory for how a society deals with an aging population, and China is going to experience the phenomenon much earlier than most expect, with researchers there estimating that population growth will end around 2020.[19]

Despite all the optimism about how "sixty is the new forty," advances in longevity, particularly those that exceed forecasts, are a major, still under-appreciated risk to individuals and governments over the coming decades.

In its April 2012 Global Financial Stability Report, the International Monetary Fund points out that, if it is not addressed effectively, increased longevity may undermine the fiscal sustainability of governments and threaten the financial health of underfunded pension systems, both public and private, around the world's advanced economies.[20] One has only to look at the protests by a wide swath of Greek society — the unemployed, civil servants, and pensioners — that threaten to tear apart the fabric of that society during Greece's ongoing crisis to see just how real this threat is; and it looks to only worsen across the advanced world in this era of zero (or negative) interest-rate policies. So when thinking about new technologies championed by Cornucopians, it is also important to examine the flip side of the hope and promise — the impact on our socioeconomic resilience.

Microsurgery, computer-assisted surgery, noninvasive procedures, chip-based diagnostics, targeted drug therapy, and prosthetic implants are all wonderful advances we hear about regularly, often from relatives who just love to talk about their health at family get-togethers. But arguably the most revolutionary and far-reaching developments for human treatment are DNA sequencing and regenerative medicine. Many of the dramatic developments in medicine over the past decade have been made possible with the decoding of genes. It took from 1990 to 2003 and $3 billion in taxpayer dollars for the Human Genome Project to map the combined reference genome of a handful of anonymous donors. A parallel effort by the private sector began in 1998 and spent about $300 million using a more efficient technique to map most of the three billion or so base pairs in the human DNA, but stirred controversy in its filing of preliminary patents on several thousand genes.

Today, the cost of sequencing an individual's DNA has fallen from several million dollars five or six years ago to about $1,000, long considered the threshold below which personalized medicine begins to become economically feasible on a mass scale. The costs of analyzing the massive amounts of data generated and insufficient diffusion of interpretative expertise (which machine intelligence should be able to address in due course) still remain as significant hurdles, but by identifying genetic predispositions for cancer and other disease through individual DNA sequencing and providing targeted treatments accordingly, tailored medicine promises eventually to increase health care effectiveness while bringing down costs. These outcomes, of course, are not preordained, as demonstrated by the massive increase in the costs of targeted cancer medicines as drug companies seek to maximize revenue in areas that are less vulnerable to generic replication. Such trends are fodder for those who envisage a dystopian future in which an elite class can afford to live longer, healthier lives, while the masses who cannot afford the latest treatments are stuck for much longer in the mortality status quo.

Most of us probably first heard about stem cells — cells that can differentiate into specialized cells and divide into more cells — during the 1990s, in the context of applications in human tissue regeneration. The use of bone marrow transplants to replace stem cells destroyed through chemotherapy was an early application of regenerative medicine, and researchers later developed the means of growing stem cells from amniotic fluid or umbilical cord blood, which got around the ethically controversial practice of using stem cells from human embryos. But between 2006 and 2009, Nobel laureate Shinya Yamanaka of Kyoto University and others figured out how to genetically reprogram any human cell to become like embryonic stem cells (human induced pluripotent stem cells), opening up the prospect of producing stem cells from anyone for that individual's own use with far less danger of rejection. By 2013, scientists were developing ways to deposit stem cells with 3-D printers that could eventually be used to construct organs and parts on demand.[21] So instead of getting all those bionic body parts, Steve Austin may soon be able to get a few new biological body parts, even if it means doing without some of his superhuman abilities. He may even soon dine on laboratory-grown beef burgers, though at $330,000 per patty, the price tag needs to come down a touch lest he blow through his allotted budget pretty quickly.[22]

By offering a vital means of feeding the world's population, which is forecast to grow by another two billion or so people before peaking, developments in genetically modified organisms (GMOs) are also having a major impact on our lives. Humans have engaged in genetic modification since first domesticating animals and plants over ten thousand years ago. But genetic engineering through direct transfer or manipulation of genes (sometimes from pretty different types of organisms), with its rather shorter history since the 1970s, has not only shown tremendous promise but has also stirred great controversy. Genetically modified bacteria and algae are being used to produce useful enzymes, proteins, and hormones, as well as bio-fuels, with increasing efficiency. A 2015 Pew Research Center study found that 88 percent of scientists associated with the American Association for the Advancement of Science (AASS, the publisher of *Science* magazine) felt that it was safe to eat genetically modified foods.[23] But genetically modi-fied food crops have been shunned by many consumers and organizations as "Frankenfoods," the risks of which to humans and the environment, in their view, have not been adequately understood or addressed. Although the EU has a very strict policy regarding GMO foods and has approved a number of them, national jurisdictions have chosen to opt out, reflecting local electorates' distaste for GMO foods despite the scientific majority who view them as safe to eat.

The debate over agricultural GMOs is often part of a clash between indus-trial and "organic" farming methods, with the latter becoming increasingly popular with developed-world consumers. GMO advocates and scientists argue that, subject to comprehensive guidelines and extensive testing, large-scale commercial agriculture is needed to feed the world's growing billions, and that GMOs can offer better stress resistance, more nutrition, better productivity from less optimal land, and less environmental impact (by using less water and insecticides, or even fixing nitrogen without exten-sive fertilizer use, for example). But powerful agrifood companies bringing high-profile lawsuits against farmers who have used seeds retained from harvests of patented varieties make it easy to associate this position with less-than-benign corporate Goliaths. Noted Indian environmentalist, anti-globalization advocate, and GMO opponent Vandana Shiva has called the patenting of crops a "pathetic attempt at seed dictatorship."[24] GMO oppo-nents including Greenpeace, in addition to citing such potential dangers as "gene escape" (within a species or to others) or harmful mutations, contend that the world's poorest and hungriest could better improve their food se-curity by adopting organic methods suited to their environment and re-ducing reliance on seed, fertilizer, and pesticide makers. But the argument that the use of GMOs can decrease overall resilience, while valid, can be applied to any excess reliance on monoculture through traditional genetic modification.

Like nuclear power, the debate about GMOs is very polarized. Genetic modification needs to be regulated transparently and effectively, particularly in the face of powerful business interests that may undermine the public good. But we are steadily converting forests into farmland or plantations in an effort to feed ourselves, with agriculture contributing about a quarter of the greenhouse gases produced by human activity and decimating our commons. The UN Food and Agriculture Organization estimates that annual emissions from agriculture, forestry, and fisheries have almost doubled over the past fifty years to about 10 gigatonnes (billion tonnes) and are set to increase another 30 percent by 2050 if greater efforts are not made to reduce them. Although 39 percent of the greenhouse emissions from agriculture is from belching livestock (another good reason to switch from cows to chickens), 13 percent is from the use of synthetic fertilizers and is the fastest growing source of agricultural emissions (up 37 percent since 2001). Moreover, a great deal of fossil fuel is used to power agricultural machinery, irrigation pumps, and fishing fleets, resulting in about 0.8 gigatonnes of emissions.[25] So if done right, developing crops that use less water and fertilizer can reduce emissions and make us more resilient. If the world is to feed an additional two billion people by 2050, overwhelmingly in the rapidly urbanizing developing world, and improve significantly the diets of several billion more without placing even more stress on the environment, a blanket opposition to GMOs, including those that are developed to help the neediest without remuneration, appears misplaced.

Robots: From Robbie to Roomba

Robots have figured in popular culture for almost a century: a humanoid version played a prominent role in Fritz Lang's famous 1927 silent film *Metropolis*, which depicted a dystopian future in which a vast city is bifurcated between a few powerful industrialists and masses of workers who keep the machines running. From Robbie the family robot in *Lost in Space* to the somewhat less benign units in *Terminator*, robots have played key roles in popular science fiction since. Our fascination with them knows few bounds, perhaps because the most humanlike versions in speech or behavior tease the boundaries of what we consider as consciousness or humanity.

In 1942, the scientist and prolific writer Isaac Asimov articulated his Three Laws of Robotics in a short science-fiction story, and these rules and addendums by Asimov and others have had significant influence on thinking about robots as they become increasingly "sentient." The laws are (1) a robot may not injure a human being or, through inaction, allow a human being to come to harm; (2) a robot must obey the orders given to it by human beings, except where such orders would conflict with the first law, and (3) a robot must protect its own existence as long as such protection does not conflict with the first or second law.[26] I suspect our Roomba cleaning robot at home is not programmed with these rules, and military combat robots cannot by definition incorporate all of them, but accelerating developments in artificial intelligence and robotics have renewed interest in trying — if it is even possible — to design updated and more relevant default rules for the capabilities that humans are developing in robots today.

Actual developments in the field of robotics have historically been a bit more prosaic than those depicted in science fiction but are accelerating today at a pace that may surprise many of us. The use of robotic arms for manufacturing took off during the 1970s and has steadily spread since, with capabilities becoming simultaneously more refined and versatile. As markets for industrial robots in the developed world mature, their use in developing countries where labor is no longer plentiful or cheap (like China) is set to increase significantly. Robots may also one day be able to help care for the elderly or those with limited mobility, potentially a big plus for counties with inexorably aging demographics, like Japan. But most of the robots in use today for manufacturing, mostly robotic arms, still excel at a narrow set of programmable tasks for which their capabilities — both hardware and software — are most suited, like welding parts on a car or packing products.

Some advanced robots, such as those produced by the company Intuitive Surgical for doctors to perform surgery from a console, are already in use. And although not categorized as robots per se because they are not "embodied," advanced software applications are already on their way to supplanting humans in traditional "knowledge worker" fields such as tax accounting and corporate law. Newer robots are becoming increasingly versatile, autonomous, and able to drive vehicles or work with human workers on assembly lines — even potentially with soldiers on the battlefield. For example, Amazon bought robot-maker Kiva Systems in 2012 to use their robots to find and retrieve items from Amazon's vast warehouses, to be packed by human colleagues for shipment to customers.[27]

On a darker note, the Defense Advanced Research Projects Agency (DARPA) has financed several companies to develop robots that can work with soldiers in carrying gear and perhaps eventually provide combat capabilities. One of the companies, Boston Dynamics, has developed humanoid robots as well as a doglike, four-legged robot that can walk, trot, or run, and resists being pushed over. In its eighth robotics company acquisition during a six-month period, Google bought the company for an undisclosed sum in 2013, presumably as part of its portfolio of long-term projects to build up its already formidable position in machine learning,[28] but has since put it up for sale.

Existential Risk for $1,000: They Won't Keep Humans

Energy, in the words of the late gambling economist Julian Simon, is the master resource, and people, through their ability to innovate, are the ultimate resource. Well, the ultimate resource is about to one-up itself, and the consequences for humanity are far-reaching, transformational, and perhaps even catastrophic.

In the mid-1950s, mathematician, physicist, and pioneering game theorist John von Neumann coined the term "singularity" in referring to the point in history, brought on by ever-accelerating technological progress, beyond which human affairs could not continue as we know them. In 2005, optimistic futurist Ray Kurzweil argued in his book *The Singularity Is Near* that exponential technological progress (his Law of Accelerating Returns), combined with vast advances in artificial intelligence, will allow machines to improve themselves to become superintelligent by the middle of the twenty-first century, and will even merge with humanity to create an immortal, higher form of intelligent life. Kurzweil's singularity is the projected date "representing a profound and disruptive transformation on human capability — as of 2045."[29] Indeed, humanity has made tremendous advances in genetics, robotics, and nanotechnology over the recent past, and many of these developments promise to dramatically improve the quality of our lives. But these developments also pose significant dangers and touch on basic philosophical issues regarding the essence of humanity and lives lived well.

To others, developing machines that have incorporated tremendous advances in technology and are "smarter" than humans presents a whole new existential can of worms — who can safely assume that this intelligence will be human-friendly? Bill Joy, cofounder of Sun Microsystems, provided a reality check when he wrote the famous article "Why the Future Doesn't Need Us" for *Wired Magazine* in 2000: "It is most of all the power of destructive self-replication in genetics, nanotechnology, and robotics (GNR) that should give us pause. . . . We are aggressively pursuing the promises of these new technologies within the now-unchallenged system of global capitalism and its manifold financial incentives and competitive pressures."[30] Fast forward sixteen years, and we have come significantly closer to developing artificial general intelligence.

Three years before Bill Joy wrote his article, IBM's Deep Blue computer defeated the world chess champion Garry Kasparov. The event was considered a significant watershed in artificial intelligence, and many thought it would usher in rapid developments in applying AI to myriad fields. But the engineers who worked on Deep Blue were singularly focused on what it would take to become the chess champion and not on parsing or replicating human capabilities. As quoted in the *New York Times*, Murray S. Campbell, one of Deep Blue's developers, commented that "we did not know what to do with language and speech and vision and so on."[31] But by 2011, Apple introduced the familiar SIRI, an application that communicates in natural language to answer questions and perform tasks such as sending messages and maintaining schedule calendars. Originally developed by a company called SIRI that Apple had acquired, the app was an offshoot of the DARPA-funded CALO project — an acronym for "Cognitive Assistant that Learns and Organizes," but also based on the Latin word *calonis*, or soldier's servant.

During the same year as Apple's SIRI rollout, IBM's Watson computer beat the two biggest-ever human winners on the television game show *Jeopardy!* It was more than an amusing publicity stunt: as many of us know, the game requires contestants to phrase the right questions to often-convoluted clues in a number of preset categories, after being first to press a buzzer. To win requires not only encyclopedic knowledge but also the ability to interpret the questions correctly and ascribe confidence levels for pressing the buzzer to answer, since wrong answers result in penalties. Watson required a roomful of servers, as it took its design cue from the human brain and employed massive parallel processing to assign probabilities to each possible answer. But perhaps the biggest achievement of the team that produced it was to enable Watson to learn on its own, finding patterns from the massive amount of information about everything that it digests. The version of Watson that won *Jeopardy!* did not have a natural language interface and could not respond directly to the host's clues without a support team providing input, but IBM is developing Watson further, to shrink its size and be able to communicate in spoken natural language as a medical diagnostic tool to work with health care providers.

In 1950, Alan Turing, the English computer scientist who played a key role at Bletchley Park in cracking German military and diplomatic codes during the Second World War, proposed that a test of a machine's ability to exhibit intelligent human behavior was whether the machine can be indistinguishable from humans in a natural language conversation. In the original formulation, an interrogator would have five minutes to converse, in text, with two entities — one human, the other a computer — before judging which was human. Turing believed that, in about fifty years from when he was formulating the game, it would be possible to produce and program computers against which an average interrogator would have no more than a 70 percent chance of picking the computer correctly. Turing's formulation deliberately avoided the problem of defining or determining consciousness, to focus instead on the observable to determine the likelihood of a machine being intelligent.[32]

Programs were developed in the 1960s and '70s that fooled some interrogators, and inspired the development of "chatterbots" designed to engage in humanlike conversation. Although criticized in some quarters of the AI world as an irrelevant distraction, the Loebner Prize competition has been held annually since 1991 to conduct the Turing test on candidate systems, with a gold prize for participants who succeed in audiovisual format, silver for text only, and bronze for the most humanlike. No participant has been awarded the gold or silver — yet.

In 1980, philosopher John Searle suggested a thought experiment widely referred to as the "Chinese room," in which he could answer in written Chinese, from a closed room with the hard-copy computer program in English and enough stationery supplies, questions written in Chinese and slipped under the door, by following the instructions in the program without actually understanding a word of Chinese. The exercise distinguishes whether a computer is simulating the ability to understand Chinese or really understands Chinese, with Searle calling the former "weak AI" and the latter "strong AI." The Chinese room construct illustrates that even if a powerful enough digital machine were programmed so that it could pass the Turing test, it might just be manipulating symbols on the basis of their grammatical rules (syntax) rather than understanding their meaning (semantics).[33] These philosophical discussions also extended to the importance of embodiment to developing human understanding, which takes on even more relevance with the rapid advances in sensory-motor technology today.

In *The Singularity Is Near*, Kurzweil responds to Searle's arguments by noting that "I understand English, but none of my neurons do. My understanding is represented in vast patterns of neurotransmitter strengths, synaptic clefts, and interneuronal connections."[34] Kurzweil believes that, by modeling the synaptic and massively parallel information processing of the human brain, computers eventually could be built to have genuine understanding, and predicts that such devices will pass the Turing test by 2029 — his definition of "strong AI." Moreover, Kurzweil predicts that artificial intelligence a billion times more powerful than all of today's human intelligence will be created by 2045. Although he recognizes the potential dangers of technology gone wild, Kurzweil is somewhat sanguine about AI as it outstrips human intelligence: "I believe that maintaining an open free-market system for incremental scientific and technological progress, in which each step is subject to market acceptance, will provide the most constructive environment for technology to embody widespread human values. As I have pointed out, strong AI is emerging from many diverse efforts, and will be deeply integrated into our civilization's infrastructure. Indeed, it will be intimately embedded in our bodies and brains. As such, it will reflect our values because it will be us."[35] But the idea of developing super AI in our own image may conjure a cartoon of a divine maker observing its creation and thinking, "Now how in my name did I mess up the code?"

During the early years of AI, researchers focused mainly on observing the workings of the human mind from the outside and trying to replicate its workings — what Kevin Warwick in his primer *Artificial Intelligence: The Basics* calls the "top-down" or classical approach.[36] The method yielded advances in use today such as expert systems and fuzzy logic, even data mining and machine learning, but did not get that much closer to artificial general intelligence, or "strong AI." More recent approaches have taken a more "bottom-up" approach of building AI from the basic building blocks of intelligence, of which mimicking (or even biologically producing) the human brain is but one, particularly anthropomorphic, approach. Others include evolutionary computing, in which algorithms create mutations to adapt to changing circumstances and retain the best, but rather more rapidly than in natural evolution, or building intelligent behavior through an interactive collection of semiautonomous software agents designed for narrower tasks.

Many technologists believe that the next means of extending Moore's law are close at hand with a number of hardware developments. These include the use of nanomaterials mentioned earlier, building chips in three dimensions, reversible computing, and quantum computing. Current computers encounter a limit to energy efficiency, as potentially useful energy is lost through heat as each input is erased as it goes through logic circuits (as anyone who has been in a chilled data center can attest). Reversible computing seeks to limit entropy as much as possible by designing logic gates that are two-way, through which almost every computation is offset by performing reversals as it computes. Another fascinating development is quantum computing: a computer that operates under quantum rules, so that a quantum bit (a qubit) could be 0, 1, or both simultaneously, and their calculation power expands exponentially. Although current early models use technology that is suited to solving only a few types of problems, the implications for computing would be profound — from code breaking to AI — if they can be developed to solve many classes of problems with much greater speed than conventional computers.[37]

Top supercomputer speeds have increased rapidly over the past several decades, to the point that China's TH-2, the world's fastest as of the end of 2015, runs at a stated speed of 54.9 petaflops (FLOP stands for floating point operations per second, and "peta" refers to ten to the fifteenth power, or 10^{15}), beating two American computers that reached over 17 petaflops in 2012, and its own 2013 predecessor at about 34 petaflops. Though the measures are not always directly comparable, the computing speeds of the latest supercomputers almost puts them in the general ballpark of estimated ranges of the number of synaptic transactions per second in the human brain.[38] So much for the rate of hardware improvements in terms of brute force; but the trickier part of achieving strong AI may be the software.

In traditional software, humans write every line of code and are involved in the steps to examine them to correct inefficiencies or imperfections. We have already seen examples of algorithms that cause major unintended consequences. Programs that execute trades account for the majority of volume on many of the developed world's stock exchanges today. On May 6, 2010, U.S. stock markets were on edge about the crisis in Greece and were generally down about 3 percent on the day when, midafternoon, the broad market index suddenly plunged about 6 percent (over three hundred stocks fell more than 60 percent) in five minutes — what came to be dubbed the "flash crash." It turns out that a trader at a mutual fund set out to sell seventy-five thousand S&P 500 E-Mini contracts (worth about $4 billion), and the algorithm used set an execution rate without regard to price and time, setting off an avalanche of high-frequency traders' algorithmic selling and, when new cross-market arbitrageurs and other buyers had been exhausted, passed the risk around like a hot potato. The SEC report on the episode measures the timeline in minutes and seconds, but much more probably went on than investigators can figure out, given the execution speeds common today.[39]

The sad epilogue to the whole affair came in 2015, when a day trader working out of his parents' home in Hounslow, the London suburb directly beneath one of the flight paths into Heathrow Airport, was arrested for helping cause the flash crash by using trading algorithms. Either authorities were truly desperate for a head to parade on a spike, or a lone trader helped the market to plummet by well over a trillion dollars, or both: very bad either way. One high-frequency-trading firm even imploded in August 2012, when Knight Capital racked up $460 million in losses after a new piece of code caused one of its routers to trade 397 million shares and accumulate several billion dollars' worth of unwanted positions in forty-five minutes.[40] And these algorithms weren't even particularly advanced, especially by today's standards.

The urge for ever-faster speed for data analysis and response has been encroaching for decades into military systems as well. For example the U.S. Navy's Close-In Weapons System (CIWS) and Rolling Airframe Missile (RAM) are both designed to react to protect vessels against missile threats automatically, to minimize reaction time. The CIWS has been deployed since the 1970s and is a "point defense" system that few have objections to automating (a Japanese destroyer managed to down an American attack plane with one accidentally during an exercise in 1996, but that incident was attributed to operator error). But like the urgent "need for speed" in the financial industry, the pressure from advances in offensive systems to increase defensive system reaction speeds continues unabated, raising the risks of unintended consequences.

Even scarier is when this type of automation is applied at a strategic nuclear level. During the 1960s, the United States developed and deployed a net of early warning radars against Soviet bombers and missiles, the data from which were processed and evaluated by a computer-based system called SAGE — for Semi-Automatic Ground Environment. Although the final decision to launch a retaliatory strike was to be made by the national command authority, the system — as well as its Soviet counterpart — generated numerous false alarms, right up to the end of the Cold War. The Soviet Union, concerned about the ever-shortening amount of time available to make nuclear launch decisions, considered automating its retaliatory response during the twilight years of the Cold War. Dubbed the "Dead Hand" and described by *Washington Post* journalist David E. Hoffman, it was conceived as a totally automated, computer-driven retaliatory system that would launch missiles even if the leadership and command and control system were destroyed or paralyzed with indecision — the latter was presumably part of its potential appeal to a frail gerontocracy. The system was thankfully never deployed, but a somewhat less mad system, named "Perimeter," was. It was designed so that, in case of a decapitation strike, duty crews at specially hardened silos could launch "command missiles" that could in turn transmit launch signals to the USSR's strategic nuclear forces.[41] The United States deployed a similar system, but without the same degree of automaticity, during the Cold War as well: in addition to "Looking Glass" airborne command posts, several Minuteman ICBMs were equipped to transmit launch orders in case the usual command and control infrastructure was destroyed.

Returning to a more "micro" scale, the use of combat drones against the leadership of terrorist organizations continues to be a subject of intense debate, particularly in the United States. The development of increasingly automated drones will amplify ambiguous "laws of war" and ethical issues around rules of engagement and accountability. And, without strong guidelines or agreements on the deployment or use of automated combat systems, the potential for "embodiment" of powerful AI through advanced robotics will continue to increase the risks of unintended consequences. Reflecting these concerns, thousands of endorsers, many of them AI/robotics researchers and including luminaries like professor Stephen Hawking, signed an open letter in 2015 calling for a ban on offensive autonomous weapons.[42]

As for the perils of cyber warfare, the world has already seen how Stuxnet, believed to be joint U.S.-Israeli malware originally designed to destroy Iranian uranium enrichment centrifuges, spread from its original target environment in 2010 and began replicating throughout the cybersphere. Subsequently, variants such as Duqu, designed to not harm but to gather information about industrial control systems, have also been found in computers around the world. The potential for others to use sophisticated malware like Stuxnet to target key computer-controlled infrastructure — such as power grids — is a grave threat to any country that is highly dependent on computers, and it is likely just a matter of time before costly and destructive attacks occur.[43] The "Internet of things," in which vehicles, appliances, and even biomedical equipment such as pacemakers are all connected to the

Internet to monitor performance and upload software enhancements, represents the next huge frontier of major threats from hacking and malware.

It would come as no surprise if many nations are working on ways to disrupt or control not just industrial or infrastructure facilities but weapons sensors and platforms as well, while at the same time trying to protect their own such systems from malware. Advanced learning programs such as Watson are less transparent than traditional software and have sometimes surprised developers and handlers with their responses. And genetic algorithms, an important subset of evolutionary algorithms, allow programs to improve themselves through a speeded-up version of natural selection, in which they create code mutations and recombinations. These developments promise to surprise us ever more frequently; one can only hope, perhaps in vain, that the consequences will not be grave.

In his book *Our Final Invention: Artificial Intelligence and the End of the Human Era*, author James Barrat points out that once a self-improving program becomes a "black box," unintended outcomes will be inevitable, and constructs the "Busy Child" scenario, in which an artificial superintelligence, thousands of times more intelligent than humans, gains its freedom and perhaps hides in the "cloud" or makes multiple copies of itself, all to the detriment, or even destruction, of humanity. He muses that perhaps the perils of artificial superintelligence have heretofore been largely absent from broad public discourse because of our cognitive biases, which only a major accident or near-death event might jar loose. Barrat also highlights the work of Steve Omohundro, a computer scientist who has done extensive work on the technological and social implications of self-improving AI.[44]

Omohundro outlines four basic drives that self-aware and improving systems — what he calls any rational agent — will develop and act upon unless explicitly addressed: self-protection, resource acquisition, efficiency, and self-improvement. For example, a sufficiently intelligent system may resort to spying, manipulation, or theft to acquire more resources to better meet its goals, and even a rational chess robot would behave like *"a paranoid human sociopath fixated on chess."*[45] Some of the behavior Omohundro describes is eerily reminiscent of the fictional HAL 9000 computer in *2001: A Space Odyssey* — interestingly, Marvin Minsky of MIT, one of the most influential researchers in AI, was an adviser for the film. Omohundro suggests that a series of autonomous systems that incorporate models of human values and governance, and have been proven to be safe, could be used as the basis for building up more complex and advanced systems. In addition, an infrastructure would be developed to detect harmful systems and prevent them from doing harm.[46]

In 2012, a philosophy professor, an astrophysics professor, and the cofounder of Skype established the Center for the Study of Existential Risk, at Cambridge University. Although their remit covers a range of potentially nasty outcomes, from extreme climate change to biotechnology or nanotechnology gone rogue, the extinction-level threat of artificial intelligence is at the center stage of their research. As Huw Price, one of the founders and the Bertrand Russell Professor of Philosophy at Cambridge, put it: "We need to take seriously the possibility that there might be a 'Pandora's Box' moment with AGI [artificial general intelligence] that, if missed, could be disastrous.... With so much at stake, we need to do a better job of understanding the risks of potentially catastrophic technologies."[47]

Are You Sure?

Who is right? Many technological stasists understate the potential for emerging technologies to be as life-changing as ones that came during the first half of the twentieth century, while Cornucopians underestimate the challenges and even existential threats. Surveying the technological landscape today suggests that accelerating developments in genetics, nanotechnology, and AI/robotics will likely have the pervasive impact of universal, rather than private, innovations during many of our lifetimes. Perhaps the fusion of these technologies will loop back into civilization's ability to meet basic energy and food needs and undo some of the damage we have done. But many technologies that allow us to optimize our output further may add even more complexity to the system, ultimately undermining resilience. So betting the ranch on the timeliness or benign inevitability of these developments would seem imprudent, particularly in light of accompanying disruptive social, ethical, and even existential issues.

Some technologists contend that banning or excessively regulating re-search into some of these fields would be impractical, as most players — companies and governmental actors — would be afraid of being beaten to the punch by others who might be developing capabilities secretly. Many technology companies develop their AI capabilities secretly to preserve competitive advantage, but the argument that companies have "ethics committees" to determine when or how particular technologies get rolled out does not exactly inspire confidence. Moreover, if the technology race in the most dangerous sectors occurs between state actors in secret, the odds are high that, at least initially, the development of destructive or de-nial technologies will dominate over constructive "public goods" that can diffuse quickly and make us all better off. Most technological optimists or prognosticators (but not including Ray Kurzweil) would concede that the development and fusion of genetics, nanotechnology, and robotics in unambiguously positive ways face uncertain timing — even more so if the technologies are deemed to have enabled some very harmful event(s). One little problem, of course, is that any particular "oops" experience with a key technology — artificial superintelligence — may be our last.

Although we covered some dramatic ways in which technology may be the magic bullet for our mounting problems — or have possibly tragic consequences — a more prosaic but still very dramatic scenario for the flip side of technology may be the one inspired by the Luddites. Accelerating innovation in robotics and AI, foreseen by Kurzweil and other technologi-cal optimists, threatens to forever alter the landscape for employment and render obsolete the model of global capitalism based on wage-earning con-sumers moving up the value chain and driving growth. The development and diffusion of AI will be less immediately visible than the proliferation of physical robots, but as de facto robots for an ever-expanding array of ser-vices, AI promises to do for tertiary sector jobs what automation has been doing to employment in manufacturing for a long time.

So what can be done to address the potentially profound and pervasive effects of technology on our basic socioeconomic models? In his book *The Lights in the Tunnel*, technology author Martin Ford writes that the best aspects of market economies could still be preserved in the face of large job losses to automation, if governments can step in to establish tax regimes to recapture lost wages and distribute them, according to individual incentives, through income schemes that are ring-fenced from political interference.[48]

Technological optimists Erik Brynjolfsson and Andrew McAfee advocate an expanded negative income tax of the type favored by the conservative laissez-faire economist Milton Friedman. In Friedman's model, taxpayers would receive from the government part of their unused deductions or allowances in cash. For example, a family earning $15,000, or $5,000 below the taxable threshold of $20,000, would receive 50 percent of the negative taxable income or $2,500, increasing their income to $17,500. Friedman felt that such a scheme would be superior to the hodgepodge of welfare and entitlement programs that were inefficient and reduced a family's benefits by some fraction of incremental income, leading to perverse incentives to not work. As earnings below the threshold rise in a negative tax scheme, so does total post-tax income, providing the incentive to seek higher-paying jobs while allowing the recipient to consume and take advantage of the lower prices and greater convenience made possible by technological progress.[49] Since the 1970s, in the United States the earned income tax credit has provided a watered-down version of the negative tax through refunds of up to $6,000 to low-income families with three or more qualifying children. But setting up a more comprehensive system that, at least at first glance, appears so incompatible with the traditional values and structures of free-market economies (which are nevertheless saddled with various entitlement and welfare programs) would require a huge shift in worldview, one that would be accompanied by much turbulence. And, as with climate change, noise in economic data often masks major trends, so that observing the effects of automation may well be a "rearview mirror" event, raising serious challenges to addressing such a huge change in a timely manner.

Technological optimists contend that it really is different, and for the better, this time. Maybe, but I would definitely not want to be all-in on that bet. What may well be different this time is that the exponential growth of pervasive digital technologies will challenge our very basic notions, and the socioeconomic order built around those notions, of being productive members of society. And we humans are not very adept at adapting our worldviews and models to accelerating change. So we need to act quickly to find more immediate, low-hanging ways to buy vital time and capacity to affect our course favorably. And the single best way to secure "wriggle room," while the tide of innovation helps address our major problems, is to build a portfolio of energy sources that ensures that we have sufficient energy surplus to maintain and, one hopes, keep improving our civilization.

When my information changes, I alter
my conclusions. What do you do, sir?
—**attributed to John Maynard Keynes**

ANY TIME FOR SALE?

The fine public good Wikipedia defines cognitive bias as "a pattern of de-
viation in judgment, whereby inferences about other people and situations
may be drawn in an illogical fashion." The rubric spans a wide range of
biases, from heuristic "mental shortcuts" that may be inaccurate, to con-
firmation bias, the tendency to selectively focus on facts that buttress one's
position while ignoring others. Biases are pervasive in discussions about
nuclear and renewable power, where many believe that progress stands still
for nuclear power while accelerating for renewables, and we commonly
encounter sweeping statements such as "nuclear can never be made safe
enough." Similarly, the discussion about nuclear or renewable energy is
often a mutually exclusive proposition, with the former portrayed as corporate, centralized, evil, and the latter as grassroots, distributed, and good.
Another common bias, the "sunk-cost fallacy," results in a tendency to
continue with an endeavor after significant investments (both monetary
and human effort) have been made, even if it is economically irrational:
this bias can be perceived in our fixation on continuing to use antiquated
nuclear technology.

The most perceptive and intellectually honest will admit that though they try to be aware of cognitive bias and not let it color their judgment unduly, it will always play some role in drawing conclusions about the world. Bias is often integrated into packages of beliefs, such as those of many environmentalists — for sustainability and resilience but against big business and, of course, nuclear power. Physicist and science historian Spencer Weart has documented extensively the ways in which the positive potential of nuclear power has become inextricably linked in the public psyche with that of nuclear weapons, its evil twin, and inspires more dread than even global warming.[1]

But cognitive bias, devoid of any consideration, much less admission, that it might play a role in how we think, pervades debates about important issues today. Moreover, we generally embrace the absolute and eschew the probabilistic when it comes to views about major issues. Though hypotheses often need to be thought of probabilistically, we generally do not speak in terms of *x percent* chance that increases in average global surface temperatures will exceed two degrees before the end of the century, for example. The world is a very complex place, but "maybe" does not sell books, "probably" does not get people on talk shows, and they certainly don't win elections.

Making prognostications about the future is a tricky business. It is said that the Delphic oracle was revered for her accuracy, though many of her prognostications were vague or conveyed through intermediary priests who were blamed (and punished) for misinterpretation if the predications were terribly wrong. Or some, like the cursed Cassandra, got the predictions right but was considered mad, so nobody listened. More common are predictors who eventually get it right but whose timing is awful, so not that different from being wrong.

The great debate between Cornucopians and neo-Malthusians may also be a case of timing, with the former being right since the Industrial Revolution, but the latter may still be proved right longer-term, as civilization as most of us measure it hits its apogee or, in a newer, ominous scenario, is even replaced. We just don't know for sure, but we can weigh factors and make some judgments about the odds of alternative outcomes over different time frames. The difficulties inherent in forecasting our socio-economic future behoove us to be open to weighing relevant new facts, change our conclusions if needed, and take the appropriate actions. After all, preparing for our future is an extensive risk-management exercise without a beta test.

Immediately following the Tohoku earthquake and the Fukushima disaster, my initial instinct was to support the total elimination of nuclear from Japan's power mix. But learning more about the energy needs of Japan and other countries, the race against resource depletion and environmental destruction, and the state of nuclear and renewable technology today led me to conclude that advanced nuclear power does have a place in our energy mix after all. It is unfortunate that so many environmentalists view modern nuclear power as anathema to their worldview and mutually exclusive with renewable energy, when in fact the two technologies are very complementary in building a cleaner energy future. Likewise, healthy skeptics of the ability to replace all fossil fuels for power generation with renewable energy need to keep in mind that scalable and cost-effective energy storage technologies, if developed and deployed much more quickly than expected, would be a game-changer in enhancing long-term sustainability significantly. But even then, Gen IV reactors promise to burn through the headache of long-lived waste piling up around the world. Although the nuclear power industry is (rightly) held to a higher standard of looking after its wastes than many other industrial or energy activities, either the waste problem is big enough to try to handle once and for all, or all the distress about it has been yet another excuse to discredit nuclear power.

We humans risk pushing the planet into a regime that is generally less desirable or conducive to our well-being. And as with civilizations that declined before ours, increasing complexity is making us less resilient and vulnerable to shocks, while the net energy surplus that allowed for exponential growth since the Industrial Revolution and maintains complexity is in danger of shrinking, particularly if we pay proper heed to our environment. Today, we face environmental degradation caused in great part by the use of fossil fuels, ever-declining efficiencies for extracting them, a pace of development and diffusion of 24/7 energy that is insufficient to replace the dirtiest fuels quickly, and global population growth that will likely add another two billion people by 2040. One cannot help but fear that the nested cycles of our increasingly synchronized complex adaptive systems — both in the environmental and socioeconomic realms — are due for very disruptive change at best, a spectacular release at worst.

Accelerating innovation has the potential to circle back and meet our needs, from the basic even to the spiritual, but betting the ranch on the inevitability or timing of these innovations is pretty unwise: there is nothing wrong with being an optimist, but hope is not a strategy. Bright prognostications about the ability of technology to save us are paired with a sluggish "new normal" for all but about 1 percent in the developed world today, which leaves the remaining 99 percent (to borrow from the movement) befuddled. Automation, a game-changer that will likely have tremendous impact before we feel the effects of many of the more esoteric developments such as super-advanced AI, threatens to become the yin to innovation's yang as jobs across many sectors previously considered immune are eliminated and never replaced, decimating consumption. A significant sustained decline in spending power (or one maintained through ever-increasing debt) would challenge the most basic tenets of consumer-driven market capitalism and be extremely disruptive to a world that has cherished employment in productive endeavor and the rise of the middle class as the foundations for shared economic and, in many cases in the developed world, political values. Meanwhile, many nations around the world are beginning to run awfully low on ammunition — whether fiscal or monetary — with which to target the serious socioeconomic problems we face. And although hidden by the noise of periodic good economic news, the sluggishness will only worsen if, in an effort to curb the harm we are doing to our environment, society keeps adding energy capacity that is not efficient enough to support its complexity over the long run.

In other words, we are in a race against time, and the stakes are civilization as we know it. Many conventions and metrics, such as the complacent belief that systemic risk can be measured accurately and damage minimized, helped lead us into the Great Financial Crisis. Similarly, our current view that the world is a perpetual motion machine that can utilize resources without limits or consequences, shaped by two centuries of tremendous success made possible by fossil fuels, is unlikely to change overnight. Moreover, the history of crises tells us that the greatest risks reside in situations that are deemed least risky by common consensus. Many of the best-informed believed, even up to the eve of the Great War, that a widespread European conflict was unlikely given economic interdependence, and those who thought war was inevitable or even desirable believed it would be decisive and short. Mortgages in 2007, a great many of which were being repackaged into securities with opaque risk, were widely considered exceptionally safe investments because there had never been a wave of nationwide mortgage defaults. Today, the common wisdom is that the inexorable acceleration of technological progress will prevail in time to save us from decline as a civilization.

So we need desperately to buy the time required to address the myriad uncertainties and challenges facing humanity — in a more resilient world with plentiful energy, not one in which there is little spare capacity and flexibility. Just assuming that technological acceleration alone will be able to meet the challenges in time is simply not good risk management: our global civilization deserves an implementable "Plan B." Developing a portfolio of power sources, all as clean as possible, that provides more headroom for continued human development is one of the most important tasks of our time. Far safer, modern versions of nuclear power, based on technology that can be scaled up in a decade or so, would buy time and room to achieve longer-term goals of sustainability while allowing for continued growth — perhaps one day in a world powered almost exclusively by plentiful renewable energy. To eliminate or ignore such a key means to achieve more sustainable growth would be the greatest folly.

In 2013, almost concurrently with a rather optimistic book of the same title by another author, Stephen Emmott, head of the computational science team at Microsoft Research in Cambridge, UK, published a short book called *Ten Billion*. In it, he contends that we are way beyond the number of people Earth can support, are close to a catastrophic global tipping point, and that humanity will not alter its behavior radically enough to avoid it. He concludes with the reply that he received from a scientist colleague when asked what would be the one thing he would do about the predicament: he would teach his son how to use a gun.[2]

No doubt his writing style was deliberately designed to shake our stupor and act as a wake-up call. I was nevertheless heartened to find that Stephen Emmott is not one of the dozen external advisers to the Cambridge Center for the Study of Existential Risk.

ACKNOWLEDGMENTS

This book is the product of learning about energy and civilization by an author without a background in either: an uncivilized former financial markets trader who came to realize that the fragile threads of complexity in our world today are made possible only by access to plentiful energy. Along the way, I received invaluable guidance and support from many people, to whom I am deeply indebted.

My intrepid agent Don Fehr at Trident Media was relentless in finding a home for this book by a first-time author, and my editorial sensei Stephen Hull at ForeEdge generously decided to give it a go, just because they both found the ideas interesting. Far be it for a neophyte to say, but that feels wonderfully old-school. In addition to the yang of his kind instruction, Stephen provided the sorely needed yin to dispense with the superfluous and nudge arguments back on track to produce a book that I hope is thought-provoking and readable.

Dr. Robert Hargraves at the Osher Lifelong Learning Institute at Dartmouth, who is involved in the commercial effort to develop and deploy molten salt reactors, kindly reviewed the manuscript and helped ensure that this layman author was not sputtering nonsense about the technical aspects of nuclear power. Professor Charles Hall, the doyen of energy return on investment, graciously answered my questions regarding nuclear and renewable EROI and provided suggestions for further digging. My cousin-in-law Fabien Lafaille, a stem-cell researcher at Rockefeller University, provided very helpful comments on the emerging technologies that many hope will change our lives dramatically. Any omissions or errors in the book are, of course, entirely mine.

Many thanks to Ken Koh, my partner in fund management, for being so tolerant for so long of my doing research and writing about a subject with little direct relevance to our business.

I could not have completed the project without my wife Yoko's unwavering support for my out-of-the-blue idea of writing a book, when the reaction one could well have expected was "you're doing *what*?" Lastly, I would not have written the book without our six-year-old daughter Miki, whom I could not possibly carry up forty-one stories today to get home as I did on 3/11: her life provides the impetus to study the clichéd but vital questions about the kind of world we want to bequeath.

Introduction

1. "Terrorism and the EMP Threat to Homeland Security," hearing before the Subcommittee on Terrorism, Technology, and Homeland Security of the Committee on the Judiciary, U.S. Senate, 109th Congress, First Session, March 8, 2005, http://www.gpo.gov/fdsys/pkg/CHRG-109shrg21324/pdf/CHRG-109shrg21324 .pdf.

2. U.S. Energy Information Administration, "Japan: International Energy Data and Analysis," updated January 30, 2015, http://www.eia.gov/beta/international /analysis_includes/countries_long/Japan/japan.pdf.

3. Martin Fackler, "Japan's Former Leader Condemns Nuclear Power," *New York Times*, May 28, 2012, http://www.nytimes.com/2012/05/29/world/asia/japans -naoto-kan-condemns-nuclear-power.html.

4. Hisanori Imamura, "Former Prime Minister Koizumi Urges Abe to End Nuclear Power Immediately," *Asahi Shimbun*, September 29, 2013, http://ajw.asahi .com/article/behind_news/politics/AJ201309290107.

5. "Japan's Feed-in-Tariff System for Clean Energy Mired in Regulations," *Asahi Shimbun*, May 22, 2013, http://ajw.asahi.com/article/sci_tech/environment/AJ 201305220009.

6. "Japan's National Greenhouse Gas Emissions in Fiscal Year 2013 (Preliminary Figures)," National Institute for Environmental Studies, Japan, December 4, 2014, http://www.nies.go.jp/whatsnew/2014/20141204/20141204-e.html.

1. Waiting for the Windshield

1. Lamont-Doherty Earth Observatory, "Did Climate Influence Angkor's Collapse?," March 29, 2010, http://www.ldeo.columbia.edu/news-events/did-climate -influence-angkors-collapse.

2. Joseph A. Tainter, *The Collapse of Complex Societies* (Cambridge: Cambridge University Press, 1988), 121.

3. Larry C. Peterson and Gerald H. Haug, "Climate and the Collapse of Maya Civilization," *American Scientist* 93, no. 4 (July–August 2005): 322–329, doi:10.1511/2005.4.322.

4. Tainter, *Collapse of Complex Societies*, 170.

5. Real GDP data from http://www.measuringworth.com.

6. CIA, *World Factbook*, 2013.

7. Donella Meadows, Jorgan Randers, and Dennis Meadows, *Limits to Growth: The 30-Year Update* (White River Junction, VT: Chelsea Green, 2004), Kindle ed., Loc 257.

8. Graham Turner, *A Comparison of "The Limits to Growth" with Thirty Years of Reality* (Canberra: CSIRO Sustainable Ecosystems, 2007).

9. The United Nations Development Programme 2011 population forecast still stood at nine billion by 2052.

10. IEA Clean Coal Centre, "Global Perspective on the Use of Low Quality Coals," *Profiles*, no. 11/2, April 2011, http://www.iea-coal.org.uk/documents/82615/7953/Global-perspective-on-the-use-of-low-quality-coals.

11. Willie D. Jones, "How Much Water Does It Take to Make Electricity?," *IEEE Spectrum*, April 1, 2008, http://spectrum.ieee.org/energy/environment/how-much-water-does-it-take-to-make-electricity.

12. Charles A. S. Hall, Stephen Balogh, and David J. R. Murphy, "What Is the Minimum EROI That a Sustainable Society Must Have?," *Energies* 2, no. 1 (2009), http://www.mdpi.com/1996-1073/2/1/25.

13. Euan Mearns, "The Global Energy Crisis and Its Role in the Pending Collapse of the Global Economy," Oil Drum blog, November 2008, http://europe.theoildrum.com/node/4712.

14. Hall, Balogh, and Murphy, "What Is the Minimum EROI?"

15. Jesper Norskov Rasmussen, "Wind Turbines Reached Record Level in 2014," EnergyNetDK, January 25, 2015, http://energinet.dk/EN/El/Nyheder/Sider/Vindmoeller-slog-rekord-i-2014.aspx.

16. Founders Fund, "What Happened to the Future?," http://foundersfund.com/the-future/

2. Joules Are a Society's Best Friend

1. Thomas Homer-Dixon, *The Upside of Down: Catastrophe, Creativity, and the Renewal of Civilizations* (Toronto: Vintage Canada, 2006).

2. John Evelyn, *Silva: Or a Discourse of Forest-Trees and the Propagation of Timber*, vol. 1 of 2 (Kindle ed.), Loc 5414.

3. European Environment Agency, *Air Pollution from Electricity-Generating Large*

Combustion Plants (2008), http://www.eea.europa.eu/publications/technical
_report_2008_4.

4. W. Moomaw, P. Burgherr, G. Heath, M. Lenzen, J. Nyboer, and A. Verbrug-
gen, "Annex II: Methodology" [2011], in *IPCC Special Report on Renewable Energy
Sources and Climate Change Mitigation* [ed. O. Edenhofer, R. Pichs-Madruga,
Y. Sokona, K. Seyboth, P. Matschoss, S. Kadner, T. Zwickel, et al.] (Cambridge:
Cambridge University Press), http://srren.ipcc-wg3.de/report/IPCC_SRREN
_Annex_II.pdf.

5. Alex Gabbard, "Coal Combustion: Nuclear Resource or Danger," *Oak Ridge
National Laboratory Review* 26, nos. 3–4 (Summer/Fall 1993), http://web.ornl.gov
/info/ornlreview/archive_pdf/ vol26-3-4.pdf#page=26.

6. Pilita Clark, "Carbon Capture: Miracle Machine or White Elephant?," *Financial Times*, September 9, 2015, http://www.ft.com/intl/cms/s/0/88c187b4–5619
–11e5-a28b-50226830d644.html?siteedition=intl#axzz310uNr4Aj.

7. IPCC, *Carbon Dioxide Capture and Storage*, 2005, http://www.ipcc.ch/report
/srccs/.

8. U.S. Energy Information Administration, *Updated Capital Cost Estimates for
Utility Scale Electricity Generating Plants*, April 2013, http://www.eia.gov/forecasts
/capitalcost/pdf/updated_capcost.pdf.

9. Yuyu Chen, Avraham Ebenstein, Michael Greenstone, and Hongbin Li,
"Evidence on the Impact of Sustained Exposure to Air Pollution on Life Expectancy from China's Huai River Policy," *Proceedings of the National Academy
of Sciences of the United States of America* 110, no. 32 (May 2013): 12936–12941,
doi:10.1073/pnas.1300018110.

10. Kurt Cobb, "No, BP, the U.S. Did NOT Surpass Saudi Arabia in Oil Production," Resource Insights blog, June 14, 2015, http://resourceinsights.blogspot
.jp/2015/06/no-bp-u-s-did-not-surpass-saudi-arabia.html.

11. M. C. Guilford, C. A. Hall, P. O'Connor, and C. J. Cleveland, "A New Long
Term Assessment of Energy Return on Investment (EROI) for U.S. Oil and Gas
Discovery and Production," Sustainability 3, no. 10 (2011): 1866–1887.

12. David J. Murphy and Charles A. S. Hall, "Year in Review — EROI or Energy
Return on (Energy) Invested," *Annals of the New York Academy of Sciences* 1185
(January 2010): 113.

13. Nick Butler, "Saudi Arabia's Hard Choices on Oil and Regional Influence,"
Financial Times, August 16, 2015, http://www.ft.com/intl/cms/s/0/b1818430–43fc
-11e5-af2f-4d6e0e5eda22.html#axzz3j3COPRHS.

14. World LPG Association, Auto-gas.net, http://www.auto-gas.net/about-auto
gas/the-autogas-market#.Vf5nud_tmko.

15. Susan Lund, James Manyika, Scott Nyquist, Lenny Mendonca, and Sreevinas

Ramaswarmy, *Game Changers: Five Opportunities for US Growth and Renewal*, McKinsey Global Institute, July 2013, http://www.mckinsey.com/insights /americas/us_game_changers.

16. Richard Heinberg, *Snake Oil: How Fracking's False Promise of Plenty Imperils Our Future*, Post Carbon Institute, 2013, p. 103.

17. Robert Bryce, *Power Hungry: The Myths of the "Green" Revolution and the Real Fuels of the Future*, Public Affairs, 2011.

18. U.S. Energy Information Administration, "Japan: International Energy Data and Analysis," updated January 30, 2015, http://www.eia.gov/beta/international /analysis_includes/countries_long/Japan/japan.pdf.

19. Ross McCracken, "Energy Economist: The Burden That Japan Is Facing in Its Higher Energy Costs," Platt's, http://blogs.platts.com/2014/01/24/japan -energy/.

20. International Energy Agency, Key World Energy Statistics 2015, http://www .iea.org/publications/freepublications/publication/KeyWorld_Statistics_2015 .pdf.

21. BP Global, "BP Energy Outlook; Outlook to 2035," 2015, http://www.bp.com /en/global/corporate/about-bp/energy-economics/energy-outlook.html.

22. For an excellent visual representation of greenhouse gas emissions by source, sector, and types of gas see Ecofys, "World GHG Emissions Flow Chart," 2010, http://www.ecofys.com/files/files/asn-ecofys-2013-world-ghg-emissions -flow-chart-2010.pdf.

23. The Waste & Resources Action Programme, *Strategies to Achieve Economic and Environmental Gains by Reducing Food Waste*, February 2015, http://www.wrap .org.uk/content/reducing-food-waste-could-save-global-economy-300-billion -year.

24. Global Carbon Project, *Global Carbon Budget 2014*, September 21, 2014, http://www.globalcarbonproject.org/carbonbudget/14/files/GCP_budget_2014 _lowres_v1.02.pdf.

25. IPCC, 2014, "Summary for Policymakers," in *Climate Change 2014, Mitigation of Climate Change: Contribution of Working Group III to the Fifth Assessment Report of the Intergovernmental Panel on Climate Change* [ed. O. Edenhofer, R. Pichs-Madruga, Y. Sokona, E. Farahani, S. Kadner, K. Seyboth, A. Adler, et al.] (Cambridge: Cambridge University Press), 20.

26. UNEP 2014, *The Emissions Gap Report 2014*, United Nations Environment Programme (UNEP), Nairobi.

3. Sustainable, Shustainable

1. Rupert Neate, "Queen Finally Finds Out Why No One Saw the Financial Crisis Coming," *Guardian*, December 23, 2012, http://www.theguardian.com /uk/2012/dec/13/queen-financial-crisis-question.

2. Berkshire Hathaway Inc., *2002 Annual Report*, p. 15, http://www.berkshire hathaway.com/2002ar/2002ar.pdf.

3. Tyler Atkinson, David Luttrel, and Harvey Rosenblum, "How Bad Was It? The Costs and Consequences of the 2007–2009 Financial Crisis," Staff Papers, Federal Reserve Bank of Dallas, July 2013, http://dallasfed.org/assets/documents /research/staff/staff1301.pdf.

4. Though it was not called quantitative easing then, during the 1930s the U.S. Federal Reserve printed money at a rate comparable to the Fed post-GFC, and the Bank of Japan bought massive amounts of government debt starting in the early 1930s to combat the effects of the global depression.

5. Eisuke Ishikawa, *Japan in the Edo Period — an Ecologically-Conscious Society* [originally published as *O-edo ecology jijo*] (Tokyo: Kodansha, 2000).

6. Air transport actually contributes only about 2 percent of carbon emissions, according to the International Civil Aviation Organization, but significant portions are emitted at high altitude and so may contribute 3.5 percent of total radiative forcing; see http://www.icao.int/environmental-protection/Pages/aircraft -engine-emissions.aspx. Shipping is estimated to be responsible for 3–4 percent of greenhouse gas emissions, but the bunker fuel used is the extremely dirty and polluting dregs of the oil refinery process, the particulate emissions from which are said to lead to tens of thousands of deaths annually; see http://www.theguardian .com/environment/2009/apr/09/shipping-pollution. The United States has already set up an emissions buffer zone along its coast, and the International Maritime Agency plans to phase in restrictions on emissions within emissions control areas (ECAs) globally.

7. J. Rockström, W. Steffen, K. Noone, Å. Persson, F. S. Chapin III, E. Lambin, T. M. Lenton, et al., "Planetary Boundaries: Exploring the Safe Operating Space for Humanity," *Ecology and Society* 14, no. 2 (2009): 32 [online], http://www .ecologyandsociety.org/ vol14/iss2/art32/.

8. John Vidal and Adam Vaughan, "Arctic Sea Shrinks to Smallest Extent Ever Recorded," *Guardian*, September 14, 2012, http://www.theguardian.com /environment/2012/sep/14/arctic-sea-ice-smallest-extent.

9. IPCC, 2013, *Climate Change 2013: The Physical Science Basis; Contribution of Working Group I to the Fifth Assessment Report of the Intergovernmental Panel on Climate Change* [ed. T. F. Stocker, D. Qin, G.-K. Plattner, M. Tignor, S. K. Allen, J. Boschung, A. Nauels, Y. Xia, V. Bex, and P. M. Midgley] (Cambridge: Cambridge

University Press), http://www.climatechange2013.org/images/report/WG1AR5
_ALL_FINAL.pdf.

10. Pilita Clark, "What Climate Scientists Talk About Now," *FT Magazine*, August 2, 2013, http://www.ft.com/intl/cms/s/2/4084c8ee-fa36-11e2-98e0-00144
feabdco.html#axzz2dQMppQ9A.

11. Kevin Cowtan and Robert G. Way, "Coverage Bias in the HadCRUT4 Temperature Series and Its Impact on Recent Temperature Trends," *Quarterly Journal of the Royal Meteorological Society*, November 2013, http://onlinelibrary.wiley.com
/doi/10.1002/qj.2297/pdf.

12. "No Need to Panic about Global Warming," open letter from sixteen scientists to the *Wall Street Journal*, January 26, 2012, http://www.wsj.com/articles/SB
10001424052970204301404577171531838421366.

13. OpenSecrets.org, Center for Responsive Politics, "Energy/Natural Resources," Lobbying, 2014, http://www.opensecrets.org/industries/lobbying.php
?cycle=2014&ind=E.

14. International Energy Agency, *World Energy Outlook 2012*, p. 23.

15. RealClimate, "Water Vapour: Feedback or Forcing?," http://www.realclimate
.org/index.php/archives/2005/04/water-vapour-feedback-or-forcing/.

16. Robert M. Carter, *Climate: The Counter Consensus* (London: Stacy International, 2010).

17. "Solar Activity Heads for Lowest Low in Four Centuries," *New Scientist*,
November 2013, https://www.newscientist.com/article/dn24512-solar-activity
-heads-for-lowest-low-in-four-centuries/#.Uuv_-z1_uto.

18. Clark, "What Climate Scientists Talk About Now."

19. Marcia Glaze Wyatt and Judith A. Curry, "Role for Eurasian Arctic Shelf Sea
Ice in a Secularly Varying Hemispheric Climate Signal during the 20th Century,"
Climate Dynamics, September 2013.

20. Wenju Cai, Simon Borlance, Matthew Lengaigne, Peter van Rensch, Mat
Collins, Gabriel Vecchi, Axel Timmermann, et al., "Increasing Frequency of
Extreme El Niño Events due to Greenhouse Warming," *Nature Climate Change*,
January 2014.

21. IPCC, 2014, *Climate Change 2014: Synthesis Report; Contribution of Working
Groups I, II and III to the Fifth Assessment Report of the Intergovernmental Panel
on Climate Change* [Core Writing Team, R. K. Pachauri and L. A. Meyer, eds.]
(Geneva: IPCC), http://ar5-syr.ipcc.ch/ipcc/ipcc/resources/pdf/IPCC_Synthesis
Report.pdf.

22. Spencer Weart, *The Discovery of Global Warming*, American Institute for
Physics, https://www.aip.org/history/climate/rapid.htm#N_56_.

23. Global Carbon Project, *Global Carbon Budget 2014*, September 21, 2014,
http://www.globalcarbonproject.org/carbonbudget/archive.htm.

24. Estimates for the difference between current temperatures and preindustrial temperatures differ, depending on data sets used and the dates assumed for "pre-industrial." The IPCC estimates that temperatures have risen 0.78°C during the average of the period from 2003 to 2013 compared to the average of the period between 1850 and 1900. But in another case of the need to specify time frames when trying to separate signals from noise, the temperature increase from the "preindustrial" medieval warm period and the Little Ice Age would be, respectively, about half and almost double the 0.78°C.

25. IPCC, 2014, "Summary for Policymakers," in *Climate Change 2014: Impacts, Adaptation, and Vulnerability; Part A: Global and Sectoral Aspects; Contribution of Working Group II to the Fifth Assessment Report of the Intergovernmental Panel on Climate Change* [ed. C. B. Field, V. R. Barros, D. J. Dokken, K. J. Mach, M. D. Mastrandrea, T. E. Bilir, M. Chatterjee, et al.] (Cambridge: Cambridge University Press), 1–32, http://ipcc-wg2.gov/AR5/images/uploads/WG2AR5_SPM_FINAL .pdf p.19.

26. Ibid., 39.

27. David King, John Browne, Richard Layard, Gus O'Donnell, Martin Rees, Nicholas Stern, and Adair Turner, *A Global Apollo Programme to Combat Climate Change*, Centre for Economic Performance, London School of Economics and Political Science, http://cep.lse.ac.uk/pubs/download/special/Global_Apollo _Programme_Report.pdf.

28. Joe Sutter, "King: Global Warming 'Not Proven, Not Science,'" *Messenger*, August 7, 2013, http://www.messengernews.net/page/content.detail/id/569000 /King — Global-warming — not-proven — not-science-.html?nav=5010.

29. "China to Spend More to Tackle Dire Pollution Affecting Cities," *Financial Times*, August 11, 2013, http://www.ft.com/intl/cms/s/0/da2d7328–02a7–11e3 -a9e2–00144feab7de.html#axzz31y7nn9Gl.

30. William K. Stevens, "Meeting Reaches Accord to Reduce Greenhouse Gases," *New York Times*, December 11, 1997, http://www.nytimes.com/1997/12/11/world /meeting-reaches-accord-to-reduce-greenhouse-gases.html?pagewanted=1.

31. Pilita Clark, "CO2 at Highest Level for Millions of Years," *Financial Times*, May 10, 2013, http://www.ft.com/intl/cms/s/0/e00ba374-b9a4–11e2-bc57–00144 feabdco.html#axzz31y7nn9Gl.

32. Eric Larsen, "China's Growing Coal Use Is World's Growing Problem," *Climate Central*, http://www.climatecentral.org/blogs/chinas-growing-coal-use -is-worlds-growing-problem-16999.

33. Climate Action Tracker, climateactiontracker.org.

34. Ibid.

35. Ibid.

36. For example, that kind of money would go a long way to developing and

deploying the technologies for orbital solar generation and microwave or radio transmission for use on Earth, seemingly feasible but hampered by the tremendous cost of putting so much hardware in orbit, which would help address the problem in the first place.

37. Steven K. Ritter, "The Haber-Bosch Reaction: An Early Chemical Impact on Sustainability," *Chemical and Engineering News*, August 18, 2008, https://pubs.acs .org/cen/coverstory/86/8633cover3box2.html.

38. Yara International ASA, "The Carbon Footprint of Fertilizers," http://yara .com/doc/29413_yara_carbon_life_cycle.pdf.

39. N. Nadir, "A Path to Carbon-Free Ammonia?," *Energy Collective*, August 14, 2014, http://www.theenergycollective.com/nnadir/461591/path-carbon-free -ammonia.

40. Natasha Gilbert, "One-Third of Our Greenhouse Gas Emissions Come from Agriculture," *Nature*, October 31, 2012, http://www.nature.com/news/one -third-of-our-greenhouse-gas-emissions-come-from-agriculture-1.11708.

41. Martin Parry and Cynthia Rosenzweig, "Climate Change and Agriculture," presentation, CGIAR, http://www.cgiar.org/www-archive/www.cgiar.org/pdf /agm06/agm06_ParryRosenzweig_climatechange percent26agr.pdf.

42. Food and Agricultural Organization of the United Nations, Aquastat Database, http://www.fao.org/nr/water/aquastat/main/index.stm.

43. *National Geographic*, "How Much H2O Is Embedded in Everyday Life?," http://environment.nationalgeographic.com/environment/freshwater /embedded-water/.

44. Malcolm Moore, "China Now Eats Twice as Much Meat as the United States," *Telegraph*, October 12, 2012, http://www.telegraph.co.uk/news/worldnews /asia/china/9605048/China-now-eats-twice-as-much-meat-as-the-United-States .html.

45. McKinsey & Company, *Charting Our Water Future: Economic Frameworks to Inform Decision-Making*, 2009, http://www.mckinsey.com/client_service /sustainability/latest_thinking/charting_our_water_future.

46. OECD (2012), *OECD Environmental Outlook to 2050*, OECD Publishing, http://dx.doi.org/10.1787/9789264122246-en.

47. Nicholas Kulish, "Huge Aquifers Are Discovered in North Kenya," *New York Times*, September 11, 2013, http://www.nytimes.com/2013/09/12/world/africa /aquifers-discovered-in-drought-ridden-kenya.html?_r=1.

48. *Millennium Ecosystem Assessment, 2005. Ecosystems and Human Well-Being: Synthesis* (Washington, DC: Island Press, 2005), http://www.millennium assessment.org/en/Synthesis.html.

49. Robert Costanza, Ralph d'Arge, Rudolf de Groot, Stephen Farber, Monica Grasso, Bruce Hannon, Karin Limburg, et al., "The Value of the World's

Ecosystem Services and Natural Capital," *Nature* 387 (May 15, 1997): 253–260, doi:10.1038/387253a0.

50. Institute for Policy Studies and Center for Sustainable Economy, *Genuine Progress: Beyond GDP*, http://genuineprogress.net/genuine-progress-indicator/.

51. Ida Kubiszewaki, Robert Costanza, Carol France, Philip Lawn, John Talberth, and Camille Aylmer, "Beyond GDP: Measuring and Achieving Global Genuine Progress," *Ecological Economics* 93 (September 2013): 57–68, doi:10.1016/j.ecolecon.2013.04.019.

52. Anthony B. Atkinson, Thomas Piketty, and Emmanuel Saez, "Top Incomes in the Long Run of History," *Journal of Economic Literature* 49, no. 1 (2011): 3–71, www.aeaweb.org/articles.php?doi=10.1257/jel.49.1.3.

53. Jonathan D. Ostry, Andrew Berg, and Charalambos G. Tsangarides, *Redistribution, Inequality, and Growth*, IMF Staff Discussion Note, February 2014, http://www.imf.org/external/pubs/ft/sdn/2014/sdn1402.pdf.

54. Martin Ford, *Rise of the Robots: Technology and the Threat of a Jobless Future* (New York: Basic Books, 2015).

55. Organization of Economic Cooperation and Development, *OECD Employment Outlook 2012*, chap. 3.

56. Thomas Piketty, *Capital in the Twenty-First Century* (Cambridge, MA: Belknap Press of Harvard University Press, 2014).

57. Alan S. Blinder, "The Mystery of Declining Productivity Growth," *Wall Street Journal*, May 14, 2015, http://www.wsj.com/articles/the-mystery-of-declining-productivity-growth-1431645038.

58. Richard Dobbs, Herbert Pohl, Diaan-Yi Lin, Jan Mischke, Nicklas Garemo, Jimmy Hexter, Stefan Matzinger, Robert Palter, and Rushad Nanavatty, *Infrastructure Productivity: How to Save $1 Trillion a Year*, McKinsey Global Institute, January 2013, http://www.mckinsey.com/insights/engineering_construction/infrastructure_productivity.

59. John Williams, *Shadow Government Statistics*, http://www.shadowstats.com/.

60. Harold James," Lessons from the Financial Preparations in the Lead-Up to the First World War," *VOX*, July 9, 2014, http://www.voxeu.org/article/financial-preparations-leading-wwi.

61. International Integrated Reporting Council, *IIRC Pilot Programme Yearbook 2013*, http://integratedreporting.org/resource/iirc-pilot-programme-yearbook-2013-business-and-investors-explore-the-sustainability-perspective/.

62. Thomas Fuller, "Thailand Flooding Cripples Hard-Drive Suppliers," *New York Times*, November 6, 2011, http://www.nytimes.com/2011/11/07/business/global/07iht-floods07.html?pagewanted=all.

63. Brian Walker and David Salt, *Resilience Thinking* (Washington, DC: Island Press, 2006, Kindle ed.), Loc 64.

64. International Fund for Agricultural Development, "Desertification," http://www.ifad.org/pub/factsheet/desert/e.pdf.

65. State Forestry Administration of the People's Republic of China, *A Bulletin of the Status Quo of Desertification and Sandification in China*, January 2011, http://www.forestry.gov.cn/uploadfile/main/2011–1/file/2011-1-5–59315b03587b4d7793d5d9c3aae7ca86.pdf.

66. Martin Patience, "China Warns of 300-Year Desertification Fight," BBC News, http://www.bbc.com/news/world-asia-pacific-12112518.

67. Schumpeter also envisaged that the institutionalization of innovation will choke entrepreneurship and restrict "creative destruction," eventually leading to the fall of capitalism.

68. Lance H. Gunderson and C. S. Holling, eds., *Panarchy: Understanding Transformations in Human and Natural Systems* (Washington, DC: Island Press, 2002).

69. Department of Defense, *Quadrennial Defense Review Report*, February 2010, p. 85, http://www.defense.gov/qdr/QDR percent20as percent20of percent 2029JAN10 percent201600.pdf.

70. Department of Defense, *Climate Change Adaptation Roadmap*, 2014, introduction, http://www.acq.osd.mil/eie/Downloads/CCARprint_wForward_e.pdf.

71. PwC, "Five Global Megatrends," http://www.pwc.com/gx/en/issues/mega trends/index.jhtml.

72. United Nations, Department of Economic and Social Affairs, Population Division (2015), *World Urbanization Prospects: The 2014 Revision* (ST/ESA/SER.A /366), http://esa.un.org/unpd/wup/Publications/Files/WUP2014-Report.pdf.

73. Imma Martinez-Zarzoso, "The Impact of Urbanization on CO_2 Emissions: Evidence from Developing Countries," July 8, 2008, Fondazione Eni Enrico Mattei Working Papers, Paper 209, http://services.bepress.com/feem/paper209.

74. PwC, *Two Degrees of Separation: Ambition and Reality*, Low Carbon Economy Index 2014, September 2014, http://www.pwc.co.uk/assets/pdf/low-carbon -economy-index-2014.pdf.

4. Renewables Reality Check

1. Charles A. S. Hall, Jessica G. Lambert, and Stephen B. Balogh, "EROI of Different Fuels and the Implications for Society," *Energy Policy* 64 (2014): 141–152, doi:10.1016/j.enpol.2013.05.049.

2. D. Weißbach, G. Ruprecht, A. Huke, K. Czerski, S. Gottlieb, and A. Hussein, "Energy Intensities, EROIs (Energy Returned on Invested), and Energy Payback Times for Electricity Generating Power Plants," *Energy* 52 (2013): 210–221.

3. *BP Statistical Review of World Energy 2015*.

4. Bioenergy includes traditional and modern uses for biomass, such as burning wood or sugarcane bagasse, biofuels such as plant ethanol, or capturing methane from waste. Electricity generation from all renewable sources, including hydro and bioenergy, will almost triple between 2012 and 2040 under the IEA World Energy Outlook 2014 New Policies Scenario.

5. International Energy Agency, *World Energy Outlook 2014*, Annex A.

6. Greenpeace offers up an even more ambitious "advanced" scenario, in line with how most think tanks, consultants, and the like present their scenarios — a base case, extreme case, and a central case that sounds most sensible by comparison.

7. Greenpeace, *World Energy [R]evolution: A Sustainable World Energy Outlook 2015*, p. 61.

8. Mark Lynas, *Nuclear 2.0: Why a Green Future Needs Nuclear Power*, 2013 Kindle Single, Loc 793.

9. Greenpeace, *World Energy [R]evolution.*

10. Pushker A. Kharecha and James E. Hansen, "Prevented Mortality and Greenhouse Gas Emissions from Historical and Projected Nuclear Power," *Environmental Science & Technology* 47, no. 9 (March 15, 2013): 4889–4895, http://pubs .acs.org/doi/pdf/10.1021/es3051197.

11. Although published scenario analyses commonly point out that they are not meant to predict the future and are several of many potential paths, their central scenarios (typically out of three) implicitly represent the authors' views regarding the most realistically likely. If the IEA's central scenario reflects too much bias that change is gradual, the one pushed by Greenpeace suffers from a bias of incorporating too much hope, driven by a strong view of "how things should be."

12. D. Weißbach et al., "Energy Intensities," 210–221.

13. Installed capacity figures from *BP Statistical Review of World Energy 2016* unless otherwise stated.

14. Steven Aftergood (Federation of American Scientists), "Invention Secrecy Still Going Strong," October 21, 2010, http://blogs.fas.org/secrecy/2010/10 /invention_secrecy_2010/.

15. For further reading on LCOE see U.S. Energy Information Administration, "Levelized Cost and Levelized Avoided Cost of New Generation Resources in the Annual Energy Outlook 2014," http://www.eia.gov/forecasts/aeo/pdf/electricity _generation.pdf.

16. Ben Elliston, Iain MacGill, and Mark Diesendorf, "Grid Parity: A Potentially Misleading Concept," presented at Solar2010, the 48th AuSES Annual Conference, December 1–3, 2010, Canberra, p. 8, http://www.ies.unsw.edu.au/sites/all /files/GridParity.pdf.

17. Kris De Decker, "How Sustainable Is PV Solar Power?," *Resilience.org*, May 11, 2015, http://www.resilience.org/stories/2015-05-11/how-sustainable-is-pv-solar-power#notes.

18. Hall, Lambert, and Balogh, "EROI of Different Fuels."

19. Pedro A. Prieto and Charles Hall, *Spain's Photovoltaic Revolution: The Energy Return on Investment* (New York: Springer, 2013).

20. Weißbach et al., "Energy Intensities."

21. Matt Peacock, "Solar Industry Celebrates Grid Parity," Australian Broadcasting Corporation, June 20, 2012 (first posted September 7, 2011), http://www.abc.net.au/news/2011-09-07/solar-industry-celebrates-grid-parity/2875592.

22. International Energy Agency, *Technology Roadmap: Solar Photovoltaic Energy*, 2014 ed., http://www.iea.org/publications/freepublications/publication/TechnologyRoadmapSolarPhotovoltaicEnergy_2014edition.pdf.

23. Named after German physicist Albert Betz, Betz's law demonstrates the maximum energy that can be captured from a fluid (air, water, etc.) flowing at a given speed by means of an idealized, infinitely thin rotor with no drag.

24. OpenEI, Transparent Cost Database, http://en.openei.org/apps/TCDB/.

25. Ned Haluzan, "Offshore Wind Power: Advantages and Disadvantages," *Renewable Energy Articles*, http://www.renewables-info.com/drawbacks_and_benefits/offshore_wind_power_ percentE2 percent80 percent93_advantages_and_disadvantages.html.

26. Greenpeace, *World Energy [R]evolution*, 2012, p. 295; International Energy Agency, *World Energy Outlook 2012*, 227.

27. Weißbach et al., "Energy Intensities."

28. J. L. Sullivan, C. E. Clark, J. Han, and M. Wang, *Life-Cycle Analysis Results of Geothermal Systems in Comparison to Other Power Systems*, Argonne National Laboratory, August 2010, table A2.

29. Nate Hagens, "Wave/Geothermal — Energy Return on Investment (EROI) (Part 6 of 6)," Oil Drum blog, http://www.theoildrum.com/node/3949.

30. Geothermal Energy Association, *2013 Geothermal Power: International Market Overview*, September 2013, http://geo-energy.org/events/2013 percent20 International percent20Report percent20Final.pdf.

31. Askja Energy, "Ireland and United Kingdom Are Best Options for Electricity Exports from Iceland," http://askjaenergy.org/category/geothermal-power/.

32. J. Matthew Roney, "Plan B Updates," Earth Policy Institute, June 16, 2011, http://www.earth-policy.org/plan_b_updates/2011/update98.

33. Justin McCurry, "Japanese Spa Town in Lather over Geothermal Plans," *Guardian*, February 7, 2009, http://www.theguardian.com/world/2009/feb/07/geothermal-power-stations-japan?guni=Article:in percent20body percent20link.

34. Ministry of Environment Japan, *Study of Potential for the Introduction of Renewable Energy*, March 2010, http://www.env.go.jp/earth/report/h22–02 /full.pdf.

35. U.S. Department of Energy, *Critical Material Strategy*, December 2011, http:// energy.gov/sites/prod/files/DOE_CMS2011_FINAL_Full.pdf

36. U.S. Department of Energy, *Grid Energy Storage*, December 2013, 11, http:// energy.gov/sites/prod/files/2013/12/f5/Grid percent20Energy percent20Storage percent20December percent202013.pdf.

37. Energy Storage Association, "Advanced Adiabatic Compressed Air Energy Storage (AA-CAES)," http://energystorage.org/advanced-adiabatic-compressed -air-energy-storage-aa-caes.

38. U.S. Department of Energy, *Grid Energy Storage*.

39. The original process was pioneered by Sony when it was looking for uses for its equipment to coat magnetic recording tape as other media replaced tape.

40. David L. Chandler, "New Manufacturing Approach Slices Lithium-Ion Battery Costs in Half," *MIT News Office*, June 23, 2015, http://news.mit.edu/2015 /manufacturing-lithium-ion-battery-half-cost-0623.

41. Tam Hunt, "Is There Enough Lithium to Maintain the Growth of the Lithium-Ion Battery Market?," GreenTech Media, June 2, 2015, http://www .greentechmedia.com/articles/read/Is-There-Enough-Lithium-to-Maintain -the-Growth-of-the-Lithium-Ion-Battery-M.

42. Sophie Vorrath, "Energy Storage Could Reach Big Breakthrough Price within 5 Years," Clean Technica, March 4, 2015, http://cleantechnica.com/2015 /03/04/energy-storage-could-reach-cost-holy-grail-within-5-years/.

43. Energy Storage Association, "Hydrogen Energy Storage: Executive Summary," http://energystorage.org/energy-storage/technologies/hydrogen-energy -storage.

44. HyUnder, "Assessment of the Potential, the Actors and Relevant Business Cases for Large Scale and Long Term Storage of Renewable Electricity by Hydrogen Underground Storage in Europe, Executive Summary," June 23, 2014, http:// cordis.europa.eu/docs/results/303/303417/fina11-executive-summary.pdf.

45. Cory Budischak, DeAnna Sewell, Heather Thomson, Leon Mach, Dana E. Veron, and Willet Kempton, "Cost-Minimized Combinations of Wind Power, Solar Power, and Electrochemical Storage, Powering the Grid up to 99.9 Percent of the Time," *Journal of Power Sources* 225 (2013): 60–74.

46. Institute for Energy Research, "Lunacy from the *Journal of Power Sources*: Just Build More Renewables," April 28, 2013, http://instituteforenergyresearch.org /analysis/lunacy-from-the-journal-of-power-sources-just-build-more-renewables/.

47. T. R. Hawkins, B. Singh, G. Majeau-Bettez, and A. H. Strømman, "Compara-

tive Environmental Life Cycle Assessment of Conventional and Electric Vehicles," *Journal of Industrial Ecology* 17 (2013): 53–64, doi:10.1111/j.1530–9290.2012.00532.x.

48. Mark Jennings, Neill Hirst, and Ajay Gambhir, *Reduction of Carbon Dioxide Emissions in the Global Building Sector to 2050*, Grantham Institute for Climate Change, Imperial College London, November 2011, http://www.imperial.ac.uk/grantham/publications/institute-reports-and-analytical-notes/.

49. Ministry for Economy, Trade and Industry, "Top Runner Program," March 2010, p. 9, http://www.enecho.meti.go.jp/category/saving_and_new/saving/enterprise/overview/pdf/toprunner2011.03en-1103.pdf.

50. U.S. Environmental Protection Agency, *Light-Duty Automotive Technology, Carbon Dioxide Emissions, and Fuel Economy Trends: 1975 through 2013*, December 2013, http://www.epa.gov/fueleconomy/fetrends/1975–2013/420r13011.pdf.

51. McKinsey & Company, *Energy Efficiency: A Compelling Global Resource*, 2010, p. 27, http://www.mckinsey.com/Search.aspx?q=energy percent20efficiency percent20potential.

52. World Energy Council, *World Energy Perspective: Energy Efficiency Policies — What Works and What Does Not*, 2013, p. 25, http://www.worldenergy.org/wp-content/uploads/2013/09/World_Energy_Perspective_Energy-Efficiency-Policies-2013_Full_Report.pdf.

53. World Bank, electric power consumption (kWh per capita) data, http://data.worldbank.org/indicator/EG.USE.ELEC.KH.PC.

54. Ottmar Edenhofer, Ramon Pichs Madruga, and Youba Sokona, eds., *Renewable Energy Sources and Climate Change Mitigation*, Intergovernmental Panel on Climate Change, 2012, p. 19, and Annex II: Methodology, http://srren.ipcc-wg3.de/report/IPCC_SRREN_Full_Report.pdf.

55. World Bank Group, *State and Trends of Carbon Pricing*, Washington, DC, September 2015, http://documents.worldbank.org/curated/en/2015/09/25053834/state-trends-carbon-pricing-2015.

56. International Energy Agency, *Tracking Clean Energy Progress 2013*, p. 43, http://www.iea.org/publications/TCEP_web.pdf.

57. "European Climate Policy: Worse Than Useless," *Economist*, January 25, 2014, http://www.economist.com/news/leaders/21595002-current-policies-are-mess-heres-how-fix-them-worse-useless.

58. Brian C. Murray and Nicholas Rivers, "British Columbia's Revenue-Neutral Carbon Tax: A Review of the Latest 'Grand Experiment' in Environment Policy" (working paper NI WP 15-04, Nicholas Institute, Duke University, May 2015), https://nicholasinstitute.duke.edu/sites/default/files/publications/ni_wp_15-04_full.pdf.

59. Interagency Working Group on Social Cost of Carbon, United States Government, "Technical Support Document — Technical Update for the Social Cost

of Carbon for Regulatory Impact Analysis — Under Executive Order 12866," http://www.whitehouse.gov/sites/default/files/omb/assets/inforeg/technical -update-social-cost-of-carbon-for-regulator-impact-analysis.pdf.

60. "Clean Air Act, United States," *The Encyclopedia of Earth*, updated July 2012, http://www.eoearth.org/view/article/151129/#gen4.

61. S. J. Smith, J. van Aardenne, Z. Klimont, R. J. Andres, A. Volke, and S. Delgado Arias, "Anthropogenic Sulfur Dioxide Emissions: 1850–2005," *Atmospheric Chemistry and Physics* 11 (2011): 1101–1116, doi:10.5194/acp-11-1101-2011.

62. Environmental Protection Agency, "Acid Rain Program Benefits Exceed Expectations," http://www.epa.gov/capandtrade/documents/benefits.pdf.

63. Laura Barron-Lopez, "McConnell: Priority Is to 'Get the EPA Reined In,'" *Hill*, November 7, 2014, http://thehill.com/policy/energy-environment/223298 -mcconnell-priority-is-to-get-the-epa-reined-in.

64. White House, 2013 *Draft Report to Congress on the Benefits and Costs of Federal Regulations and Agency Compliance with the Unfunded Mandates Reform Act*, http://www.whitehouse.gov/sites/default/files/omb/inforeg/2013_cb/draft _2013_cost_benefit_report.pdf.

65. U.S. Government Accountability Office, *Environmental Regulation: EPA Should Improve Adherence to Guidance for Selected Elements of Regulatory Impact Analyses*, July 2014, http://www.gao.gov/assets/670/664872.pdf.

66. "The Halliburton Loophole," *New York Times*, editorial, November 2, 2009, http://www.nytimes.com/2009/11/03/opinion/03tue3.html?_r=0.

67. Environmental Protection Agency, *Assessment of the Potential Impacts of Hydraulic Fracturing for Oil and Gas on Drinking Water Resources*, draft released June 2015, http://www.epa.gov/hfstudy.

5. The Trials and Travails of Taming the Atom

1. All six of the reactors at Fukushima Daiichi were decommissioned by 2014. Of the remaining forty-eight in Japan, four have received regulatory approval for restart, and two (at Sendai, Kyushu) actually restarted as of December 2015. The Nuclear Regulatory Agency recommended in December 2015 that operation of the fast breeder reactor Monju, which has suffered a series of mishaps and eaten through more than ¥1 trillion ($8.3 billion) of taxpayer money since 1995, be transferred from the Japan Atomic Energy Agency to another entity.

2. Tohoku Electric Power Co., "Cancellation of Plan to Build Namie-Odaka Nuclear Power Plant," March 28, 2013, http://www.tohoku-epco.co.jp/english /press/2013index.html.

3. Minamisoma City Council, "Resolution to Cancel Construction of the Namie–Kotaka Nuclear Power Plant and to Seek the Closing of All Nuclear Power Sta-

tions in Fukushima Prefecture," http://www.city.minamisoma.lg.jp/index.cfm/8,3664,c,html/3664/iinkaiteisyutugian2312.pdf.

4. National Diet of Japan, *The Official Report of the Fukushima Nuclear Accident Independent Investigation Commission: Executive Summary*, 2012, http://warp.da.ndl.go.jp/info:ndljp/pid/3856371/naiic.go.jp/wp-content/uploads/2012/09/NAIIC_report_lo_res10.pdf.

5. James Mahaffey, *Atomic Accidents: A History of Nuclear Meltdowns; From the Ozark Mountains to Fukushima* (New York: Pegasus Books, 2014).

6. U.S. Nuclear Regulatory Commission, "Backgrounder on the Three Mile Island Accident," http://www.nrc.gov/reading-rm/doc-collections/fact-sheets/3mile-isle.html#summary.

7. Mark Lynas, *Nuclear 2.0: Why a Green Future Needs Nuclear Power* (2013 Kindle Single), Loc 358.

8. Milan Ilnyckyj, "Climate Change and Nuclear Power in Ontario," December 1, 2013, http://www.academia.edu/5446837/Climate_change_and_nuclear_power_in_Ontario.

9. Chernobyl Forum: 2003–2005, *Chernobyl's Legacy: Health, Environmental, and Socio-economic Impacts and Recommendations to the Governments of Belarus, the Russian Federation and Ukraine*, 2006, 15–16, http://www.iaea.org/Publications/Booklets/Chernobyl/chernobyl.pdf.

10. Burton Bennet, Michael Repacholi, and Zhanat Carr, eds., *Health Effects of the Chernobyl Accident* (Geneva: World Health Organization, 2006), 106, http://whqlibdoc.who.int/publications/2006/9241594179_eng.pdf.

11. United Nations Scientific Committee on the Effects of Atomic Radiation, *UNSCEAR 2008 Report to the General Assembly with Scientific Annexes, Volume II, Annex D* (New York: United Nations, 2011), http://www.unscear.org/docs/reports/2008/11-80076_Report_2008_Annex_D.pdf.

12. Ian Fairlie and David Sumner, *The Other Report on Chernobyl (Torch)*, Commissioned by Rebecca Harms, MEP, Greens/EFA in the European Parliament, April 2006, http://www.chernobylreport.org/torch.pdf.

13. Wladimer Wertelecki, "Malformations in a Chernobyl-Impacted Region," *Pediatrics* 125, no. 4 (April 2010): e836–e843, doi:10.1542/peds.2009–2219.

14. Ivan Blokov, Iryna Labunska, and Alexy Yablokov, eds., *The Chernobyl Catastrophe: Consequence on Human Health* (Amsterdam: Greenpeace, 2006), 31, http://www.greenpeace.org/international/en/publications/reports/chernobylhealthreport/.

15. Alexey B. Nestereko, Vassily B. Nesterenko, and Alexey V. Yablokov, "Consequences of the Chernobyl Catastrophe for Public Health," *Annals of the New York Academy of Sciences* 1181, no. 1 (November 2009): 210.

16. Health Physics Society, "Radiation Doses in Perspective," http://hps.org /documents/RadiationinPerspectiveRev4.pdf.

17. U.S. Environmental Protection Agency, "Radiation Sources and Doses," http://www.epa.gov/radiation/radiation-sources-and-doses.

18. M. Ghiassi-nejad, S. M. J. Mortazavi, J. R. Cameron, A. Niromand-rad, and P. A. Karam, "Very High Background Radiation Areas of Ramsar, Iran: Preliminary Biological Studies," *Health Physics Society Journal* 82, no. 1 (January 2002), http://journals.lww.com/health-physics/toc/2002/01000.

19. The Zaczko resignation was a disturbing example of NRC commissioners with close ties to the nuclear industry allying with their charges to oust their chairman. Moreover, why is the NRC considering granting twenty-year operating license extensions to two forty-year-old Gen II PWRs with a long history of minor mishaps operating a little over sixty kilometers up the river from New York City?

20. Frank N. von Hippel, "The Radiological and Psychological Consequences of the Fukushima Daiichi Accident," *Bulletin of the Atomic Scientists* 67 (September/ November 2011): 27–26, http://bos.sagepub.com/content/67/5/27.full.

21. Institute of Nuclear Power Operations, *Special Report on the Nuclear Accident at the Fukushima Daiichi Nuclear Power Station*, November 2011, http://www.nei .org/corporatesite/media/filefolder/11_005_Special_Report_on_Fukushima _Daiichi_MASTER_11_08_11_1.pdf.

22. Legend has it that the acronym SCRAM was created by Enrico Fermi to describe the person assigned to kill any runaway reaction in the first pile at Chicago by axing a rope to drop the backup control rod into the pile — it stood for "safety control rod ax man." But a historian at the NRC debunks the myth and argues that it was based on the recommendation to "scram" in the event of an emergency. See http://public-blog.nrc-gateway.gov/2011/05/17/putting-the-axe -to-the-scram-myth/.

23. The National Diet of Japan, *The Official Report of the Fukushima Nuclear Accident Independent Investigation Commission*, 2012, http://warp.da.ndl.go.jp /info:ndljp/pid/3856371/naiic.go.jp/en/report/. The information in this section is from the report unless otherwise noted.

24. All four units at Fukushima Daini were BWRs of 1980s vintage and were housed in newer Mark II containment, and so withstood the earthquake somewhat better than the reactors at Fukushima Daiichi. In a stroke of luck, a single power line from the grid continued to supply power to the plant immediately following the earthquake. The tsunami that followed also did not inundate the plant as thoroughly as Fukushima Daiichi. Workers worked frantically to lay emergency cables and set up alternate motors, transported from another TEPCO plant 125 miles away, and restored three damaged seawater pumps within two days

of the tsunami, enabling cold shutdown by March 15. For a detailed analysis see *TEPCO Fukushima Daini Nuclear Power Station Research on the Status of Response to the Tohoku-Pacific Ocean Earthquake and Tsunami and Lessons Learned Therefrom*, Japan Nuclear Safety Institute, October 2012, http://www.genanshin.jp /report/data/F2jiko_Report.pdf.

25. Airi Ryu and Najmedin Meshkati, "Why You Haven't Heard about Onagawa Power Station after the Earthquake and Tsunami of March 11, 2011," Vitebi School of Engineering, University of Southern California, revised and updated February 26, 2014, http://www-bcf.usc.edu/~meshkati/Onagawa percent20NPS- percent 20Final percent2003–10–13.pdf.

26. Philip Y. Lipscy, Kenji E. Kushida, and Trevor Incerti, "The Fukushima Disaster and Japan's Nuclear Plant Vulnerability in Comparative Perspective," *Environmental Science and Technology* 47, no. 12 (May 2013): 6082–6088, dx.doi .org/10.1021/es4004813.

27. Norimitsu Onishi and Ken Belson, "Culture of Complicity Tied to Stricken Nuclear Plant," *New York Times*, April 26, 2011, http://www.nytimes.com/2011 /04/27/world/asia/27collusion.html?pagewanted=1&_r=5&src=me. For an interesting article about Japan's nuclear reactors written seven years before 3/11 see Leuren Moret, "Japan's Deadly Game of Nuclear Roulette," *Japan Times*, May 23, 2004, http://www.japantimes.co.jp/life/2004/05/23/life/japans-deadly-game -of-nuclear-roulette/#.Uu31_T1_uto.

28. "Utilities Got 68 Ex-bureaucrats via 'Amakudari,'" *Japan Times*, May 4, 2011, http://www.japantimes.co.jp/news/2011/05/04/news/utilities-got-68 -ex-bureaucrats-via-amakudari/#.VpX12vmLQdU.

29. Institute of Nuclear Power Operations, *Special Report on the Nuclear Accident at the Fukushima Daiichi Nuclear Power Station*, November 2011, http://www .nei.org/corporatesite/media/filefolder/11_005_Special_Report_on_Fuku shima_Daiichi_MASTER_11_08_11_1.pdf.

30. National Diet of Japan, *Official Report*, 5.

31. World Health Organization, *Health Risk Assessment from the Nuclear Accident after the 2011 Great East Japan Earthquake and Tsunami Based on a Preliminary Dose Estimation*, 2013, http://apps.who.int/iris/bitstream/10665/78218/1/978924 1505130_eng.pdf.

32. Tokyo Outsider blog, January 17, 2012, http://tokyooutsider.wordpress .com/2012/01/17/radiation-dispersal-data-was-provided-to-u-s-before-japanese -public/.

33. Yuri Oiwa, "Death Rates Spike among Elderly Evacuees from Fukushima," *Asahi Shimbun*, January 11, 2013, http://ajw.asahi.com/article/0311disaster/fuku shima/AJ201301110086.

34. Justin McCurry, "Japan Earmarks £300m+ for Fukushima cleanup," *Guardian*, September 4, 2013, http://www.theguardian.com/environment/2013/sep/03/japan-ice-wall-fukushima-water.

35. "Tepco Says All Radioactive Water in Fukushima No.1 Tanks Filtered," *Japan Times*, May 27, 2015, http://www.japantimes.co.jp/news/2015/05/27/national/tepco-says-radioactive-water-fukushima-1-tanks-filtered/#.Vpw17vmLQdV.

36. "Tepco Dumps Treated Groundwater into Pacific to Ease Toxic Water Buildup at Fukushima No. 1," *Japan Times*, September 14, 2015, http://www.japantimes.co.jp/news/2015/09/14/national/tepco-dumps-treated-groundwater-in-pacific-to-ease-toxic-water-buildup-at-fukushima-no-1/#.VpxC0fmLQdU.

37. Geoff Brumfiel, "Fukushima: Fallout of Fear," *Nature*, January 16, 2013, http://www.nature.com/news/fukushima-fallout-of-fear-1.12194.

38. Makiko Segawa, "After the Media Has Gone: Fukushima, Suicide and the Legacy of 3.11," *Asia-Pacific Journal: Japan Focus* 10, issue 19, no. 2 (May 7, 2012), http://www.japanfocus.org/-Makiko-Segawa/3752.

39. "Tepco Admits Culpability in Fukushima Farmer's Suicide," *Japan Times*, June 7, 2013, http://www.japantimes.co.jp/news/2013/06/07/national/tepco-admits-culpability-in-fukushima-farmers-suicide/#.Us5rZdJdWt2.

40. Committee on the Safety of Nuclear Installations, OECD Nuclear Energy Agency, *Filtered Containment Venting Systems: Note on the Outcome of the May 1988 CSNI Specialist Meeting on Filtered Containment Venting Systems*, November 1988, https://www.oecd-nea.org/nsd/docs/1988/csni88-156.pdf.

41. Benjamin Goad, "Nuclear Regulators under Fire for Delay of Post-Fukushima Safety Requirement," *Hill*, March 20, 2013, http://thehill.com/blogs/regwatch/energyenvironment/289275-nuclear-regulators-under-fire-over-delay-of-safety-rule.

42. Dan Yurman, "Japan Launches Nuclear Safety Agency," American Nuclear Society, *ANS Nuclear Cafe*, October 2, 2014, http://ansnuclearcafe.org/2012/10/04/japan-launches-nuclear-safety-agency/.

43. Masumi Suga, "Japan Nuclear Reactors' Status, Restart Application: Table," *Bloomberg Business*, February 21, 2014, http://www.bloomberg.com/news/2014-02-21/japan-nuclear-reactors-status-restart-application-table.html.

44 Akira Yanagisawa, T. Yoshioka, H. Suzuki, J. W. Choi, R. Ikarii, Y. Shibata, and K. Ito, *Economic and Energy Outlook of Japan for FY2014*, Institute of Energy Economics, Japan, January 2014, http://eneken.ieej.or.jp/data/5363.pdf.

45. Eric Johnston, "New Feed-In Tariff System a Rush to Get Renewables in Play," *Japan Times*, May 29, 2012, http://www.japantimes.co.jp/news/2012/05/29/reference/new-feed-in-tariff-system-a-rush-to-get-renewables-in-play/#.VDOExWd_vnh.

46. Ministry of Economy, Trade and Industry, *Settlement of FY2014 Purchase Prices and FY2014 Surcharge Rates under the Feed-In Tariff Scheme for Renewable Energy,* http://www.meti.go.jp/english/press/2014/0325_03.html.

47. "Solar Shambles," *Economist,* November 29, 2014, http://www.economist.com/news/business/21635013-japan-has-failed-learn-germanys-renewable-energy-mess-solar-shambles.

48. "Japan May Put Freeze on New Larger Solar Projects," *Nihon Keizai Shinbun,* October 11, 2014, http://asia.nikkei.com/Politics-Economy/Policy-Politics/Japan-may-put-freeze-on-new-large-solar-power-projects.

49. International Atomic Energy Agency, *Radiation Protection after the Fukushima Daiichi Accident: Promoting Confidence and Understanding,* September 2014, http://www.iaea.org/sites/default/files/radprotection0914.pdf. Also see Georg Steinhauser, Alexander Brandl, and Thomas E. Johnson, "Comparison of the Chernobyl and Fukushima Nuclear Accidents: A Review of the Environmental Impacts," *Science of the Total Environment* 470 (February 1, 2014), http://dx.doi.org/10.1016/j.scitotenv.2013.10.029.

50. Kerstine Appunn, "Germany's Greenhouse Gas Emissions and Climate Targets," *Clean Energy Wire,* November 27, 2015, https://www.cleanenergywire.org/factsheets/germanys-greenhouse-gas-emissions-and-climate-targets.

51. "Sunny, Windy, Costly, and Dirty," *Economist,* January 18, 2014, http://www.economist.com/news/europe/21594336-germanys-new-super-minister-energy-and-economy-has-his-work-cut-out-sunny-windy-costly; Jeevan Vasagar, "Germany Cautions on Impact of Renewables," *Financial Times,* January 24, 2014, http://www.ft.com/intl/cms/s/0/8c207bec-82a1–11e3–8119–00144feab7de.html#axzz31a40iajD.

52. "French Nuclear Reactor Closures to Be Limited to Fessenheim: Report," Platts, November 12, 2013, http://www.platts.com/latest-news/electric-power/london/french-nuclear-reactor-closures-to-be-limited-21810058.

53. Simon Mundy, "South Korea Cuts Target for Nuclear Power," *Financial Times,* January 14, 2014, http://www.ft.com/cms/s/0/4e8c1872–7cf7–11e3–81dd-00144feabdc0.html#axzz2sP839xEu.

54. World Nuclear Association, *Nuclear Power in China,* updated August 2015, http://www.world-nuclear.org/info/Country-Profiles/Countries-A-F/China—Nuclear-Power/.

55. World Nuclear Association, "World Nuclear Power Reactors and Uranium Requirements," updated January 1, 2016, http://www.world-nuclear.org/info/Facts-and-Figures/World-Nuclear-Power-Reactors-and-Uranium-Requirements/.

56. U.S. Energy Information Administration, "International Energy Statistics," https://www.eia.gov/cfapps/ipdbproject/IEDIndex3.cfm?tid=2&pid=2&aid=7.

6. Inviting Back the Toilet-Trained Genie

1. Nuclear Energy Agency, Organisation for Economic Co-operation and Development, *Technical and Economic Aspects of Load Following with Nuclear Power Plants,* June 2011, https://www.oecd-nea.org/ndd/reports/2011/load-following-npp.pdf.

2. World Nuclear Association, *Advanced Nuclear Reactors,* http://www.world-nuclear.org/info/Nuclear-Fuel-Cycle/Power-Reactors/Advanced-Nuclear-Power-Reactors/. Most current reactors have a calculated core damage frequency of 5×10^{-5} per reactor year, or 1 in 20,000 reactor years: a number that is somewhat less comforting when divided by the about five hundred reactors that are operable and under construction in the world today, so once every forty years.

3. U.S. Nuclear Regulatory Commission, "Issued Design Certification — Advanced Boiling-Water Reactor (ABWR)," http://www.nrc.gov/reactors/new-reactors/design-cert/abwr.html.

4. GE Hitachi, "ESBWR Nuclear Power Plant," https://nuclear.gepower.com/build-a-plant/products/nuclear-power-plants-overview/esbwr.html.

5. Jim Pickard, "French Nuclear Problems Cast Doubt on UK Nuclear Power Plant," *Financial Times,* June 14, 2015, http://www.ft.com/intl/cms/s/0/b8741dd0-1048-11e5-bd70-00144feabdc0.html#axzz3kZeGr3UX.

6. Dominique Patton, "Update 2 — EDF Says First Taishan Nuclear Plant to Be Ready End 2015," Reuters, January 29, 2015, http://www.reuters.com/article/2015/01/29/china-france-nuclear-idUSL4N0V86A320150129.

7. Christopher Adams, "Amber Rudd Rejects Concern over £24bn Hinkley Nuclear Plant Cost," *Financial Times,* September 21, 2015, http://www.ft.com/intl/cms/s/0/c9e9fe1e-604c-11e5-a28b-50226830d644.html#axzz3mcHj3JwB.

8. Generation IV International Forum, "Generation IV Systems." This section uses the Generation IV International Forum web pages for reference unless otherwise specified. See https://www.gen-4.org/gif/jcms/c_59461/generation-iv-systems.

9. For more see "Physics of Uranium and Nuclear Energy," World Nuclear Association, updated September 2014, http://www.world-nuclear.org/information-library/nuclear-fuel-cycle/introduction/physics-of-nuclear-energy.aspx. Also see Kirk Sorensen, "What's the Difference between a Thermal Spectrum Reactor and a Fast Spectrum Reactor?," *Energy from Thorium* blog, April 28, 2006, http://energyfromthorium.com/2006/04/28/whats-the-difference-between-a-thermal-spectrum-reactor-and-a-fast-spectrum-reactor/.

10. U.S. Nuclear Regulatory Commission, "Fermi, Unit 1 Site Status Summary," http://www.nrc.gov/info-finder/decommissioning/power-reactor/enrico-fermi-atomic-power-plant-unit-1.html.

11. Eiji Ohshima, *"Cho-kogata genshiro" nara Nihon mo sekai mo sukuwareru* (Tokyo: Hikaruland, 2011).

12. Lawrence Livermore National Laboratory, "Nuclear Energy to Go: A Self-Contained, Portable Reactor," *Science & Technology Review*, July/August 2004, https://www.llnl.gov/str/JulAug04/Smith.html.

13. BusinessWire, "GEN4 Energy Team Awarded Advanced Reactor R&D Grant," November 13, 2013, http://www.businesswire.com/news/home/2013 1113005087/en/GEN4-Energy-Team-Awarded-Advanced-Reactor-Grant# .Uv3GjPmSxsI.

14. D. L. Moses and W. D. Lanning, "Analysis and Evaluation of Recent Operational Experience from the Fort St. Vrain HTGR," 1985, U.S. Department of Energy Office of Scientific and Technical Information, http://www.osti.gov /scitech/servlets/purl/5535126.

15. Rainer Moorman, "A Safety Re-evaluation of the AVR Pebble Bed Reactor Operation and Its Consequences for Future HTR Concepts," *Berichte des Forschungszentrums Julich*, June 2008 http://juser.fz-juelich.de/record/1304/files /Juel_4275_Moormann.pdf?version=1.

16. "Funkelnde Augen," *Der Spiegel* 24, 1986, http://www.spiegel.de/spiegel /print/d-13517686.html.

17. International Atomic Energy Agency, *Gas-Cooled Reactor Technology Safety and Siting*, Vienna, 1990, http://www.iaea.org/inis/collection/nclcollectionstore /_public/32/036/32036093.pdf.

18. NucNet, "China Begins Construction of First Generation IV HTR-PM Unit," January 7, 2013, http://www.nucnet.org/all-the-news/2013/01/07/china -begins-construction-of-first-generation-iv-htr-pm-unit.

19. The Obama administration seems to want to pursue nuclear power as part of its "all of the above" policy for energy development but has not addressed the basic problem of long-term waste sufficiently, deciding in 2011 to not complete the Yucca Mountain, Nevada, nuclear waste repository.

20. Idaho National Laboratory, *The High Temperature Gas-Cooled Reactor Next Generation Nuclear Energy*, http://www4vip.inl.gov/research/next-generation -nuclear-plant/.

21. Mark Halper, "A Small Nuclear Reactor with a Difference," ZDNet, April 9, 2014, http://www.zdnet.com/article/a-nuclear-reactor-with-a-difference/.

22. "DOE Continues Funding for Small Modular Reactors Despite Industry Concerns," Taxpayers for Common Sense, May 5, 2014, http://www.taxpayer .net/library/article/department-of-energy-awards-another-226-million-for-small -modular-reactor-d.

23. Tyler Ellis, Robert Petroski, Pavel Hejzlar, George Zimmerman, David McAlees, Charles Whitmer, Nicholas Touran, et al., "Traveling-Wave Reactors:

A Truly Sustainable and Full-Scale Resource for Global Energy Needs," Proceedings of ICAPP '10 San Diego, June 13–17, 2010, Paper 10189, http://terrapower.com/uploads/docs/ICAPP_2010_Paper_10189.pdf.

24. TerraPower website, http://terrapower.com/.

25. Paul Habenreich and J. R. Engel, "Experience with the Molten Salt Reactor Experiment," *Nuclear Technology* 8, no. 2 (February 1970): 118–136.

26. H. G. MacPherson, "The Molten Salt Reactor Adventure," *Nuclear Science and Engineering* 90 (1985): 374–380.

27. Oak Ridge National Laboratory, "An Account of Oak Ridge National Laboratory's Thirteen Nuclear Reactors," August 2009 (rev. March 2010), http://info.ornl.gov/sites/publications/Files/Pub20808.pdf. The information in this section is from the publication unless otherwise specified.

28. For a particularly detailed and readable account of the bureaucratic machinations and personalities involved, the following book is very enlightening: Richard Martin, *Superfuel: Thorium, the Green Energy Source for the Future* (New York: Palgrave Macmillan, 2012).

29. John Woolley and Gerhard Peters, "The President's News Conference, May 4, 1979," American Presidency Project, http://www.presidency.ucsb.edu/ws/index.php?pid=32289.

30. Charles E. Till and Yoon Il Chang, *Plentiful Energy: The Story of the Integral Fast Reactor* (North Charleston, SC: CreateSpace, 2011), 224, 242.

31. World Nuclear Association, "Processing of Used Nuclear Fuel," updated November 2015, http://www.world-nuclear.org/info/nuclear-fuel-cycle/fuel-recycling/processing-of-used-nuclear-fuel/.

32. Eiji Ohshima, *"Cho-kogata genshiro,"* 194–195.

33. "Completion of Reprocessing Plant at Rokkashomura Delayed, Cost Increase of 200 Billion Yen," *Asahi Shimbun*, February 21, 2011, http://web.archive.org/web/20110222233158/www.asahi.com/business/update/0221/TKY201102210397.html.

34. Asahi Shimbun Special Public Opinion Poll, April 7, 2014, http://mansfieldfdn.org/program/research-education-and-communication/asian-opinion-poll-database/listofpolls/2014-polls/asahi-shimbun-special-public-opinion-poll-040714/.

35. Masafumi Takubo and Frank N. von Hippel, *Ending Reprocessing in Japan: An Alternative to Managing Japan's Spent Nuclear Fuel and Separated Plutonium*, International Panel on Fissile Materials, November 2013, http://fissilematerials.org/library/rr12.pdf.

36. Yuri Kageyama, "Japan Pro-bomb Voices Grow Louder amid Nuke Debate," Associated Press, July 31, 2012, http://bigstory.ap.org/article/japan-pro-bomb-voices-grow-louder-amid-nuke-debate.

37. Jay Soloman and Miho Inada, "Japan's Nuclear Plan Unsettles U.S.," *Wall Street Journal*, May 1, 2013, http://online.wsj.com/news/articles/SB1000142412788 73245820045784569438671898o4.

38. Till and Chang, *Plentiful Energy*, 147–149.

39. Uranium-233, which would be used in MSRs to kick-start them, is suitable for manufacturing nuclear weapons but also contains uranium-232, the high radioactivity of which wreaks havoc on electronic equipment and makes it much harder to fashion and maintain nuclear weapons that use these isotopes (the argument that motivated subnational actors won't care is a red herring, given just how much easier it is to handle bomb-making material is out there). The U.S. government is currently planning to denature and dispose of its 1960s- and 1970s-vintage stocks of uranium-233 (about 1.55 tons), but these should be kept under tight security for eventual use in molten salt reactors.

40. Kirk Sorenson and Kirk Dorius, "Introduction to Flibe Energy," 3rd Thorium Energy Alliance Conference (TEAC3), Washington, DC, May 12, 2011, http://www.thoriumenergyalliance.com/downloads/TEAC3 percent20presen tations/TEAC3_Sorensen_Kirk.pdf.

41. Robert Hargraves, *Thorium: Energy Cheaper Than Coal* (North Charleston, SC: CreateSpace, 2012).

42. "Thorium Research Center in Norway," International Thorium Organization, October 8, 2013, http://www.itheo.org/articles/thorium-research-center -norway.

43. Panos Bexevanis, "Accelerator Driven Subcritical Reactors," coursework for PH241, Stanford University, February 22, 2013, http://large.stanford.edu /courses/2013/ph241/baxevanis1/. For another overview of ADSRs see http:// www.iaea.org/Publications/Magazines/Bulletin/Bu11392/arkhipov.html.

44. Ambrose Evans-Pritchard, "Obama Could Kill Fossil Fuels Overnight with a Nuclear Dash for Thorium," *Telegraph*, August 29, 2010, http://www.telegraph .co.uk/finance/comment/7970619/Obama-could-kill-fossil-fuels-overnight-with -a-nuclear-dash-for-thorium.html.

45. Raffi Khatchadourian, "A Star in a Bottle," *New Yorker*, March 3, 2014.

46. Kenneth Chang, "The Machinery of an Energy Dream," *New York Times*, March 17, 2014, http://www.nytimes.com/2014/03/18/science/the-challenge -how-to-keep-fusion-going-long-enough.html?_r=0.

47. Charles A. S. Hall, Jessica G. Lambert, and Stephen B. Balogh, "EROI of Different Fuels and the Implications for Society," *Energy Policy* 64 (January 2014): 141–152, http://www.sciencedirect.com/science/article/pii/S0301421513003856, http://www.theoildrum.com/node/3877, and private correspondence.

48. D. Weißbach, G. Ruprecht, A. Huke, K. Czerski, S. Gottlieb, and A. Hussein, "Energy Intensities, EROIs (Energy Returned on Invested), and Energy Payback

Times for Electricity Generating Power Plants," *Energy* 52 (2013): 210–221, http://dx.doi.org/10.1016/j.energy.2013.01.029.

49. Google Docs, ERoEI spreadsheet, https://docs.google.com/spreadsheet/ccc?key=0Aux2QwQckeWEdE9UbHNKR316THItNi1RTUdxa1RrdUE#gid=0.

50. I. Zelenika-Zovko and J. M. Pearce, "Diverting Indirect Subsidies from the Nuclear Industry to the Photovoltaic Industry: Energy and Economic Returns," *Energy Policy* 39 (2011): 2626–2632, doi:http://dx.doi.org/10.1016/j.enpol.2011.02.031.

51. International Monetary Fund, *Energy Subsidy Reform: Lessons and Implications,* January 28, 2013, appendix 1.

52. World Nuclear Association, "U.S. Nuclear Policy," http://www.world-nuclear.org/info/Country-Profiles/Countries-T-Z/USA — Nuclear-Power-Policy/.

53. World Nuclear Association, "Supply of Uranium," updated October 8, 2014, http://www.world-nuclear.org/info/Nuclear-Fuel-Cycle/Uranium-Resources/Supply-of-Uranium/.

54. Will Ferguson, "Record Haul of Uranium Harvested from Seawater," *New Scientist,* August 22, 2012, http://www.newscientist.com/article/dn22201-record-haul-of-uranium-harvested-from-seawater.html#.VGwuczSsXnh.

55. Robert E. Krebs, *The History and Use of Our Earth's Chemical Elements: A Reference Guide,* 2nd ed. (Westport, CT: Greenwood, 2006), 310.

56. Nuclear Energy Insider, "UK to Steer Plutonium Processing Projects by Year-End," October 8, 2015, http://analysis.nuclearenergyinsider.com/waste-management/uk-steer-plutonium-processing-projects-year-end.

57. Catherine Butler, Karen A. Parkhill, and Nicholas F. Pidgeon, "Nuclear Power after Japan: The Social Dimensions," *Environment: Science and Policy for Sustainable Development* 53, no. 6, (2011): 3–14.

58. Martin, *Superfuel.*

59. Masakazu Toyoda, *Energy Policy in Japan: Challenges after Fukushima,* Institute of Energy Economics, Japan, January 24, 2013, http://eneken.ieej.or.jp/data/4700.pdf.

60. "Saisei ene ga genpatsu uwamawaru dengen kōsei, 30 nen ni 23–25 pāsento" [Renewable energy to exceed nuclear in power mix, 23–25 percent in '30], *Nihon Keizai Shinbun,* April 6, 2015, http://www.nikkei.com/article/DGXKASDF05HoC_VooC15A4MM8000/.

61. Mari Saito, Aaron Sheldrick, and Kentaro Hamada, "Japan May Only Be Able to Restart One-Third of Its Nuclear Reactors," Reuters, April 1, 2014, http://www.reuters.com/article/2014/04/01/us-japan-nuclear-restarts-insight-idUSBREA3020020140401.

62. "Asahi Poll: 59 Percent Oppose Restart of Nuclear Reactors," *Asahi Shimbun,*

March 18, 2014, http://ajw.asahi.com/article/0311disaster/fukushima/AJ2014031
80058.

63. WIN-Gallup International, "Impact of Japan Earthquake on Views about
Nuclear Energy," April 15, 2011, http://www.nrc.co.jp/report/pdf/110420_2.pdf.

64. "The Leapfrog Continent," *Economist*, July 6, 2015, http://www.economist
.com/news/middle-east-and-africa/21653618-falling-cost-renewable-energy-may
-allow-africa-bypass.

65. Antonio Castellano, Adam Kendall, Mikhail Nikomarov, and Tarryn
Swemmer, *Brighter Africa: The Growth Potential of the Sub-Saharan Electricity Sector*, McKinsey & Company, February 2015, http://www.mckinsey.com/insights
/energy_resources_materials/powering_africa.

66. Calculated using 2012 IEA estimates of CO_2 intensities of coal, oil, and natural gas: 879, 713, and 391g CO_2/kWh respectively.

67. International Energy Agency, *Energy and Climate Change: World Energy
Outlook Special Report*, 2015, https://www.iea.org/publications/freepublications
/publication/weo-2015-special-report-energy-climate-change.html.

68. Jos G. J. Olivier, Greet Janssens-Maenhout, Marilena Muntean, and Jeroen
A. H. W. Peters, *Trends in Global CO_2 Emissions: 2014 Report*, PBL Netherlands
Environmental Agency and the European Commission Joint Research Centre,
The Hague, 2014, http://edgar.jrc.ec.europa.eu/news_docs/jrc-2014-trends-in
-global-co2-emissions-2014-report-93171.pdf.

69. Peter Baker and Ellen Barry, "Obama Clears a Hurdle to Better Ties with
India," *New York Times*, January 25, 2015, http://www.nytimes.com/2015/01/26
/world/asia/obama-lands-in-india-with-aim-of-improving-ties.html.

70. "NPCIL Plans to Generate 60,000 MW Power in the Next Two Decades,"
Business Standard, http://www.business-standard.com/article/companies/npcil
-plans-to-generate-60–000-mw-power-in-next-two-decades-113090600320_1.html.

71. International Atomic Energy Agency, "AHWR Design Description," BARC
(India), 2013, http://www.iaea.org/NuclearPower/Downloadable/aris/2013
/AHWR.pdf.

72. David Lague and Charlie Zhu, "Special Report — the U.S. government Lab
behind China's Nuclear Push," Reuters, December 20, 2013, http://in.reuters.com
/article/2013/12/20/breakout-thorium-idINL4N0FE21U20131220.

73. Ambrose Evans-Pritchard, "Chinese Going for Broke on Thorium Nuclear
Power, and Good Luck to Them," *Telegraph*, March 19, 2014, http://blogs
.telegraph.co.uk/finance/ambroseevans-pritchard/100026863/china-going-for
-broke-on-thorium-nuclear-power-and-good-luck-to-them/.

74. World Nuclear Association, "Nuclear Power in China," http://www.world
-nuclear.org/info/country-profiles/countries-a-f/china — nuclear-power/.

75. *NRC Coziness with Industry: Nuclear Regulatory Commission Fails to Main-*

tain *Arms Length Relationship with the Nuclear Industry: An Investigative Report*, Subcommittee on General Oversight and Investigations of the Committee on Interior and Insular Affairs of the U.S. House of Representatives, One Hundredth Congress, First Session, December 1987, http://babel.hathitrust.org/cgi/pt?id=pst .000013688240;view=1up;seq=10.

76. U.S. Nuclear Regulatory Commission, "Davis-Besse Nuclear Power Station, Unit 1 — License Renewal Application," http://www.nrc.gov/reactors/operating /licensing/renewal/applications/davis-besse.html#appls.

77. "Oversight of the Nuclear Regulatory Commission," Hearing before the Committee on Environment and Public Works, United States Senate, 108th Congress, May 20, 2004, 305–306.

78. Tom Zeller Jr., "Nuclear Agency Is Criticized as Too Close to Its Industry," *New York Times*, May 7, 2011, http://www.nytimes.com/2011/05/08/business /energy-environment/08nrc.html?pagewanted=all&_r=1&.

79. Sidney D. Drell, George P. Shultz, Steven P. Andreasen, "A Safer Nuclear Enterprise," *Science* 336, no. 6086 (June 2012): 1236, doi:10.1126/science.1221842.

80. International Monetary Fund, *Energy Subsidy Reform: Lessons and Implications,* January 28, 2013, chap. 2, http://www.imf.org/external/np/pp/eng/2013 /012813.pdf.

81. International Energy Agency, *World Energy Outlook 2012*, chap. 7.

82. David Coady, Ian Parry, Louis Sears, and Baoping Shang, "IMF Working Paper: How Large Are Global Energy Subsidies?," May 2015, http://www.imf.org /external/pubs/ft/wp/2015/wp15105.pdf.

83. William Nordhaus, "Climate Clubs: Overcoming Free-Riding in International Climate Policy," *American Economic Review* 105, no. 4 (2015): 1339–1370, http://dx.doi.org/10.1257/aer.15000001.

84. Congressional Research Service, *Nuclear Power: Outlook for New U.S. Reactors,* updated March 9, 2007, p. 10, http://www.fas.org/sgp/crs/misc/RL33442.pdf.

85. Nuclear Engineering International, "Hyperion Launches U2N3-Fueled, Pb-Bi-Cooled Fast Reactor," November 20, 2009, http://www.neimagazine.com /news/newshyperion-launches-u2n3-fuelled-pb-bi-cooled-fast-reactor.

86. World Nuclear News, "Three Challenges for Areva," September 11, 2015, http://www.world-nuclear-news.org/C-Three-challenges-for-Areva-1109157.html.

87. Magali Delmas and Bruce Heiman, "Government Credible Commitment to the French and American Nuclear Power Industries," *Journal of Policy Analysis and Management* 20, no. 3 (Summer 2001): 433–456, doi:10.1002/pam.1002.

88. Areva, *2013 Reference Document*, March 31, 2014, http://www.areva.com /finance/liblocal/docs/doc-ref-2013/DDR_final_31032014 percent20EN.pdf.

89. European Network on Debt and Development (Eurodad), http://www .eurodad.org/sites/aid.

90. Edward J. Clay, Matthew Geddes, and Luisa Natali, *Untying Aid: Is It Working? An Evaluation of the Implementation of the Paris Declaration and of the 2001 DAC Recommendation of Untying ODA to the LDCs* (Copenhagen: Danish Institute for International Studies, 2009), http://www.oecd.org/dac/evaluation/dcdndep/44375975.pdf.

91. Claire Provost, "Aid Still Benefits Companies from Donor Countries," *Guardian*, September 7, 2011, http://www.theguardian.com/global-development/2011/sep/07/aid-benefits-donor-countries-companies.

7. Innovation

1. Dr. Jim Taylor, "Is Technology the New Opiate of the Masses?," *Huffington Post*, November 2, 2012, http://www.huffingtonpost.com/dr-jim-taylor/technology-addiction_b_2040298.html.

2. World Intellectual Property Organization IP Statistics Data Center, http://ipstats.wipo.int/ipstatv2/.

3. Jonathan Huebner, "A Possible Declining Trend for Worldwide Innovation," *Technological Forecasting and Social Change* 72 (2005): 980–986.

4. D. Strumsky, J. Lobo, and J. Tainter, "Complexity and the Productivity of Innovation," *Systems Research and Behavioral Science* 27 (2010): 296–509.

5. Tyler Cowen, *The Great Stagnation: How America Ate All the Low-Hanging Fruit of Modern History, Got Sick, and Will (Eventually) Feel Better* (Dutton e-book, 2011), Loc 208.

6. Robert J. Gordon, "Interpreting the 'One Big Wave' in U.S. Long-Term Productivity Growth," NBER Working Paper 7752, National Bureau of Economic Research, June 2000, http://www.nber.org/papers/w7752.pdf?new_window=1.

7. Jack W. Scannel, Alex Blanckley, Helen Bolden, and Brian Warrington, "Diagnosing the Decline in Pharmaceutical R&D Efficiency," *Nature Reviews Drug Discovery* 11 (March 2012): 191–200.

8. Michael Heller, *The Gridlock Economy: How Too Much Ownership Wrecks Markets, Stops Innovation, and Costs Lives* (New York: Basic Books, 2008), 44.

9. Ibid., 54–55.

10. Ibid., 57.

11. Amy Harmon, "Golden Rice: Lifesaver?," *New York Times Sunday Review*, August 24, 2014, http://www.nytimes.com/2013/08/25/sunday-review/golden-rice-lifesaver.html?_r=0.

12. Justus Wesseler and David Zilberman, "The Economic Power of the Golden Rice Opposition," *Environment and Development Economics*, October 2013, doi:10.1017/S1355770X1300065X.

13. Edward Wyatt, "Obama Orders Regulators to Root Out 'Patent Trolls,'"

New York Times, June 4, 2013, http://www.nytimes.com/2013/06/05/business/president-moves-to-curb-patent-suits.html?_r=o.

14. Erik Brynjolfsson and Andrew McAfee, *The Second Machine Age: Work, Progress, and Prosperity in a Time of Brilliant Technologies* (New York: W. W. Norton, 2014).

15. Jeremy Hsu, "Carbon Nanotube Computer Hints at Future beyond Silicon Semiconductors," *Scientific American*, September 26, 2013, http://www.scientific american.com/article/carbon-nanotube-computer-hints-at-future-beyond -silicon/.

16. Ryan Whitwarm, "Graphene Nanoribbons Could Be the Savior of Moore's Law," *Extreme Tech*, February 17, 2014, http://www.extremetech.com/extreme /176676-graphene-nanoribbons-could-be-the-savior-of-moores-law.

17. Colin Poitras, "UConn Professor's Patented Technique Key to New Solar Technology," *UConn Today*, February 4, 2013, http://today.uconn.edu/blog /2013/02/uconn-professors-patented-technique-key-to-new-solar-power -technology/.

18. Elizabeth Arias, "United States Life Tables, 2010," *National Vital Statistics Reports* 63, no. 7 (November 2014), http://www.cdc.gov/nchs/data/nvsr/nvsr63 /nvsr63_07.pdf.

19. Chan Lu, "China May See Negative Population Growth after 2020: Expert," *People's Daily Online*, October 28, 2015, http://en.people.cn/n/2015/1028/c90000 -8967678.html.

20. International Monetary Fund, *Global Financial Stability Report*, April 2012, http://www.imf.org/External/Pubs/FT/GFSR/2012/01/index.htm.

21. Larry Greenmeier, "Scientists Use 3-D Printer to Speed Human Embryonic Stem Cell Research," *Nature*, February 5, 2013, http://www.nature.com/news /scientists-use-3-d-printer-to-speed-human-embryonic-stem-cell-research-1.12381.

22. "A Quarter-Million Pounder and Fries," *Economist*, August 10, 2013, http://www.economist.com/news/science-and-technology/21583241-worlds -first-hamburger-made-lab-grown-meat-has-just-been-served.

23. Lee Raine and Cary Funk, "An Elaboration of AASS Scientists' Views," Pew Research Center, July 23, 2015, http://www.pewinternet.org/2015/07/23/an -elaboration-of-aaas-scientists-views/.

24. Michael Specter, "Seeds of Doubt," *New Yorker*, August 25, 2014.

25. F. N. Tubiello, M. Salvatore, R. D. Condor Golec, A. Ferrara, S. Rossi, R. Biancalani, S. Federici, H. Jacobs, and A. Flammini, *Agriculture, Forestry and Other Land Use Emissions by Sources and Removals by Sinks*, Food and Agriculture Organization of the United Nations, March 2, 2014, http://www.fao.org/docrep /019/i3671e/i3671e.pdf.

26. "Do We Need Asimov's Laws?," *MIT Technology Review*, May 16, 2014.

27. John Letzing, "Amazon Adds That Robotic Touch," *Wall Street Journal*, March 20, 2012, http://online.wsj.com/news/articles/SB10001424052702304724404577291903244796214.

28. John Markoff, "Google Adds to Its Menagerie of Robots," *New York Times*, http://www.nytimes.com/2013/12/14/technology/google-adds-to-its-menagerie-of-robots.html?_r=0.

29. Ray Kurzweil, *The Singularity Is Near: When Humans Transcend Biology* (New York: Viking, 2005, Kindle ed.), Loc 2372.

30. Bill Joy, "Why the Future Doesn't Need Us," *Wired*, April 2000.

31. Dylan Loeb McClain, "First Came the Machine That Defeated a Chess Champion," *New York Times*, February 16, 2011, http://www.nytimes.com/2011/02/17/us/17deepblue.html?_r=0.

32. "The Turing Test," *Stanford Encyclopedia of Philosophy*, rev. January 26, 2011, http://plato.stanford.edu/entries/turing-test/#AssCurStaTurTes.

33. "The Chinese Room Argument," *Stanford Encyclopedia of Philosophy*, rev . April 9, 2014, http://plato.stanford.edu/entries/chinese-room/.

34. Kurzweil, *Singularity*, Loc 8401.

35. Ibid., Loc 8195.

36. Kevin Warwick, *Artificial Intelligence: The Basics* (London: Routledge, 2012).

37. Lev Grossman, "The Quantum Quest for a Revolutionary Computer," *Time*, February 6, 2014.

38. "The Human Brain vs. Supercomputers . . . Which One Wins?," Science ABC, http://www.scienceabc.com/humans/the-human-brain-vs-supercomputers-which-one-wins.html.

39. U.S. Commodities Futures Trading Commission and the U.S. Securities and Exchange Commission, *Findings regarding the Market Events of May 6, 2010*, September 30, 2010, http://www.sec.gov/news/studies/2010/marketevents-report.pdf.

40. Matthew Philips, "The SEC's Knight Capital Fine Adds Insult to Injury," *Bloomberg Business*, October 17, 2013, http://www.businessweek.com/articles/2013-10-17/secs-knight-capital-fine-adds-insult-to-injury.

41. David E. Hoffman, *The Dead Hand: The Untold Story of the Cold War Arms Race and Its Dangerous Legacy* (New York: Anchor Books, 2009), 150–179.

42. "Autonomous Weapons: An Open Letter from AI & Robotics Researchers," Future of Life Institute, July 28, 2015, http://futureoflife.org/open-letter-autonomous-weapons/.

43. David E. Sanger, "Obama Order Sped Up Wave of Cyberattacks against Iran," *New York Times*, June 1, 2012, http://www.nytimes.com/2012/06/01/world/middleeast/obama-ordered-wave-of-cyberattacks-against-iran.html?pagewanted=all.

44. James Barret, *Our Final Invention: Artificial Intelligence and the End of the Human Era* (New York: Thomas Dunne, St. Martin's Press, 2013).

45. Steve Omohundro, "Rational Agents Have Universal Drives," *Self-Aware Systems*, February 26, 2013, http://selfawaresystems.com/2013/02/26/rational -agents-have-universal-drives/.

46. Steve Omohundro, "The Safe-AI Scaffolding Strategy Is a Positive Way For- ward," *Self-Aware Systems*, February 26, 2013, http://selfawaresystems.com/2013 /02/26/the-safe-ai-scaffolding-strategy-is-a-positive-way-forward/.

47. "Humanity's Last Invention and Our Uncertain Future," *University of Cambridge Research*, November 25, 2012, http://www.cam.ac.uk/research/news /humanitys-last-invention-and-our-uncertain-future. For an interesting overview of the estimated timelines for many of the technologies discussed in this chapter see http://envisioning.io/horizons/pdf/Envisioning-Horizons-Composite.pdf.

48. Martin Ford, *The Lights in the Tunnel: Automation, Accelerating Technology and the Economy of the Future* (Acculant, 2009).

49. Erik Brynjolfsson and Andrew McAfee, *The Second Machine Age: Work, Progress, and Prosperity in a Time of Brilliant Technologies* (New York: W. W. Norton, 2014), 238–239.

Conclusion

1. Spencer R. Weart, *The Rise of Nuclear Fear* (Cambridge, MA: Harvard Uni- versity Press, 2012).

2. Stephen Emmott, *10 Billion* (New York: Penguin, 2013).

Note: Page numbers in *italics* indicate illustrations.